It's all about
thinking

It's all about
thinking

Collaborating to Support All Learners

IN ENGLISH, SOCIAL STUDIES, AND HUMANITIES

FAYE BROWNLIE AND LEYTON SCHNELLERT

PORTAGE & MAIN PRESS

Portage & Main Press gratefully acknowledges the financial support of the Province of Manitoba through the Department of Culture, Heritage, Tourism & Sport and the Manitoba Book Publishing Tax Credit and the Government of Canada through the Book Publishing Industry Development Program (BPDIP) for our publishing activities.

Printed and bound in Canada by Friesens

Cover and interior design by Relish Design Ltd.

LIBRARY AND ARCHIVES CANADA CATALOGUING IN PUBLICATION

Brownlie, Faye
    It's all about thinking : collaborating to support all learners / Faye Brownlie and Leyton Schnellert.—In English, social studies, and humanities.

Includes bibliographical references.
ISBN 978-1-55379-221-5

    1. Critical thinking. I. Schnellert, Leyton II. Title.

LB2395.35.B765 2009   153.4′2   C2009-905522-8

PORTAGE & MAIN PRESS

100–318 McDermot Ave.
Winnipeg, MB Canada R3A 0A2
Email: books@portageandmainpress.com
Toll-free: 1-800-667-9673
Fax-free: 1-866-734-8477

www.pandmpress.com

FSC
www.fsc.org
MIX
Paper from
responsible sources
FSC® C016245

Dedication
To all those teachers who have taken a risk to work with colleagues.

Acknowledgments
Our thinking and practices continue to develop through our collaborations with teachers and students in classrooms. This book came together because a group of teachers accepted our invitation to collaborate with us and publicly share their learning journeys.

Special thanks to Lisa Chang, Mehjabeen Datoo, Krista Ediger, Dave Giesbrecht, Julie Anne Mainville, Catriona Misfeldt, Joanne Panas, Kathy Pantaleo, Terry Taylor, Linda Watson, and Stacey Wyatt.

Faye Brownlie has worked in staff development with teachers, schools, and districts across Canada, the United States, and internationally. Her recent multi-district, multi-year projects in British Columbia include the Leadership for Learning Academy, the DART (District Assessment of Reading Team), the Early Primary Reading Assessment Consortiums, and the Reading and Writing for Critical Thinking Project in Latvia. Faye continues to teach one day a week in the Richmond School District in British Columbia. She has co-authored many books for teachers.

Leyton Schnellert has been a classroom teacher and a learning resource teacher in middle, junior high, and secondary schools. Currently, he teaches at Simon Fraser University where he supports teachers as they inquire into their practice through graduate diplomas and the Master of Education in Educational Practice program. He continues to collaboratively plan, teach, and reflect with colleagues and students through research and consulting activities.

Table of Contents

Introduction

Picture this scenario: a staff development consultant; eight secondary teachers; their first meeting; a 75-minute block of time to plan together before the consultant leads a class of grade-8 students in a demonstration lesson for another 75 minutes; and the lesson that has just been co-planned with the teachers. Following the demonstration, the teachers and the staff-development consultant meet together to discuss the lesson, consider what worked, what did not work, and what to do next. The consultant opens by asking, "What do you hope to learn today?" There is a moment of silence, then one of the teachers, with crossed arms, responds, "How long have you been doing this new kind of teaching?"

There is the rub. What is "this new kind of teaching"? What does this teacher expect is going to happen? When she signed on to participate in this professional-development sequence, what was the phrase that caught her attention?

We believe that this is a scenario that is common for many teachers. There is no shortage of good and great ideas to help us become more effective teachers. Opening publishers' catalogues, scanning conference programs, taking courses at university all offer a wide range of possibilities—learning strategies, differentiation, assessment for learning, backward design, inquiry, professional learning communities. What is the right focus? What makes the greatest difference? How do you choose? What makes one approach different from another? What is good teaching?

It's All About Thinking attempts to address these questions. We believe that the glue that holds our classes together is "thinking"—thoughtful teachers and thoughtful students. Teachers have to make countless decisions based on their knowledge of their students, their knowledge of curriculum, and their knowledge of instruction. Their ultimate goal is to help students develop as thinkers who use their knowledge to problem solve, to act wisely.

It's All About Thinking will show you ways to get to know your students. It will show you how to use this knowledge in planning your instruction. It will show you ways to use the curriculum in Social Studies, Humanities, and English Language Arts, alone or together in grades 5 to 12, to nurture thinking.

Chapters 1 to 4 explain our big ideas and beliefs. These beliefs have been developed through our work in classrooms rich in diversity, in heterogeneous classrooms with students who have a wide range of abilities, and in classrooms that include many English-language learners. To best address the learning needs of these students, we believe in collaboration—teachers working together, co-planning, co-teaching, and co-assessing. We believe that it is necessary for teachers to develop a personal mental model of learning that they use to filter the plethora of good ideas available for their teaching.

Chapters 5 to 12 offer classroom scenarios. In each chapter, a teacher or teacher team presents a series of lessons or a unit of study. Woven throughout each lesson are instructional choices they have made. These include differentiated instruction, backward design, assessment for learning, open-ended strategies, gradual release of responsibility, cooperative learning, literature circles and information circles, and inquiry. No one chapter includes all the options, yet each includes Universal Design for Learning, assessment for learning, and open-ended strategies. This is the strength of our profession. Teachers making personal choices, based on their students, their curriculum, and their instruction preferences. There is no one right way. Teachers, too, are thinking. *It's All About Thinking* will help you browse conference programs and courses of study to make personal, professional choices that will have the greatest impact on your students' learning. How you put together your blend of approaches for your students is what creates the impact.

We invite you to use and adapt the ideas, units, and lessons we offer in this book. The scenarios described take place in BC classrooms in which teachers use the BC curriculum and BC Performance Standards. Although the curriculum and performance standards we mention may differ somewhat from those in your school district, consider them a jumping-off point.

Let us return to the scenario. After some questions and answers, we discovered that the teacher with crossed arms thought that we were "doing" *differentiation* that day and wondered if it was different from the *diversity* that they had "done" last year. We are not "doing" any approach. *It's All About Thinking* shows what happens when teachers draw different frameworks and approaches together in order to create the best of teaching—for them, at this time, with this particular group of students. Good luck with your teaching!

Chapter 1

Meeting the Needs of All Learners

Nothing can be taught unless it has the potential of making sense to the learner, and learning itself is nothing but the endeavour to make sense. (Frank Smith 1978)

Teaching is complex and intriguing. Each semester and each school year begins a new journey, often toward a familiar destination but never along the same route. It is the learners who determine our route, who cause us to revise our travel plans and detour toward unexpected surprises, to hurry through known territory, and to linger longer in other areas. It is the learners who help us visit known sights with fresh eyes and expand our horizons. It is the learners who engage with our curriculum, who engage and develop because of our relationship with them, who make teaching worthwhile. Today's learners are more diverse than they have ever been. They hold the promise of tomorrow, and they are today's challenge.

Who Are the Learners?

Today's classrooms are diverse. Yet students have *always* had different learning styles and different rates of learning. In the past, to address different learning needs, students were often segregated based on their differences. Students who learned at a slower pace were placed in a class with similar students. Students who had learning difficulties or disabilities may have been placed in a separate class. Students who had difficulty with impulse control and behaviour management could have been in yet a different class. Sometimes, these classes were in the home school of the student; sometimes they were not. Sometimes the placement was for part of a day; sometimes it was a full-time placement. One of the challenges was Who is in and who is out, and what is the cut-off? The intent was to better address the learning needs of all students and leave the teacher with a more homogeneous and, thus, more teachable group, but classroom teachers recognized that diversity still remained in their classes. There were still students who learned differently and at different rates.

In recent years, other groups of students have added to the diversity in our classrooms. One emerging group is made up of students whose first language is not English, those who may be learning English as a second, a third, or even a fourth, language. In the past, more students tended to share a common first language and a common culture. Canada's 2006 Census data show that one in five Canadians is born abroad, the highest foreign-born population since the Depression. Canada is now home to citizens from 200 different countries who still speak 150 different languages (Statistics Canada 2006). Children from all these countries arrive in our schools.

Within this group, there is wide disparity. Some of the students have attended schools, but some have not. Some students have been living in refugee camps for several years and might even have been born there. The experience of just entering a school building is new to them.

Another group of students whose unique learning needs are becoming more recognized are Aboriginal learners. From 1951 to 2001, Canada's population doubled; in the same 50 years, the Aboriginal population increased seven times. Although the Aboriginal population makes up 3.5 per cent of the population in Canada, 30 per cent of Aboriginal children live in homes on welfare; this figure is 50 per cent in British Columbia, and 80 per cent in both Manitoba and Saskatchewan (Calvin Helin, Rural Schools Conference, Vancouver, BC, October 2008). Across Canada, there is great disparity between the graduation rates of Aboriginal and non-Aboriginal populations. In BC, 80 per cent of non-Aboriginal students graduate but only 48 per cent of Aboriginal students graduate; across Canada, 71.5 per cent of non-Aboriginals graduate from high school, but only 57.7 per cent of Aboriginals graduate from high school. Not graduating correlates with poorer health and lower economic prosperity. We are failing this group of students. They, too, must be recognized and included in our discussions of diversity.

Finally, children of poverty make up a third group of diverse students. They often go hungry; they lack the background experiences that align easily with the curriculum; and they feel disenfranchised. To help break the cycle of poverty, they, too, need access to a quality curriculum. According to Mary Ellen Turpel-Lafond, British Columbia's Representative for Children and Youth, a recent study in that province found that children whose families were on welfare were more likely to become involved in crime than they were to graduate (Making Connections Conference, Richmond, BC, November 2008). This research and the research of Doug Willms suggest that this trend can be broken if students form attachments with adults at school, if they learn meaningful pro-social behaviour, and if they have access to equality in their school curriculum, that is, if they are exposed to and can access the same high-quality content and courses as their peers (Willms 2002).

As a consequence of policies of inclusion and of recognition that all students have the right to be educated in the least restrictive environment and to be with their peers, all these students are now found in regular classrooms. We believe that all students belong in regular classrooms, engaged in high-quality, thoughtful learning experiences with their peers while pursuing a complex, meaningful curriculum. We begin our planning with all students in mind and with the conviction that our planning for a full range of learner strengths and styles means that more students will have opportunities to be successful more of the time, and that fewer adaptations and modifications will be required for students with special needs. This is the essence of Universal Design for Learning (which is discussed in more detail in chapter 4).

Today's classrooms present a challenge: How do we best address the wide range of learners' needs—academic, social, and emotional? How do we build a community of learners who, as a result of working together, are more individually able than they would have been working alone? How do we prepare our students to be the best they can be in a complex, ever-changing world? What can we do in the classroom to make a difference for *all* learners? To answer some of the questions, we turn to the research.

What Makes a Difference for Adolescent Learners?

What helps adolescents learn more effectively? What can we do to better meet their needs? The Carnegie Corporation Report of 2004, *Reading Next: A Vision for Action and Research in Middle and High School Literacy* (Biancarosa and Snow), outlines a collection of needs and promising practices that teachers can focus on and that, when common in classrooms, will heighten the learning of all students. This report delineates 15 attributes, nine of which are "instructional improvements" and six of which are "infrastructural improvements." Threaded through these areas are two common themes:

1. All learners can benefit from purposeful, engaging instruction.
2. More learning takes place in classrooms that focus on and nurture students as readers, writers, and thinkers.

Using the promising practices in *Reading Next* as a jumping-off point, we interpret the instructional needs of adolescents as in the following nine ways:

1. Direct, explicit comprehension instruction

Frank Smith (2006) described learning to read as an apprenticeship. Young readers are welcomed into the club by working side by side with a mentor and learning the skills of the trade. We must continue this apprenticeship beyond the primary and intermediate grades. In order to learn how to read (that is, to comprehend, respond, and analyze) complex texts of different genres in different subject areas, students in the middle and senior years should continue the apprenticeship. Teachers, as mentors, show what goes on in their minds as they read for meaning and understanding. How does a scientist, a statistician, a critic, a historian read? Students can learn this from teachers who work in those disciplines day after day. They must learn the skills of comprehension and analysis within the context of each discipline, what the skills are, what they look like, and how to do them.

Ellin Keene (2008) is a teacher-researcher who has described key comprehension strategies of effective readers and writers. Like others, she points out that good readers use these strategies to understand. Her list includes:

- monitoring meaning
- using relevant prior knowledge and schema
- asking questions
- inferring
- evoking images
- determining importance in text
- synthesizing

No list of comprehension strategies is a recipe for teaching. Keene's list of strategies can provide a helpful starting point as it sets us up to consider what we do when we are comprehending and how we will make this explicit to our students. As Wilhelm, Baker, and Dube (2001) remind us, the explicit teaching of these reading comprehension strategies is important only when the strategies help students construct personally meaningful understandings—they are not strategies for their own sake.

2. Effective instructional principles embedded in content

Students need to work with and learn effective reading, writing, and thinking strategies in all areas of the curriculum. Researchers such as Lenz and Deshler (2004) have found that students often do not generalize these thinking skills across units of study, let alone across subjects and contexts. Thus the explicit teaching of these strategies needs to happen in many settings and as part of the criteria for what successful thinkers and learners are expected to do and get better at. Students need to be taught how to make sense of all their different texts—poems in English classes, labs in science classes, recipes in home economics, primary sources in history, maps in geography, problems and applications in mathematics, images in art, and so on.

Effective instruction follows a pattern called the "gradual release of responsibility," which includes:

- model
- guided practice
- independent practice
- independent application (BCELA IRP 2006; Pearson and Gallagher 1983)

This gradual release of responsibility supports all learners:

- First the teacher models the thinking of how to make meaning from the text. This includes setting a purpose for students' reading, often in relation to a learning task. To introduce helpful ways to work with text they usually "think aloud," verbalizing for students how to determine, sort, and compare relevant information and ideas.
- Then opportunities are provided for students to think aloud with partners or in small groups, giving one another feedback on how they are working through their thinking. The teacher supports and coaches this phase.
- Then the students begin to work with the strategy or approach independently, still within the established framework for teaching and learning.
- Ultimately, the teacher looks for independent application of what has been taught. For this to happen, opportunities need to exist beyond the day's assignment, for the students to demonstrate—without teacher guidance—their independent use of the strategy.

Most importantly, students need opportunities to monitor their use of thinking strategies in gradual release and to make links between how and why they are used in different tasks and settings. (This and other key instructional principles are explained further in the next sections.)

3. Motivation and self-directed learning

Motivation affects engagement, the key to all learning. Motivation is often directly related to the quality of the relationship that a student has with the teacher. It is also related to the student's sense of voice and choice in the classroom. When all control seems to exist other than within the student, students may have difficulty maintaining their motivation for learning. For example, some approaches that inherently have more choice built in include literature and information circles, inquiry learning, teaching with and to multiple intelligences, open-ended teaching, and readers' and writers' workshops.

Within any of these instructional approaches, opportunities to set personal goals and to be involved in self-assessment make a difference in student literacy learning. This does not mean just asking the questions What do you want to learn? or How do you want to learn this? For most students, these questions are too broad.

Building opportunities for students to assess their own thinking and learning against shared criteria is one of the most effective ways to help students develop skills in metacognition—that is, thinking about their own thinking and learning. As students learn to use metacognition, they begin to make and monitor personalized plans for their growth. As teachers provide support and feedback to students, the students become greater agents of their own learning. This leads them to self-direct and to self-regulate, or monitor, their own learning.

4. Text-based collaborative learning

To build their repertoire of thinking strategies and develop content knowledge, students need opportunities to work both alone and in collaboration with others. Strategies that enable students to read together and to construct understandings of the text help move students beyond the limits of their own experience. Effective paired and group structures help students link their learning with others, pose questions, and dig more deeply as they socially construct their knowledge and understandings of text.

5. Strategic tutoring

Some students require more time and more specific teaching in order to reach the curricular outcomes. Allow time for this specific teaching to happen. Some of the additional time and specific teaching may occur in the regular class or in after-hour tutorials, while more intensive needs will be met in additional programming. In many middle and secondary schools, students view the resource centre as a place to get help with their homework. This is often just "getting through stuff" rather than building and increasing relevant skills such as how to synthesize the key ideas from information text. To narrow the achievement gap for students, structures must be created to help students learn and develop critical skills that they can then apply independently. This may range from an additional course to a tutorial, but the focus is on increasing literacy skill, not just on completing an assignment. Too many students have been heard to say, "Just help me get this assignment done. Don't teach me!"

6. Diverse texts

Richard Allington posed the question "How can you learn from texts you can't read?" (2001). This is a common concern. Far too often, students sit in classes where everyone has the same textbook. They are expected to first be interested in it, then be able to read it. However, the readability of many of our texts is far beyond the reading level of our students. These students could learn the content *if* it were presented with a more accessible text. Learning the content with accessible text would build a student's background knowledge and then allow them to tackle more challenging text. But this is a Catch-22 situation. As long as we stay tied to one text for all students, we limit the literacy and content learning of a large group of students. This is also true in English Language Arts classes, but we are seeing a strong movement toward teachers working with literature circles for part of the time, greatly increasing the amount of reading being done by students (Brownlie 2005). Information circles and inquiry learning are two approaches that teachers are using with non-fiction texts to engage students by offering a range in text complexity *and* further engaging students by offering choice.

7. Intensive writing

Students need the opportunity to write intensively, to write *connected text*—that is, text that requires them to generate ideas and to link these ideas through writing. Writing helps them clarify their thinking and hold their thinking, on paper or on the computer, while they reflect on it and polish it, alone and with others. Students need to write to make sense of what they are reading, to respond to what they are reading, and to reflect on their reading. Writing, not rote copying or filling in quick answers to someone else's questions, is a constructive, meaning-making process. In *Writing Next* (2006), Graham and Perin reviewed the scientific research on what makes a difference in improving writing for students in grades 4 to 12. Their research highlights such factors as writing strategies, summarization, collaborative writing, establishing specific product goals, word processing, sentence combining, pre-writing, inquiry, process writing, studying models of writing, and writing across the content areas.

As with any aspect of learning, engagement is the key. These factors to improve writing work in concert to increase student engagement and understanding of how to develop their own thinking and how to connect, synthesize, and apply the concepts they are learning about.

8. A technology component

Computers, web pages, and online journals are all examples of the information and communications technology that can open the world to learners. Literacy development is enhanced by the use of technology as a means of accessing, demonstrating, and expanding thinking. Technology is not simply a fancy pencil for recording or a sophisticated tool that provides drill and practice. Nor is it solely a means to fast-track a conversation, for example by twittering or blogging or instant messaging. Nor is it just for entertainment. The use of technology must be based on the same sound educational principles as in any other learning situation. And as with any other new learning situation, learning has a social aspect, so interaction, partners, and conversation should be included with technology. A group of teachers in West Vancouver were involved in a laptop research project with their grade 7 students. One teacher stated, "One of the surprises of this project has been how much more interaction time I have had with my students. They are so engaged with their work that I can move from student to student, coaching and providing specific feedback. I hadn't expected this. There are simply no management issues, and I have so much more time to teach."

9. Ongoing formative assessment of students

Black and Wiliam's (1998) study of formative assessment practices for the Assessment Research Group (ARG) clarifies how teachers are changing their assessment practices to emphasize formative assessment. With formative assessment, teachers use the information gained from classroom work, daily assignments, interviews, conferences, and snapshots of student performance to guide their teaching and their students' learning. This assessment is called assessment *for* learning. Its main purpose is to guide instruction. With formative assessment, students become more aware of the required expectations and more involved in giving feedback to themselves and others on their progress toward these expectations. Involving students in formative assessment has been shown to increase student learning and raise achievement.

We consider the following questions when we look at how assessment informs instruction from a teaching perspective:

- What can my students do?
- What is missing? *or* What do they still need to learn?
- What do I need to teach?
- Is my teaching making a difference?
- If not, what do I need to teach now? Do I teach in a different way, or move on?

As mentioned earlier, we know that student learning is greatly enhanced when teachers focus on student metacognition and goal-setting. We consider the following questions when we look at how assessment informs learning from a student's perspective:

- What am I able to do, considering the criteria for success?
- What is missing? *or* What do I need to learn?
- What is my plan for learning?
- Who can help me?

Meeting the Needs

So what do effective teachers do? What works in classrooms? These are our four key beliefs:

1. Teachers need a mental model of effective learning

The mental model of effective learning works as a lens. Through this lens, information is viewed—new strategies, new programs, new curriculum, new assessment tools, and new mandates. Teachers use their mental model to describe to others—and to themselves when planning and reflecting—what they value in learning and what works in their classrooms. They use their model to examine information to see how it fits with their beliefs. If it doesn't, they either discard the new information or rework it in order to make it fit. Consider, for example, a teacher working with literature circles in her classroom. A colleague volunteers to share a shiny, updated, levelled reading kit with her. The colleague presents the kit because she knows that the teacher is trying to work with multiple levels of texts in her room. The kit even has an assessment tool that tells her "exactly where the kids are at and monitors their progress!" The classroom teacher appreciates the multiple texts presented in the kit but does not want her students reading short passages and answering someone else's questions, especially in a multiple choice format. She does not see these as authentic or engaging reading tasks and does not see the assessment as based on her view of reading. If she uses the kit at all, it will be with a strategy focus, such as finding the key idea of a passage and having the students choose which passage they want to read in order to practise the strategy of finding the key idea.

2. Open-ended strategies support all learners

Purposeful, constructive activities that teachers engage in to link their students and their experiences with the content of the curriculum, prepare students to construct understanding. When planning instruction, the teacher takes into consideration the learners in her class and the curriculum expectations to design strategic learning sequences that will assist the learners in moving from their current learning place to another learning place as described in the curriculum. This requires knowing the learner, knowing the curriculum, and knowing how best to facilitate the learning.

To help students construct their personal understandings, we divide our strategies into three categories, based on their purpose:

1. connecting
2. processing
3. transforming and personalizing

Figure 1.1 Planning open-ended strategies

Strategy Category	Strategy Purpose
Connecting	• Connect to others and to curriculum content • Access and activate background knowledge • Acquire and build background knowledge
Processing	• Interact with new ideas, build understanding by adding on new information and revising former information
Transforming/Personalizing	• Showing acquired information in personalized, thoughtful ways

Figure 1.1 captures our view of planning. We try to work with collaborative strategies as much as possible, to capitalize on the social aspect of learning. We want all students to connect what they and others already know to the ideas and concepts they will be studying. We often start a learning sequence by asking students to predict, link, and/or compare key words, ideas, or relationships before engaging with new content. These are connecting strategies, helping students build from what they know. Next we use processing strategies to help students build the comprehension and analysis skills that they need to successfully use, link, and compare key information from the new

texts with what they knew previously. Students might be asked to record or highlight a key word for the paragraph and find three other words that provide details related to this key word. Processing strategies can be used with all kinds of texts—print, media, visual, and oral. Finally, we use transforming strategies. We want our students to take information and be able to synthesize and represent it in a way that shows that they have taken important, relevant ideas and understood them enough to transform them, and, when possible, interpret the information in their own way.

We develop and choose open-ended and collaborative strategies with all the learners in mind. These strategies are open-ended in that they do not ask students to find the "right" answer but rather require students to make connections, process information, and transform the information in a variety of ways. Working with open-ended strategies leaves room for us to scaffold learning based on the strengths and needs of the individual students within the class. The strategies are collaborative in that they require students to share their thinking at several points along the way—both teaching and learning from one another—as all ideas are welcome, and understandings are refined over time. In designing instruction this way, we find that we need to make fewer adaptations and modifications for the diverse learners in our class. This allows us more time for both whole-class teaching, small-group coaching, and individual conferencing. More students are included as members of the learning community and are exposed to quality teaching rather than working on separate packages of material designed for them as individuals and/or removed from the classroom learning context. For us, a supportive classroom is one that welcomes and celebrates learners and is designed to encourage all of its community members as strategic thinkers.

3. Collaboration counts

All teachers, no matter what their role in a school is, work in exceedingly complex jobs. We believe that such complexity is decreased when we work together. Michael Fullan (2004) says that the ability to collaborate is one of the core requirements of postmodern society. He believes that, without collaborative skills and relationships, it is not possible for students to learn and to continue to learn as much as they need in life beyond the classroom. This is as true for adults as it is for students! Collaboration can come in the form of co-planning, co-assessing, or co-teaching. In all forms, teachers work together as equals, bringing their unique and complementary skills together to create a stronger whole. Hourcade and Bauwens (2002) see the model of one educator teaching alone in one classroom for the entire day, trying to meet the needs of all students, as no longer appropriate. Professional collaboration is the way of the future, and cooperative teaching is at the forefront of professional collaboration. Collaboration opportunities include resource teacher and classroom teachers working together, or two or more classroom teachers working together. The teaching scenarios in this book have all been developed collaboratively.

4. All students belong in the regular classroom

We begin planning with all students in mind, then build in further adaptations and modifications as necessary. As much as possible, resource teachers focus on supporting the work of the regular classroom. We consider resource teachers to include all non-enrolling teachers whose job it is to support atypical learners. These may include learning assistance teachers, special education teachers, English as an Additional Language teachers, English as Second Dialect teachers, librarians. This does not preclude strategic tutoring outside the classroom but does change the focus of the program design. The initial question in planning for students with special needs is *not* Whom should I see? What should I do? It *is* Let's build a class profile, set class goals, examine our lesson design, and then see who will need additional support and how this can best be given. Whenever possible, the focus of the intervention should be in the classroom, scaffolding student learning to the curriculum content and the classroom context. Most important is that teams set shared goals for all students and work to address how teaching and learning sequences can be designed for maximum impact. Then the classroom and resource teachers think about the time they have at their disposal and their own strengths and skills, and work to build support for students accordingly. A resource teacher's role might include:

- **team teaching lessons in the class**, where both teachers have interchangeable roles leading lesson sequences, checking in with small groups, creating adaptations and modifications within the sequences to scaffold specific students' learning
- **complementary instruction**, where each teacher takes on specific aspects of the lesson, for example, one teacher prepares the strategy sequence and a graphic organizer, while the other finds a range of texts and adapts the sequence and organizer for various students
- **supplementary instruction**, where one teacher takes the lead in large-group instruction and the second teacher works with small groups to pre-teach, re-teach, or deepen understanding

These and many other configurations involve planning together with the diverse needs of all learners in mind, and they involve a commitment to giving students engaging, coherent learning opportunities. Thus, working together in the regular class ensures that all students receive foundational content, modelled strategy instruction, and collaborative learning opportunities. In instances where support occurs outside the classroom, it is still with the same goals in mind.

Chapter 2

Working Together As a School

Only through sharing ideas, materials, resources, and expertise do teachers develop, survive and thrive. (Villa, Thousand, and Nevin 2004)

Teaching is a complex endeavour. Gone are the days—if they ever truly existed—when it was assumed that one teacher, working alone, could meet the needs of all learners in a classroom. We believe that together we are better, that working as a member of a team and within a school helps us grow as professionals and supports us in being the best we can be in the classroom, and in having the greatest impact on student learning.

Many teachers work with their students to develop vibrant learning communities. Over the course of the school year, they see their students begin to thrive. But making a difference in one classroom in one academic year is only the beginning. Shared efforts among teachers and across years of schooling build the potential for making a more significant impact. When teachers work together with shared goals, they help students develop understandings and strategies that can be celebrated and thus reinforced and applied in various settings. When teachers work together as interdisciplinary teams to understand their students' strengths and challenges, they develop approaches that help students connect to, process, transform, and personalize important concepts and thinking skills. Their schools become learning communities, the most important unit of change.

All Teachers, All Subjects

Over the years, we have worked with elementary, middle, and secondary school teachers and staff to develop "thinking classrooms." We believe that every classroom should be a thinking classroom, a place where students get to

- access and use their prior knowledge
- process and make connections among ideas
- personalize and transform what they have learned

We want engaged, meaning-making, critical, and self-regulating thinkers. The behaviours developed in thinking classrooms are relevant in all disciplines and in all jobs in the world. They are used by writers, mechanics, statisticians, actors, chemists, translators, cooks, parents, taxi drivers, grocers … the list goes on.

As well, to participate in a democratic society, all citizens have to use what they know to make sense of new situations, keep their minds open to new possibilities, make decisions when considering multiple sources of information, and reflect on their beliefs and actions using their increasing understandings. We see schools and classrooms as places where students are apprenticed into this way of being in the world. We want to nurture their thinking skills, building from what they already bring us, rather than thwart their creativity and individuality. We want our students to participate in authentic learning activities that contribute to their future choices and potential to participate in the world.

To create authentic and coherent learning opportunities for diverse classrooms, teachers benefit from working together to plan lessons and units of study. Teachers focus on aligning formative assessment, instruction, learning sequences, and summative assessment. In using their combined knowledge and expertise, they can better engage and support our diverse learners to simultaneously learn key concepts and develop learning strategies (Smith and Wilhelm 2006; Wilhelm 2007).

How Can We Work Together to Best Meet the Needs of Diverse Learners?

We believe that when individual teachers make time to understand and build from the learning profiles of their students, they can make a difference in the school success of those students and thus in their life opportunities. In particular, we know that, when teachers use information from formative assessments to set goals, make plans, and involve students in developing specific strategies and practices, students and teachers get better at what they are doing.

Much of what we have learned comes from working with elementary, middle, and secondary staffs to develop approaches to better support their learners. To explain this work and situate it in research, we refer again to the Carnegie Corporation's *Reading Next: A Vision for Action and Research in Middle and High School Literacy* (2004) and the six "infrastructural improvements," or school-wide factors that it recommends.

1. Extended time for literacy

When you stop to think, it is just common sense that a person becomes better at something with practise. But someone had to describe that in detail. In fact, Malcolm Gladwell (2008) calls this general rule of success "the 10,000 hour rule." Ten thousand hours is the probable number of hours that any expert has spent in practice in order to develop expertise in his field. Reading, writing, and, yes, thinking are skills — and you become a better reader, a better writer, and a better thinker the more you engage in — that is — practise these skills.

This is particularly true for reading and writing in the content areas. None of the approaches described in chapter 1 could make much difference if students had no opportunities to read, to write, to analyze, and to discuss texts that could contribute to learning the subjects they study. You can see what teachers, teams, and schools value by what actually goes on in the classrooms. If we want students to become better readers, writers, and thinkers, then we have to set up opportunities for them to develop and practise strategies that help them learn about increasingly complex ideas by using increasingly complex texts.

The *Reading Next* experts suggest that students need two to four hours of literacy-connected learning daily. Within this time period, teachers are to focus on direct, explicit instruction in which they model particular thinking skills and embed them in content-area learning. For example, teachers might choose to focus on comparing perspectives within a Social Studies unit. They model the process by assuming first one point of view, then an opposing view, and still another that is in between. Then, they help students practise comparing perspectives on the same or a different issue. As follow-up, they ask students to help decide on the criteria for assessing this particular skill in an assignment that they will complete independently. This process is essential because it takes time to gradually release strategy instruction so that students learn to read and then write in the style of the scientists or historians or writers or actors whom they have been reading and discussing. We believe that students can develop these thinking skills while they are learning the content. The two go hand in hand. They need the thinking skills to access and explore the concepts at the heart of the discipline. In order to help develop literacy within a discipline, students need extended time to engage in reading and writing activities throughout a unit of study. Experts agree that such literacy activities help students think deeply about the concepts, themes, and issues through the differing perspectives of the disciplines (Alvermann 2001; Smith and Wilhelm 2006).

When we work together to integrate planning, assessment, and instruction, we can use our shared expertise to create engaging learning activities for students and plan how students' reading, writing, and thinking abilities will be used and developed over the course of a unit. Our collaborative efforts to build in the time for students to learn strategies and to identify the big ideas in a discipline through reading and writing help them demonstrate both their knowledge and their skills more successfully by the end of a unit of study.

In summary, research studies related to extending the time for literacy learning suggest that adolescent learners thrive when teachers

- increase the amount of reading and writing that students engage in to develop their skills as strategic learners
- organize instructional time and activities so that students are actually reading and writing in class
- develop text sets on a topic so that students have an opportunity to choose from books and resources of varying format, content, and reading level
- model and apprentice "thoughtful literacy," which requires students to think about what they have just read, what they have written, or what they have acted upon, and explain or describe their thinking
- design opportunities for students to use and demonstrate the knowledge and skills they have built over the course of a unit of study

2. Professional development

Ongoing professional development significantly helps teachers reflect on their students' learning profiles, uncover trends of strength and challenge within the class or the grade, and design a plan that incorporates approaches that build student engagement and lead to active, strategic, and self-regulated learning. Effective professional development must continue over time for teachers to develop, explore, and integrate ideas and practices that support the development of their students' literacies. One-time workshops are out. Working together over time to understand and support students and their learning is in!

We know that sustained, collaborative, inquiry-based professional development can help teachers develop new understandings and approaches. For individual schools and school districts to make a difference in student learning, the best approach is to set up ongoing professional development activities in which teachers learn collaboratively. The *Reading Next* panel advocates professional development activities that include "opportunities to implement and reflect upon new ideas ... and help school personnel create and maintain a team-oriented approach to improving instruction and structures that promote better adolescent literacy" (20). This means having many opportunities where teachers use what they know about their students, the content of the curriculum, and their research in order to plan, try out, and reflect upon approaches that they helped choose, create, and adapt. Research and research-based methods and approaches are offered as possibilities to be explored in relation to other factors. This is different from suggesting that a generic approach (i.e., an instructional strategy) will work the same way in different classrooms. Instead, teachers need opportunities to look at formative assessment information, set goals together, and select, plan, or adapt related ideas and approaches. When professional development activities also offer repeated opportunities for teachers to work together to reflect on how things are going, they are better able to make the curriculum more accessible while building students' reading, writing, and thinking skills (also see Butler and Schnellert 2008).

3. Ongoing formative and summative assessment of student learning and programs

When our formative and summative assessment activities are linked to the content and strategies we teach, we can reflect on whether or not our teaching is making a difference for our students by examining student progress against criteria. Without assessment information that focuses on key thinking skills, it is difficult to support student learning or to examine the effect of particular pedagogical approaches. When we see our students successfully learning and developing the thinking skills that we have been working on, we can target new thinking skills. When we see that things are not progressing as expected, we plan and teach new ways to help students develop the thinking skills we have been working on. Paying careful attention to our students' work helps us to be very specific in our goal-setting and to focus our planning and teaching on helping all students move forward in their learning.

Within the units we teach, we include our students in examining or developing the criteria used for assessing. Summative assessments should allow students to show what they have learned about the key content of a discipline and the skills they have developed over the course of a unit. When we focus our assessments on the most important concepts and the related thinking skills that we have targeted, the focus of instruction shifts from teachers covering content to "students making meaning and developing deep understandings." (In chapter 3, we discuss formative and summative assessments in greater detail, particularly how we can use them to support all students in their learning.)

Teaching teams and schools should engage collaboratively in cycles of assessing, planning, goal-setting, doing, reflecting, and adjusting (Schnellert, Butler, and Higginson 2008). They then can use meaningful data from formative assessment at the school level, such as a fall performance-based assessment of reading or writing (see chapter 3) to set grade- or school-wide long-term goals that are specific to the students. A teaching team focused on one grade might set one shared goal for student learning (e.g., determining importance) and the individual teachers might set another more class-specific goal (e.g., supporting responses with relevant details).

Performance-based assessments of reading and writing are often used formatively in the fall to target thinking skills, then summatively in the spring to gauge student progress. They help schools track the students' improvement, and they provide the teaching staff with specific information to help plan future professional development activities and to consider what additional goals might be set for the next year or mid-year.

Both types of assessment are meaningful at multiple levels. Teachers can use them to assess individual progress toward learning-centred goals for individuals, classes, grades, and schools. They can use them to plan appropriate supports for students and teachers. When we use formative assessments as descriptive feedback for our teaching, we teach more responsively. When we look at formative assessments, we ask ourselves What is working? What is not working? and What is the plan? Summative assessments provide information about what individual students have internalized and can do independently. The information that these assessments provide differs from that provided through formative assessments. The information provides a synthesis of the number or percentage of students achieving at different levels related to specific school, grade, and classroom goals. Grade-specific or school-wide assessments that are administered in the early spring provide teaching teams and schools with evidence of student progress, useful for establishing school goals for the fall and data to teachers in the classroom to inform their instructional goals and provide descriptive feedback to students for the remainder of the spring term.

One of the most important things that we have learned is that teachers and students are integral to making assessments meaningful and useful. Whenever possible, teachers and students need opportunities to reflect on assessments so that meaningful classroom and school decisions can be made.

4. Teacher teams

The *Reading Next* panel of experts point out that as students get older and move from primary to junior/intermediate to middle and, finally, to the secondary years, they have to relate to more and more teachers as their curriculum evolves into distinct disciplines. Students' experiences of schooling may end up fractured and confusing at an age when they crave interrelatedness. Does your school's structure support coordinated instruction? Are there interdisciplinary teams? Teachers do not have to teach in similar styles to coordinate what they do and to reinforce key thinking skills and approaches. Adolescents bring rich literacy practices and understandings into their later years of schooling because, in early years, literacy was at the forefront and lessons and units were often integrated. Yet, as students move into discrete subject areas, they often do not tap into their full skill sets. A common challenge in learning is applying and adapting what you know and are newly capable of doing to new or different settings and situations.

Teachers working in teams can identify the thinking skills that students need in order to expand or develop. By coordinating their efforts, teachers can visualize how shared goals for shared students can be refined in their specific subject classes. While teamwork promotes higher collegiality and staff communication across disciplines, it also helps ensure that the students do not receive conflicting messages about learning or fall between the cracks from class to class.

The importance of collaborating should not be underestimated. Working together to develop community-minded classrooms, where all kinds of learning styles are not only welcome but celebrated, takes flexibility and planning. We have worked with a number of schools that have focused their energies on designing learning experiences both to help students develop targeted thinking skills and to invite them to use their prior knowledge, interests, and talents as a way to connect to and personalize new content. You will see several of these examples in the later chapters of this book—from Leyton's and Linda's field books and field notes, in which students start by examining their own experiences, to Stacey's and Lisa's literature circles and Kathy's information circles within an inquiry unit. In each of these examples, teachers worked together to develop and share ideas related to increasing student engagement and learning. Working together helped sustain teachers' belief in their innovations, and sharing their expertise resulted in units of study that are more accessible for more students. Embedded within these co-planned units are key criteria or, using Hourcade and Bauwens' terminology, "high standards." We set the expectation that all students can learn and improve from wherever they start. From these expectations, teachers target their teaching while personalizing the experience for students by having them work toward the criteria and receive descriptive feedback.

Grade-wide teaching teams can make a significant difference in student learning. Teachers who meet regularly as teams increase coherence for students moving from class to class and help them make connections across subject areas (*Reading Next*). By using formative assessment information and looking for links between curricular areas, teachers can develop and reinforce the same thinking skills in all subject areas.

In classrooms where teachers work together—learning resource teachers and classroom teachers co-teaching, literacy coaches and classroom teachers working together, two classroom teachers combining their classes—we see more students getting support when they need it. In collaborative classrooms, inclusion is not a special education model; it is a school model, and it is different from pull-out models of support. The emphasis is on designing learning experiences so that more students have more success in each individual classroom. As professionals, we want to constantly examine and refine our practice. By working together, we discover what does and does not work and can adapt our instruction in real time. When collaborative teaching is ongoing (i.e., when teachers work together weekly), we always build in five to 15 minutes to debrief and to determine how a lesson went and to plan ahead. We have found that collaborative problem-solving and teaching result in new ideas, new or better thematic units, and a feeling of connection with colleagues. Working together, teachers can develop lessons and activities that reach more learners. Most importantly, we design learning sequences that better engage our students while we become more strategic in our teaching.

5. Leadership

Many an initiative lives or dies based on the support of a principal or superintendent who fulfills a key responsibility—that of instructional leader. Their participation in the school community is crucial. Collaborating with teachers in their classrooms, covering a teacher's class so that he or she can co-teach or co-plan with a colleague, and sitting in on grade-wide planning meetings are ways that administrators can help teachers as they work together to improve student learning. A leader in education has to keep up to date with practice and research by attending professional development activities with staff and taking part in professional book clubs. Principals who teach or co-teach a class and who publicly share their own process of revising and integrating their planning with instruction and formative and summative assessment support the development of the school as a learning community. The practice of principals' promoting and participating in teacher learning and development activities has a more profound impact on student learning than any other practice (Robinson 2007). To develop collaborative, community-minded classes that are focused on learning, school leaders need to participate in staff learning communities. Both formal and informal leaders play a key role in modelling learning.

Similarly, teacher-leaders must take a collaborative, learning-centred approach to professional development and curricular innovation. Literacy coaches, consultants, and department heads follow the same approach; they model and contribute to a culture of professional learning. Working in this way honours a range of teacher philosophies and styles. We recommend that leaders openly share what they are learning and how they are developing their own practices. Within this context, more opportunities arise for educators to collaboratively establish instructional goals as colleagues, allowing for each professional to have input.

6. A comprehensive and coordinated literacy program

The first five *Reading Next* "infrastructural improvements," or school-wide factors, should be part of a school's comprehensive and coordinated literacy program. Extended time for literacy requires teachers to build reading, writing, and thinking activities into their units of study. Cross-curricular teams are needed in order to make thinking skills a priority across classrooms. Targeting a few thinking skills based on formative assessment information allows students and teachers to focus on developing and integrating them into content learning. Deep-content learning is possible when these strategies are used.

Coming together regularly to share information and plans and to problem-solve is the behaviour of a learning community—that is, one that values all members as well as their efforts and questions. Developing a vision and goals for students and a range of approaches that support student learning must be a shared process. A comprehensive plan informed by research must be developed and refined over time. When teachers and leaders take part in this process, their innovation has an impact beyond a single classroom.

Final Thoughts

Experts agree that schools and cross-curricular teaching teams working together on shared goals can make a significant difference. Both the schools and the teams should establish these shared goals using data from formative assessments that

- focus on developing students as active, independent learners
- can be embedded in content teaching
- are shared by teachers across classes and subjects
- are shared with and reflected on by the students themselves
- are maintained and sustained across one or more years

The data from the end-of-year summative assessment can then be used to reflect on and refine team efforts and set new goals for the next year.

Some of the richest examples of successful implementation of shared goals involve collaborative teaching among classroom teachers and among classroom and support teachers (e.g., resource teachers, librarians, literacy coaches). These co-teaching arrangements are based on a shared ownership of the goal to improve student learning and lead to richer professional learning for the teachers involved. There are so many ways to collaborate! (Samples of collaborative scenarios, of teachers working together to support student learning in the best ways possible, are found in chapters 5 through 12.)

Chapter 3

Assessment that Supports Learning

By adopting the "assessment for learning" techniques that focus on the learners, teachers will find that their students' performance will improve because they are more likely to see themselves as learners. More students will be successful in achieving the curricular outcomes as the teachers learn how to target their lessons and help the students identify problem areas in their own work. (Clarke, Owens, and Sutton 2006)

Mention the word *assessment* and most teachers and students think of marks. Students check out their marks, compute their averages, compare their marks with each other. Unfortunately, receiving and examining marks is not what most affects student learning. We are in the business of learning. Our assessment practices should reflect this. The driving purpose of formative assessment is to inform teachers' instruction and students' learning. As Black et al. (2003) state, "formative assessment is a process, one in which information about learning is *evoked* and then *used* to modify the teaching and learning activities in which teachers and students are engaged."

To understand the two major types of assessment practices, we have adapted the summation chart below, prepared by Caren Cameron (BCELC, . Sept. 2007) that succinctly describes them.[1]

---

1. Some researchers (Earle) differentiate a third category of assessment—assessment *as* learning. We combine *for* and *as* in recognition that our ultimate goal is *for* the student to understand his role *as* a learner. We aim to involve students as much as possible in the learning process which, in our opinion, includes assessment of progress.

Figure 3.1 Assessment Practices

	Assessment OF Learning (summative assessment)	Assessment FOR Learning (formative assessment)
Purpose	Report out, summative assessment, measure learning	Guide instruction, improve learning
Audience	Parents and public	Teachers and students
Timing	At the end	Minute by minute, day by day, at the beginning
Form	Letter grades, rank order, percentages, scores	Descriptive feedback

As mentioned in chapters 1 and 2, the authors of the *Reading Next* study synthesized their findings by presenting 15 areas for educators to focus on in order to improve adolescent literacy. Our favourite quote from this study is the mathematical equation $15 - 3 = 0$ which, according to the authors, means that, without three of the 15 key focus areas, significant change in student achievement is unlikely. The three key areas are

1. **Ongoing professional development.** We must work together, over time, engaged in goal-directed, professional conversations about student work.
2. **Summative assessment.** Assessment *of* learning that helps us see whether the changes we make in our instructional practices indeed have an impact on our students' learning.
3. **Formative assessment.** Assessment *for* learning that is embedded in regular teaching practices and encourages students to develop independence as learners.

Both assessment *of* learning and assessment *for* learning are important. They serve different purposes. We have to include both in our teaching.

Assessment OF Learning

Assessment of learning (AOL) is that which takes place at the end of a unit of study when students either take a test or complete a project or performance in order to demonstrate what they have learned. This is not the assessment that most improves student learning. Teachers use the marks collected from these tests or projects to calculate a student's final grade for a report card. Like snapshots, the marks say, "At this particular point in time, based on the evidence we have collected, and against these criteria or this standard, we can say how much you have learned." Marks represent a way of telling others the measurement of a student's learning.

Different kinds of feedback

If assessment of learning is the main form of assessment used, then student learning is not maximized because the marks come too late to impact their learning. Marks describe how much has been learned, not what has been learned and what still needs to be learned. Students need this feedback about learning while they are still engaged in the learning activity so that they may use it to improve. Teachers also need feedback on how their students are doing so that they may adjust their teaching to address the gaps in their students' learning. Every experienced teacher knows that just making a lesson plan does not guarantee that the lesson will work—or that it will work in the same way with each class. The learning process varies from student to student and from class to class, and both the leaders and the learners need personal feedback along the way as part of the teaching/learning process, not the feedback that comes after the fact that was provided by marks and scores.

Assessment FOR Learning

When teachers shift to spending more time on assessment *for* learning (AFL, or formative assessment) and less time on assessment *of* learning (summative), they still collect marks, but usually fewer marks. Using the time they would normally use for marking, teachers give descriptive feedback during the learning, when students can put the information to use. They do not give marks when assessing for learning; they give descriptive feedback. The more immediate and appropriate the feedback, the more likely the student will use it.

Michael Smith and Jeff Wilhelm (2002, 2006) suggest that we think of the feedback students receive when they play a video game. The players receive exactly what they need to know in order to progress. Teachers want to give to their students feedback that is immediate (while students are still engaged in the work of learning), timely (when they need it and can use it), and personal (what they need, not what someone else might need). When the feedback is immediate, timely, and personal, student progress is enhanced.

AFL strategies

We use six specific strategies when assessing for learning based on the work of Black, et al. (2003).[2]

1. Learning Intentions

Learning intentions tell students what they can expect to learn—during this class, during the next learning sequence, during the unit. They are posted for students and teachers' reference. Teachers articulate the learning intentions and frame them as "I will…" or "I can…" statements, allowing students to more easily own the statements. For example, in a grade 6/7

---

2. Webcasts focusing on these strategies are available at <bcelc.org>.

English Language Arts classroom where students are working on reading and responding to poetry, the learning intentions are:

- I can read a variety of poems and explain my thinking in a small group discussion.
- I can write a personal response to a poem.

With this clarity of learning intention, it is possible for all students to keep their eye on the ball and work in a goal-directed way.

2. Criteria

Criteria describe to students what a powerful performance (one that works well) or product will look like. They are best developed with the students, using examples either of published work or of work produced by the students themselves. In an English Language Arts classroom where students read and respond to poetry, the process for building criteria requires several steps:

- Choose three or four student responses to poetry that the class can examine. Choose diverse student samples, each exhibiting different strengths.
- Discuss these responses with the class, focusing only on the strengths, never on criticism.
- After the discussion, ask students to write down their individual criteria for what a written response should include.
- Then have them choose their top three criteria.
- Move the students into groups of three or four to discuss and decide on three common criteria.
- Then have each small group present their top criteria to the whole class.
- Have students work with the criteria to categorize them and make a summary list.
- Add another criterion if the students have not identified an aspect of the curriculum that should be addressed.
- Work with the class for several days to ensure that their list of criteria works.
- Then have students keep a copy of the criteria in their poetry response journals.
- Have students use the criteria during their work with poetry responses to self-assess, peer-assess, and set goals.

One grade 6/7 class generated the following set of criteria:
- connections
  - relating self to poem
  - showing how the poem changes your thinking
  - asking questions of the poem or poet
- opinions
  - expressing likes and dislikes about the poem, with evidence
- emotions
  - explaining why you feel the way you do about the poem and how you think the author feels about his/her subject

- image
  - commenting on the image formed in your mind upon reading the poem
- response style
  - using descriptive words
- using quotes from the poem
  - suggesting improvements to the poem, if needed

The picture book *Charlie's Checklist* (1997), a story by Rory S. Lerman with pictures by Alison Bartlett, is a great source for introducing your students to what criteria are and how to describe them.

3. Descriptive feedback

The backbone of assessment for learning is finding out what you need to know, when you need to know it. For the learner, descriptive feedback answers these three questions:

1. What's working?
2. What's not working?
3. What's next?

These questions guide our interactions with our students as we meet with them individually in a side-by-side conference, in a small group, or as a class.

In the grade 6/7 English Language Arts class, the students receive descriptive feedback from us as we read their poetry responses. We move around the class as students work, a highlighter in hand. The students signal when they would like a quick chat for some descriptive feedback. We ask if there is something in particular they want us to notice. With their response in mind, we highlight several examples of What's working? in the student's response. Then we help him or her decide on one aspect that is not working and together we negotiate a quick plan for What's next?—that is, how to deal with What's not working?

We also collect the responses that we have not yet seen and respond to them in the same way so that all students receive descriptive feedback as quickly as possible—when they can still use the advice. If we notice a pattern in the What's not working? category, we teach a mini-lesson the next day either to the whole class or to the small group of students who need this instruction. Notice that giving descriptive feedback does not mean stopping teaching. When feedback is combined with effective instruction, student learning is enhanced (Hattie and Timperley 2007). Our response is guided by the learning intention that we established with the students and the criteria that we worked on together. Everything is explicit. Students practise responding and working with the criteria many times before any mark is assigned based on the criteria. There are no surprises.

4. Questioning

In a classroom that focuses on assessment for learning, teachers' questions are open-ended and invite reasoning. Teachers listen in a respectful way, intent on understanding the student's thinking and in engaging in real discourse. Students are invited to question themselves, to use their questions to guide their learning, and to kindle their curiosity. Questions are not used for control or for quick guess-my-thinking games. All students are included in the discourse, so strategies such as no-hands may be used—that is, students do not raise their hands to answer a question. Rather we pose a question, students discuss possible answers with a learning partner, and then we call randomly on different students to answer the question. This strategy increases student reasoning and participation in the lesson, because some students can become reliant on those students in the class who consistently raise their hands, answer the questions, and do the thinking for everyone. Just being physically present in the classroom does not ensure that a student is learning. Engagement in the learning process does.

In the grades 6/7 English Language Arts class, the students write their questions about the poem around the actual text of the poem before entering their small group conversations. Their questions are their entry into the conversation. They also pose questions about their own responses as they use the criteria. They, too, are reflecting on their work, considering What's working? What's not working? and What's next? Consider our teacher question What should I notice about your response today? This question gives ownership to the student, invites his or her participation in the assessment process, and leaves the control with the learner. The learners are leading the learning; the teacher is following the learners' lead.

5. Self-assessment and peer-assessment

Students need to be involved as much as possible in the work of becoming the best learner they can be. This requires that they clearly understand the task, the learning intention, and what achievement will look like—that is, the criteria. When these are explicit and we model how to work with the criteria, with descriptive feedback, and with open-ended questioning, students can successfully assess one another's work. They follow the same guidelines that we have been modelling:

- Work with the end in mind.
- Use the criteria as a reference point for what it should look like.
- Frame your descriptive feedback around the same three questions: What's working? What's not working? What's next?
- Invite a conversation with your peers; do not take control and tell.

As students work with peer-assessment, we are there to guide the practice and coach as necessary. Student conversations are authentic and helpful, so performance improves as each student now has many more opportunities for feedback. When all feedback comes from the teacher, the odds of getting enough and just when you need it are not great! Ultimately, the student is self-assessing as he works, which is where the real locus of learning is. Learners carry with them the ability to tell whether what they are doing is getting them what they want.

In the grade 6/7 class, we began by having all peer-assessment happen simultaneously, after each student had had two quick conferences with us and after they had examined and described our feedback conversations. Students understood the process and were able and keen to participate. With their continued practice, their responses improved, and their ability to pinpoint for us where they would like our feedback—that is, What should I notice?—became more and more precise. Instead of a student asking "Is this okay?" they began to make comments like "I think I made good connections with the poem, but I don't know if you can tell why I liked it. Is there enough evidence?"

6. Ownership

The agent of learning is the student. When students are clear about the expectations, know how to participate, and recognize that their voices are valued in the process and that they are the ultimate consumers, they work harder. All the strategies of assessment for learning are geared toward inviting students in, toward giving them informed control, toward working with them to help students be the best they can be.

In the grade 6/7 class, our question "What do you want me to notice about your work?" centres the conversation on the students. They own their learning. Our job is to help. We students and teachers are in this together.

Assessment for learning—a grand event

Most assessment for learning occurs day by day, minute by minute, in the classroom. However, we also advocate a grand event formative assessment that is not a daily occurrence. As described in *Student Diversity* (1998; 2006), the Standard Reading Assessment is a performance-based assessment that helps teachers collect information about their students' reading that they can use to inform their teaching. Many schools administer this performance-based reading assessment early in the year or early in the term. They examine the results of the assessment to find areas of strength and challenge for the group of students. This is not an assessment for marks. The trends established from the assessment are used to help target specific areas of instruction. Repeating the assessment at a later date—another grand event—helps teachers monitor the effectiveness of their instruction, get feedback, and make new teaching plans.

When conducting the assessment, teachers

- choose a passage (usually from a text they plan to use)
- build some background knowledge with their students
- set a purpose for reading
- pose several open-ended questions
- listen to students read orally and have a short interview with them

When coding the assessment, teachers

- code individual responses by highlighting descriptors
- examine individual quick scales to find a pattern common to the class
- set class goals, based on the patterns of strengths and needs of the class

When planning with the assessment information, teachers

- share the strengths and goals with the class
- choose strategies to teach that help students achieve the goals

Notice that this is another form of descriptive feedback. The assessment sets up a class picture that answers the questions for this particular snapshot.

Using the information gathered from the third descriptive feedback question What's next? informs subsequent planning. This is a curriculum-based assessment, created around the grade level expectations for proficient reading—that is, reading literature, reading for information, or reading poetry. It is a snapshot of independent, thoughtful reading. The passage is not tied directly to the content currently being taught. The intent is to see if students are independently and thoughtfully applying the skills and strategies for reading that are required—at this particular grade level, in this particular subject.

There are several different ways to use this performance-based assessment. In Tait Elementary School, the assessment is scheduled five times a year. The year-long school calendar highlights the five assessment weeks. During these weeks, teachers choose a 75-minute period in which to conduct their assessment. Resource teachers, librarians, administrators, or any other non-enrolling teachers sign up to conduct the assessment in the classroom, co-assessing with the classroom teacher. No teacher is alone in her classroom while conducting the assessment. Within the next two weeks, time is arranged for the staff members to code the assessments together. A copy of the grade-level Quick Scale of the provincial performance standard is copied for each student. Teachers meet in teams to highlight on the performance standard what they have noticed about each student's work. Once each student's work has been recorded, a class summary is also created, noting the strengths of the class and the areas of need. While the staff is together, the classroom teachers report on what they notice about their class as a whole, what their area of focus is, and what strategies they plan to use in addressing this area. The collaboration creates a climate in which shared learning is valued.

The assessments occur early in September, in November before report cards, in January, in March before report cards, and in May. Each assessment follows the same pattern: co-assessing, co-coding, and sharing the results and plans. The cycles of assessment allow teachers to see whether their teaching has made a difference in the students' learning. They can comment in the students' report cards on the growth they have perceived, but they do not record the assessment results as letter or number grades; rather, they prepare descriptive comments.

During the end-of-the-year assessment, some schools choose to change the descriptive comments to a numerical rating (depending on the rubric being used) as summative information. The staff can then examine this information to determine whether they have reduced, over time, the number of students who achieved below expectations and whether more students are achieving higher levels of proficiency. It is important to pause in our teaching to see whether we are, indeed, making a difference in our efforts to achieve our own goals.

In middle school or secondary school, the incoming group of students is typically assessed on their content-area reading. Again, a schedule is established among the teams of teachers who conduct the assessment. Together, the staff meet on a professional development morning to code the papers and to establish a profile of their incoming students—their areas of strength and their areas of need. The staff then moves into departments to choose content-specific strategies to address the chosen area of student need. Some schools repeat their assessments in January and May, others repeat them only at the end of the year as a whole school; individual teachers conduct similar assessments more frequently with their own classes. Several questions are always asked: What is working? What can these students do? What is not yet working? What do these students need? What is my plan to address this need? Then, after the first assessment, Is my teaching making a difference?

In secondary school, a department or an individual teacher along with the resource teacher may create a performance-based assessment to guide their practice. The cycle of the assessment is determined by the teacher or the department, depending on how frequently they want to examine snapshots of their students' independent work. During the repeat assessments and in regular classroom practice, teachers may want to focus only on one or two questions in order to target particular areas on which they and the students are working. For example, at MacNeill Secondary School, teachers chose to use the section "The Rise of Islam" from their Social Studies text. The students had not yet studied these three pages of text, which also featured a map, several photos with captions, text sidebars, the chapter overview and a pre-reading guide. The teachers asked their students to write out their responses to the following questions:

- **Predicting:** What do you think the text will be about? How do you know?
- **Summarizing:** In a web, or in words, diagrams, or drawings, show clearly that you understand the main ideas and details of this text.
- **Connecting:** How does what you read connect with what you already know?
- **Vocabulary:** Give a brief definition for each of the following words: *adorned, pilgrimage, convert.* Also, please write a word from the text that you found challenging. What is its meaning?

- **Strategies:** What strategies did you use to determine the meaning of the words in the point above?
- **Making inferences:** Read between the lines to find something that you believe to be true but that isn't actually said. Explain your reasoning and support your opinion with the text.
- **Reflecting:** Was this activity easy or hard? Why? What did you do to help yourself understand? (If this was easy, what do you usually do to help yourself understand something more difficult?)

While the students worked on their responses, the teachers circulated and listened to each student read a short passage from the text aloud. Using an oral reading page (see Figure 3.2), teachers recorded the miscues they heard the students make, gave them a compliment on their oral reading, and circled one of the descriptors—*halting, careful, confident/fluent,* or *expressive.* They also asked them several questions:

- When you come to a challenging word, how do you figure it out?
- If your reading does not make sense, what do you do?
- What is this selection mainly about?
- What surprised you about this selection? Why?

Upon completion, the teachers met to work together and learn about their students. They discovered that their students had strengths in predicting and making connections but were less able in summarizing and working with main ideas and supporting details. Together they brainstormed known strategies to help develop their students' abilities to summarize and identify main ideas and details; then they chose the specific strategies that they would all work on with their students. As well, they established a date (allowing about eight weeks) when they would present another piece of the text to their students, ask them to summarize it, and to identify the key ideas and supporting details. Their plan allowed them to see whether their teaching had made a difference (using the independent sample of the assessment) and whether or not they could move on to another target area, based on ongoing classroom evidence as well as the independent assessment sample.

Figure 3.2 Sample assessment of student's oral reading of a text selection

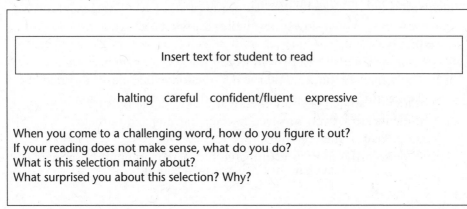

Insert text for student to read

halting   careful   confident/fluent   expressive

When you come to a challenging word, how do you figure it out?
If your reading does not make sense, what do you do?
What is this selection mainly about?
What surprised you about this selection? Why?

At Burnaby North Secondary School, teachers followed a similar process, choosing to assess their grades 8s and 9s in Social Studies. Upon completion of their descriptive coding, the administrator, Kevin Brandt, took a tally of the percentage of students in each of the four categories—Not Yet Within Expectations, Minimally Meeting Expectations, Fully Meeting Expectations, and Exceeding Expectations—in each of the bands of the performance standards: Strategies, Comprehension, and Analysis. As a literacy team, they then further broke down the areas of comprehension and analysis, and they chose one specific area in each on which to focus—Note-Taking and Making Inferences—for both grades 8 and 9. The team then took the results to the staff at a staff meeting and led a discussion of the stories behind the tally graphs they had prepared. Staff quickly noted that, in the previous year with their grade 8s, they had focused on students' personal use of the strategies Note-Taking and Making Inferences. This assessment showed that the grade 9s were able to describe the strategies that they had used three times more often when those students had been in grade 8. Teaching had made a difference! They also noticed that almost twice as many students in grade 9 as compared to this year's grade 8 students were proficient in Note-Taking and Making Inferences. They agreed with the literacy team that the results showed areas of need and that more students could improve, so they would continue with a grade-wide focus on these areas and use the six assessment-for-learning strategies (beginning page 25) in their classes on a more regular basis to improve student learning.

The research is very clear that assessment-for-learning strategies can have a profound effect on improving student learning (Black and Wiliam 1998; Black et al. 2003; Hattie and Timperley 2007). We believe that this is an area where we want to focus our energies.

A final note on AOL

It is possible to design and implement highly effective assessment-of-learning practices, practices that support all learners who are working in a differentiated environment. Having clear targets and support along the way are critical to this design if the students and teacher are to achieve these targets.

Many secondary schools have an end-of-year exam in English. For many students, this one-hour exam consists of multiple-choice questions with perhaps one or two questions requiring long answers. Johnston Heights in Surrey, BC, for example, is one school in which the teachers use a different form of final assessment—a two-week in-class project which, although it is also an assessment of learning, is based on the following learning principles:

- Students can demonstrate their learning in different ways.
- Students are actively involved in their learning and in their assessment of their learning.
- Students arrive at their learning with different amounts of support and time.

Such assessment of learning is tied to the ongoing learning in the class. Teachers report that their marking takes little time because they know their students' work so well. They have been reading over their students' shoulders and talking with them about their work for two weeks. Thus, in their classes, the learning overlap with assessment is seamless.

The teachers follow these guidelines:

- Allow five to eight 90-minute classes for the in-class project work.
- Allow one or two 90-minute classes for self-assessment and peer-assessment of the project.
- Ensure that students who have required regular additional assistance in the form of English-language support, resource support, additional time, or technological support have the same support on the project.
- Encourage the gathering of suitable short stories and poems outside of class time.

Each June after marking these final projects, the teachers reflect on the students' work and the final assessment project. They revise the project as necessary, in preparation for the students who will arrive in their classes the following September.

Barb Bathgate is one of these teachers. During the first week of school in September, she outlines for her grade-9 English class what they can expect in their final project. She explains that all the work they will do throughout the year in her class will help them show their best learning on the final project—the in-class exam. She explains that there will be no secrets or surprises. The exam has three parts: Part A—Oral Assessment; Part B—Writing Assessment; Part C—Project.

The following pages provide an example of Part C, in which the project, entitled "The Inner and Outer Self," involves the construction of a Sequence Book. The instructions for creating such a book from large-size construction paper are provided in BLM format on page 35. The second BLM on page 36, Self-Evaluation and Peer-Evaluation, provides Barb's criteria for the evaluation of the Sequence Book, first by the student writer, then by the writer's peers. This page provides room for only the first of the required five peer-evaluations. It would be best to copy the two instructional BLMs back-to-back and have the students prepare another page for the additional peer evaluations.

Pages 37–38 (BLMs) provide instructions in outline form of how students should prepare their written and representational responses to affix to the construction-paper flaps of their Sequence Book. Their responses should demonstrate what they have learned throughout the year from their reading of texts in the three genres. (Part C of the English Examination, "A Sequence Book Project," is reproduced with the permission of School District No. 36 [Surrey] BC.)

Name: _____

Class: _____

Date: _____

ENGLISH 9 FINAL EVALUATION
PART C: The Inner and Outer Self
A Sequence Book Project

Your final project in English 9 requires you to demonstrate your knowledge, understanding, and application of concepts and skills covered throughout the course. You are required to do this in the form of a Sequence Book. This book involves three genres: novels, short stories, and poetry. Each of these genres has four assignments to complete.

Follow these steps to make your Sequence Book:

Directions
1. Fold two pieces of construction paper in half lengthwise.
2. Use your ruler to measure and mark off three equal segments on each piece of construction paper.

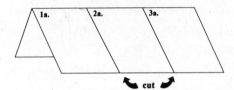

3. Cut along the marked lines to create flaps on which to paste your writing.

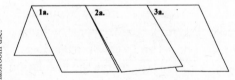

Self-Evaluation and Peer Evaluation

When evaluating a Sequence Book, take the following criteria into consideration:

- Content is original, creative, and engaging for the reader.
- Content includes required components for each section.
- Writing shows a sense of personal connection and thoughtful interpretation.
- Writing is clear and purposeful within the conventions of the form.
- Writer provides specific references to selections read.
- Writing contains few surface feature errors, which are noticeable only if looking for them.

Please give the Sequence Book a letter grade based on the above criteria and the descriptions that follow:

A   The Sequence Book is **outstanding** and meets all the criteria.

B   The Sequence Book is **very good** but could have been improved in one or two of the criteria areas.

C+ The Sequence Book is **good** but could have been improved in three of the criteria areas.

C   The Sequence Book is **satisfactory** but, with more thought and care, could have been improved in several criteria areas

C- The Sequence Book **just passes** the criteria—it is complete, but it is obvious that the writer did not put much thought and care into it.

F   The Sequence Book **does not meet any of the above criteria.**

Self-Evaluation   Name: _____

I give my project the following letter grade: _____

_____

My reasons are: _____

_____

_____

*Peer Evaluator #1   Name: _____

I give your project the following letter grade: _____

My reasons are: _____

_____

_____

* Please add another page with four more peer evaluations.

Novel		Short Stories		Poetry	
1a. Character Collage		**2a. Character Web**		**3a. Poetic Devices** (use 2-column notes)	

Make a collage of pictures that capture the essence of the character.
 	
Within the collage, include the protagonist's name, five adjectives that describe the character, and the title and author of the work.
		Include the protagonist's name, five adjectives that describe the character, and the title and author of the work.		Complete two of the devices below, with examples.
				
				                Examples
				
				Image _____
				
				              _____
				
				Mood _____
				
				              _____
				
				Symbol _____
				
				              _____	

1b. Perspectives: 2-column notes		**2b. Perspectives: 2-column notes**		**3b. Poetic Devices** Choose the two most important poetic devices used in the poem. Explain the effectiveness of the device.	
Perspective of Protagonist	Quotations (page)	Perspective of Protagonist:	Quotations (page)	#1 Quotation #1	
Perspective of Another Character	Quotations (page)	Perspective of Another Character	Quotations (page)	#2 Quotation #2	

Novel	Short Stories	Poetry
1c. BioPoem about the Character	**2c. Found Poem about the Character**	**3c. Write a Story**
1. First Name 2. Four traits that best describe character 3. Relative of _____ (brother, sister, cousin…) 4. Lover of _____ (three things or people) 5. Who feels _____ (three items) 6. Who needs _____ (three items) 7. Who fears _____ (three items) 8. Who gives _____ (three items) 9. Who would like to see _____ (three items) 10. Resident of _____ 11. Last name	Create a poem with words collected from or linked to your chosen character. Write approximately 300 words.	Write a story inspired by the poem. This could be a children's story, a fable, or a fairy tale.
1d. Personal Response to Character	**2d. Personal Response to Character**	**3d. Personal Response to Poem**
1. Tell how you feel about the character and what she/he has experienced. 2. Relate the character's experiences to something you know about from your own life or others' lives.	1. Tell how you feel about the character and what she/he has experienced. 2. Relate the character's experiences to something you know about from your own life or others' lives.	1. How does this poem relate to your own life or some other situation you know about? 2. Why would you recommend the poem to others?

The assessment in progress

Barb's students do their end-of-the-year English assessment during all class periods of the final two weeks of school. They do not take home their working papers, but they can read, research, talk, and think about what they are writing at any time out of class. In class, they work independently. Posted around the room are the examples and criteria for different response formats that the students have worked on during the year—Venn diagrams, webs and mind maps, paragraphs. As the students work, Barb moves about the room, answering questions, and providing resources and support as needed. The atmosphere is relaxed and intense. All of the students are engaged in their work. Two of the girls, who are on a week's after-school detention, take their project with them to the detention room after school. Three of the students, who have a scheduled block of time for learning assistance take their projects with them to the learning centre when they go. In both these instances, the students receive extra time and, in the latter instance, extra support.

Faye is visiting the class to observe this assessment. As she moves about the room and talks with individual students, she can uncover who might be labelled at risk for learning, who might have behaviour and/or attention issues, who is ESL, who has low written output, who thinks outside the boundaries, who is the extrovert, who is quietly hiding. The energy and productivity of the students is noticeable—it is a full class of engaged students, working to show their accomplishments. This project will reflect an authentic measure of learning.

Student feedback on the assessment

On their last day of school, students are asked to reflect on their final evaluation project (see Figure 3.3). Below, are some of their reflections:

Figure 3.3

You as a Learner

1. What part of the final assessment did you find the most challenging? Tell why.

2. What did you enjoy the most this year?

3. In your opinion, what English skills have you developed most this year? What do you need to continue working on next year?

4. What advice would you give to a student about to take this course?

5. What advice would you give to your teacher about this course?

Instead of a test, I liked the idea of a project better. I don't believe in the marking based on what we memorized instead of showing how well we can accomplish something using what we know. The whole project was okay but I felt squeezed when doing both a project and a speech at the same time.

The examples helped a lot. I didn't have to go crazy imagining what it's supposed to look like.

*The timeline was small. I believe we don't have enough time. We were not all into the project the first day. After that, I wrote at least two pages a day, which was a comfortable pace. My hand felt numb after each class.—*Amit

- *the project was fun to do—not a lot of pressure*
- *directions are easy to understand*
- *just enough time to finish*
- *overall, I think more work is being done this way, a more precise evaluation—rather than a single test—*Han

*I worked hard on this project. I didn't talk to anyone, focused and wrote till my hand hurt. I believe I connected the theme with all three genres well and chose the proper topics. The organization was all done on the first day (look at the back of direction page) and I kept up with the schedule. My written expression… I hope it got through. I spent time at home constructing the paragraphs in my head so I just had to write it down in class.—*Janelle

Chapter 4

Frameworks and Approaches to Support Diverse Learners

> If we don't insist on the value of what we teach, have faith in our students, and persist in our attempt to make the education connections, then our invitation tends to have a shallow and possibly false ring. (Liston 2004)

Teachers need to have a working model in mind when designing lesson sequences for a class of diverse learners, and there are a number of well-researched frameworks and approaches to draw on. The two frameworks we use to design lessons and units that engage and support all learners are Universal Design for Learning and Backward Design. In this chapter, we explain these two planning frameworks and six well-known and inclusive teaching approaches:

1. assessment for learning
2. open-ended strategies
3. gradual release of responsibility
4. cooperative learning
5. literature circles and information circles
6. inquiry

These approaches also address several of our key beliefs about teaching and learning:

- learning is both individual and social
- learning should be personally meaningful and authentic
- learning builds from prior experience and background knowledge
- students from grade 5 through grade 12 must learn to work with a range of different teachers who may use different instructional styles and may convey different messages

- students from grade 5 through grade 12 must learn subject content and the subject-related thinking strategies to engage with, remember, connect to, process, and synthesize the content

Universal Design for Learning

Universal Design for Learning, or UDL (Rose and Meyer 2002), is one framework we keep in mind when designing lessons and units. It can also be expressed as "designing learning to support all learners." This means that we design classroom activities that take into account the diverse strengths, challenges, and interests of all class members. We find that the accommodations we put into place for students with specific needs can benefit many other students' learning. Using the principles of UDL has moved us away from making a number of individual plans toward using approaches that offer multiple ways for all students to engage in learning, to access ideas, and to show their learning.

UDL originated in the field of architecture known as "universal design," when architects responded to the increasing demand to make the built world more accessible to all. Yes, most buildings were accessible to the majority of people, but not to all people. Although most people enter buildings by stairs, some people—people in wheelchairs, people on rollerblades, mothers pushing baby strollers—find stairs a barrier to access. The big idea of universal design is that structures, like buildings, should be planned and then built with the diverse population in mind, not just a generic, or "typical," person. By also taking into account the needs of those who are not "most people," architects can design structures that meet the needs of all people. Ramps not only help those in wheelchairs or strollers or on rollerblades but also benefit anyone who has trouble lifting with their knees, or carrying a box, or facing other unexpected and perhaps temporary challenges. When architects apply the principles of universal design, they plan multiple ways for people to access shelter, food, and water, meet with other people, or access resource people and services. Most individuals can, thus, benefit from these design features at any time in their lives.

These concepts of universal design can be applied to education as a response to the varied individual ways that students learn and the means by which they access learning. At its core, UDL is an acceptance of and respect for diversity. It goes beyond physical barriers, taking into account students' sensory and cognitive needs. Rather than the perspective that we should "fix" children because they do not learn in a particular way, UDL takes a student-centred approach, by redesigning the curriculum. This means designing many ways to engage students, many ways for them to access and process information, and many ways for them to express what they know and learn. We achieve this by using curricular materials and activities that provide multiple paths for students with differing strengths, interests, and abilities.

These alternatives are *built into* the instructional design of educational materials; they are not added on after the fact. Universal design principles can apply to assignments, classroom discussions, group work, handouts, web-based instruction, and even lectures or demonstrations.

Three guiding principles

There are three guiding principles of universal design as outlined in the paragraphs that follow. Within a particular unit of instruction and depending on the needs of our students, we might focus on one principle more than another.

1. Multiple means to tap into learners' interests and background knowledge to activate prior knowledge and increase engagement and motivation

Chapters 5 to 12 offer ways to tap into learners' interests and background knowledge; in chapter 5, for example, Linda and Leyton use a variety of connecting strategies to help students access and link their prior knowledge and experiences to the key concepts and approaches they study during a unit. The activities they devise encourage their students to use personal experience and background knowledge to engage with the content; the teachers can then tailor subsequent activities to build from what students already know and believe. For example, their process of inviting students to find, describe, and interpret personal artifacts supports both a shared and an individual process of learning and discovery. To build students' repertoire of reading, writing, and thinking strategies, they start by inviting students to draw from their individual interests and experiences, then move to the shared curriculum content. Students have a variety of their own personal experiences to draw from. Moving from personal artifacts to family artifacts and introducing concepts like *backstory*, teachers invite students to use their own personal and family artifacts to study the impact of various factors on key events in society and history.

2. Multiple means for students to acquire the information and knowledge that can help them process new ideas and information

Chapter 6 illustrates how teachers use multiple approaches to help students explore a key concept while at the same time developing thinking strategies. Mehjabeen, Krista, and Leyton planned a unit that led students to examine how hope, knowledge, or friendship can contribute to the survival and strength of the human spirit. Like Lisa's and Stacey's students in chapter 10, and Kathy's students in chapter 9, the students in Krista's and Mehjabeen's classrooms had many opportunities to learn how various characters survive difficult events and periods in their lives. By using a read-aloud text, all students had access to a shared text. Reading this text aloud reduced perceptual barriers for some students. Collecting information and ideas related to the theme of survival, then discussing them with one another, gave students another way to process ideas. Graphic organizers that students could use to organize their thoughts about the information collected offered them yet another way to acquire ideas and knowledge.

Literature circles provided a different entry into the topic. As students moved through the unit, they chose books related to the same themes and discussed how what they were learning related back to other texts. The books spanned a range of lengths, settings, and protagonists. Offering students a range of texts to choose from helped them not only to access and engage with key ideas but also to practise targeted thinking strategies many times over. (Terry's online literature circles described in chapter 12 also provide a further extension of ways into a topic.)

3. Multiple means for students to express what they know

We offer students a range of ways to show what they know. However, we also realize that we need to actually introduce and develop their ability to show their learning in this range of ways. By the midpoint of a school year, Leyton and Linda (chapter 5) have introduced and developed, and students have practised, three or four ways to show what they know—critical timelines, concept maps, dramatizations, writing-in-role. Thus, students can choose a way to demonstrate their learning in a way that works best for them. In chapter 11, Catriona helps students develop their understanding of and strategies for creating a PowerPoint presentation. Students build criteria as a class, give one another descriptive feedback, and revise their presentations using this feedback. Catriona also develops students' oral presentation strategies at the same time. She uses students' oral, visual, and written communications to assess students' thinking strategies and understanding of key geography-related concepts. Students who struggle to communicate in one modality have the opportunity to share their understandings in more than one way. Students have learned how to process information and express what they know in multiple ways and, as a result, Catriona has a better sense of what they have learned and what she should focus on next.

We use UDL because it acknowledges and accepts diversity as a reality and strength, and it helps us to plan and organize for teaching and learning with diversity in mind.

Backward Design

Planning and teaching with both students and content in mind

Teaching in the Humanities requires us to determine important ideas and enduring understandings and what thinking strategies students will need in order to demonstrate these understandings. There is much that we can focus on—for example, interesting details, layers and layers of facts and perspectives—but deep learning needs to be rooted in a few core concepts. By *core concepts* we mean a big idea that can be used to link all the information in a unit.

When we focus teaching and learning on core concepts, students can build connections between ideas and see them as interrelated components of a bigger concept. In classrooms where meaningful, authentic, and concept-oriented learning occurs, students develop enduring understandings by relating ideas from the texts they are studying to their prior knowledge and to society. To do this, we need to determine what is most important for students to learn and then design learning sequences that explicitly teach the thinking skills they need.

We find the Backward Design approach of Wiggins and McTighe (2001) to be a helpful framework to focus our planning, assessment, and instruction so that we can build both the thinking strategies and the content knowledge of all students. Backward Design involves four key elements:

1. identify key concepts from learning outcomes and organize lessons and learning sequences around the enduring understandings that we want students to develop by the end of a unit of study
2. identify what thinking strategies students need to develop and use to complete learning tasks and, in particular, for summative assessments
3. align formative and summative assessments so that students know what is expected of them
4. explicitly teach and assess thinking strategies as part of a unit of study so that students become increasingly successful learners

In chapter 8, you will meet Dave and Julie Anne. Like many teachers, they often find that their students see Social Studies as a collection of facts, dates, people, and events. Julie Anne and Dave want their students to realize that there are enduring understandings to be learned from finding and examining *connections* between the facts. Most importantly, they want their students to learn how to construct interpretations and support their ideas with logical reasoning, as experienced historians, lawyers, anthropologists, and geographers do.

The chapters that follow present examples of teachers working together. Together, they decide what is most important for students to learn and do, and then support students in developing understandings that are at the heart of the curriculum in English Language Arts and in Social Studies. Because these understandings are not grade-specific, it is easy to take the lesson sequences in the following pages and adapt them for another grade. Chapters 5, 8, 9, 11, and 12 all work with concepts and thinking strategies that span intermediate, middle, and secondary years of the curriculum. Chapters 6, 7, 10, and 12 bring the big ideas of Social Studies/Humanities into English Language Arts classrooms to anchor student learning of thinking strategies.

These big ideas are issues and understandings that require "un-coverage" —that is, when the students build their understanding bit by bit. The issues do not have simple answers. They require critical thinking. Thus, students must use thinking strategies to make sense of how real and fictional events and factors relate to each other. To develop the thinking strategies required of writers, historians, anthropologists, linguists, archivists, and geographers, we need to be engaged in a process of meaning-making. Learning in the Humanities requires these thinking strategies; teaching in the Humanities requires teachers to determine what the important ideas and enduring understandings are, what thinking strategies the students need in order to demonstrate these understandings, and then to explicitly teach students how to develop these strategies.

To begin:

- Look at the curriculum for related learning outcomes.
- Discuss what is most important for students to know and do in the unit.
- Brainstorm the big ideas to explore during the unit by linking the various things that are important for students to know and do.

We use just a few simple questions to guide our planning.

- **Planning:** What do I want my students to know and do by the end of the unit?
- **Assessment:** How will I know that they have developed these understandings and thinking strategies?
- **Instruction:** How will I engage students in constructing understandings and developing key strategies?

For example, in chapter 7, Joanne uses a memoir as a summative assessment that links to four enduring understandings for the unit—two process-based, two idea-based:

1. Effective communicators use a variety of strategies to share, construct, and clarify meaning.
2. Authors make revisions in order to clarify meaning.
3. People "draw the line" between truth and lies at different places, for different reasons.
4. We need to decide for ourselves where to draw our lines between truth and lies.

Joanne spends the unit working with her students so that they can show what they have learned about the line between truth and lies. They read many texts on this topic and engage in many activities requiring response, discussion, and analysis. She also teaches students mini-lessons related to memoirs, elements of form and style, and the writing process. All students have a chance to make meaning, develop understandings about truth and lies, and develop strategies that help them communicate these ideas through a memoir. They develop these understandings and strategies throughout the unit as they self-assess and receive feedback from Joanne and their peers in relation to shared criteria.

Formative assessment is at the heart of our approach to Backward Design. In chapter 11, Catriona first identifies the key understandings, strategies and knowledge students will need to demonstrate their understanding of the concepts in her geography unit. Then she examines the learning needs of her students. From the emerging patterns of strengths and stretches (challenges) in her class profile, she designs learning sequences to fit. She wants to promote her students' abilities in oral language and their interest in computers while accommodating their difficulties with written output, their weak attention control, and their lack of confidence in their critical thinking abilities. By identifying and planning her unit with both the key concepts and her class profile in mind, Catriona uses explicit teaching to help her students think critically about statistics and draw conclusions from their analysis about the quality of life in developing and developed countries.

Using frameworks like Backward Design helps us to develop learning-centred classrooms where all students engage in deep content learning that builds enduring understandings and thinking strategies. Using UDL helps us plan for diversity. Next we outline six approaches that help us to apply the principles of UDL while supporting students in their efforts to develop enduring understandings and to become strategic learners.

1. Assessment for learning (AFL), formative assessment

When we use assessment for learning strategies, we make sure that every student gets personalized feedback in response to a class-wide focus. In chapter 3, we introduced the AFL strategies that make a difference:

- **Learning intentions** — By identifying learning intentions, students know where they are going and what they will be able to do.
- **Creating criteria** — By including students in the development of criteria that will be applied to their work, students internalize criteria related to learning intentions.
- **Descriptive feedback** — Descriptive feedback helps students determine where they are in the process and make adjustments for further success.
- **Questioning** — Teachers use questions that are open-ended and invite and encourage students to develop their own questions.
- **Self-assessment and peer-assessment** — Opportunities to self-assess and give feedback to peers moves students toward owning and personalizing criteria and self-regulating their actions.
- **Ownership** — Students come to "own" their learning, feel a shared ownership of the learning community and its activities, and work toward making a difference in their own and others' learning.

AFL focuses on getting information about students' use of thinking strategies and understanding of essential information. The AFL information is then used to make a plan. We often say, "No plan, no point." Unless the AFL information is going to be used to set goals, to create plans to achieve those goals, and then to assess whether the goals have been achieved, it is not worthwhile collecting it. When looking at AFL information, we always focus on strengths first—What can my students do? What's working? Then we identify focus areas. We set class-wide goals that apply to *all* students and have students set personal goals. Most importantly, we make sure that there are not too many goals, because we want to stay focused and see growth. These should be goals that we practise throughout a unit and evaluate in our summative assessments. To have the greatest impact, we want students to get ongoing feedback from us—What's working? What's not working? What's next?—from each other, and ultimately from themselves, reflecting and continuing to set goals and working on them from activity to activity.

In each of the next eight chapters, we identify the AFL strategies used by teachers and how these relate to their summative assessments, assessment of learning, AOL. Backward Design helps remind us that our formative and summative assessments must line up. This helps us keep our summative assessment authentic. We may have many bullets on a rubric, but we only summatively assess those thinking strategies that we have taught and students have practised. If we didn't teach it, we won't evaluate it. Our assessment of learning aligns with what we have actually taught, and it assesses thinking strategies that students have had a chance to work on over time.

2. Open-ended strategies

We find that instruction using open-ended strategies is a key ingredient in classrooms that are learning communities. Open-ended instructional strategies are those that do not set a ceiling on what students can learn and do. Rather, they allow students to stretch as far as they can go in using language and pushing the edges of their current knowledge. At the same time, they support all learners in thinking about their learning and contributing to the learning of others. By using open-ended strategies, all students have opportunities to learn, identify, and share relevant background knowledge. To give students opportunities to use their own interests and experiences is the first principle of Universal Design. Open-ended strategies also set students up to construct their own understandings. When using Backward Design principles, we plan instruction around curriculum expectations and design opportunities for students to move from their current learning place to a learning place as described by the curriculum. We believe that all students can and should build on and from their prior knowledge, thus we use instructional strategies that ask students to find information, relate it to other information, and develop possible interpretations. Using open-ended strategies engages students in meaning-making and knowledge construction.

As mentioned in chapter 1, we divide open-ended strategies into three categories; these are strategies that help students in connecting, processing, and transforming or personalizing information. You will find an example of *connecting strategies* in chapter 5. There you will notice that Leyton and Linda often begin a lesson by asking students to connect what they already know to the ideas and concepts that they are studying. We often start a learning sequence by asking students to predict, link, or compare key words, ideas, or relationships before engaging with new content. Activating prior knowledge helps students connect what they are learning to what they already know.

For the second category—processing—we use teaching strategies that help students draw out, link, and compare key information from texts. These processing strategies can be used with all kinds of texts—print, media, visual, and oral. In chapter 12, Terry has students develop and compare their understanding of text with others online. In chapter 9, Kathy asks her students to use thinking strategies to find information related to the key questions that they are exploring. In both these examples, the teachers are focused on students using strategies to make meaning and think critically in relation to key questions, not engaging in a rote activity like finding the "right" answer. A hallmark of open-ended instructional strategies is that student thinking is used to find information, relate it, and come up with and support unique interpretations. Students have to engage in the process and can do so in ways that draw on their background knowledge and strengths as learners.

The third type of open-ended teaching strategy is one that requires students to take information and personalize and transform it. This kind of strategy is focused on figuring out what and how the elements of information go together. When possible, we ask students to take information from multiple sources, combine it, and communicate how the information can be pieced together to show a principle, a theme, or a big idea. If the information comes from a single source, it is doubly important that students go through the process of transforming the information into another form (e.g., the ideas from a novel or textbook are shown as an icon or diagram). This helps them determine the importance or relevance of certain information. Personalizing and/or transforming strategies involve synthesizing information. Synthesizing is more than summarizing; it involves showing that you have made sense of how information goes together and you have made decisions about what is important and how you can best communicate your understanding. In chapter 10, Stacey uses an ideagram as a way for students to show how they relate key ideas from a text that they are reading to other texts, to their personal experiences, and to events around the world. Similarly, Julie Anne and Dave (chapter 8) help their students personalize and transform their understandings into medicine wheels.

Open-ended instructional strategies are a powerful way to teach while keeping all the learners in mind. These strategies require students to make connections, process information, and transform information in a variety of ways. By using these strategies, we build in a range of seamless supports and prompts as we encourage students to personalize and share their responses. Students with learning challenges are included as members of the learning community, as part of the classroom conversation, and are engaged in quality teaching and learning through open-ended strategy sequences.

They construct meaning with the support of peers rather than by working on separate lessons that remove them from the learning context. For us, a supportive classroom is one that welcomes and celebrates all learners, one in which teachers use instructional strategies to help students develop their thinking and their knowledge.

3. Gradual release of responsibility

Another approach that supports diverse learners is the *gradual release of responsibility* (Pearson and Gallagher 1983). When key thinking strategies are identified for a unit of study, teachers can gradually release the development of their students' capacity as thinkers and doers, moving from modelling to guided practice to students practising in small groups, to independent practice. We watch for students' independent application of these key thinking strategies, applying them in new contexts without teacher prompting. As with open-ended strategy instruction, we focus on having students personalize and apply approaches with increasing independence.

In chapter 6, Mehjabeen and Krista gradually released the strategy of questioning into their students' control. They crafted a summative assessment that explicitly evaluated their students' questioning skills, and they taught various ways of developing questions throughout the unit. They introduced and modelled various questioning strategies using the book *Fish*. Then students tried out these strategies with a partner. Students were given multiple opportunities to practise a questioning strategy in their literature circle groups. When the teachers and their students built criteria for journal entries, one of the criteria had to do with questions. Throughout the unit, students were given explicit feedback in order to improve their questions. Finally, the summative assessment was an opportunity for students to individually demonstrate how they had developed this thinking strategy over the course of the unit.

4. Cooperative learning

Cooperation plays a key role in learning and in one's ability to contribute to and participate in society. Cooperative learning is also an instructional approach that honours and builds on student diversity. Cooperative learning involves having students work together in peer-mediated groups. Cooperative learning helps students develop thinking strategies and make meaning together. We say to students: "You should leave this group smarter than when you entered it." Cooperative learning will serve students well both during and beyond school. A key aspect of an effective workplace is the ability of co-workers to confront and resolve conflict. The most common aptitudes found in job descriptions relate to communication skills and to interpersonal skills. Working together provides students with opportunities not only to learn content but also to build their understanding through interaction.

Many researchers have shown how learning is socially constructed. Similarly, neurologists argue that talk is essential for intellectual growth.

Cooperative learning in the Humanities requires social skills, communication skills, and critical thinking skills. Within a unit of study a teacher may choose to help students develop skills in one or two of these areas. Social skills include taking turns, showing mutual respect, and encouraging others. Communication skills include paraphrasing, seeking clarification, accepting and extending the ideas of others. Critical thinking skills include suspending judgment, considering multiple perspectives related to an issue, taking into account multiple factors, and recognizing bias.

We have experienced the power of cooperative learning in K to 12 classrooms. One of the most powerful ways to engage students in active learning is to have them talk to one another about what has just been said, observed, or read. Another is to have them share and give one another feedback regarding a project or composition that they have worked on over several classes. The cooperative learning approaches used by teachers in this book are collaborative, in that they require students to share their thinking at several points along the way, as you will see in many of the chapters. In some cases, cooperative learning is a means of helping students explore ideas, develop possible understandings, share works in progress, and get feedback. In other examples, teachers teach and assess the communication and collaboration skills as part of their unit (see Kathy's and Lisa's and Stacey's chapters—9 and 10—for examples). Whether the focus is on having students scaffold one another's thinking over time, or building students' social and communications skills, or developing critical thinking skills, cooperation plays a key role in the learning community.

5. Literature circles and information circles

One of the most effective ways to engage and support all learners is to use diverse texts. Within a unit of study, we collect a range of texts on the same theme but with as wide a range of reading levels and genres as possible. Texts may include picture books, novels at a range of reading levels, short stories, short articles, and visual texts such as art, advertisements, and online texts. We often start a new unit by building students' background knowledge using a common text or several short pieces of text, then we ask students to dig deeper into a topic by choosing from and reading several more related texts.

For example, in chapter 10 you will see how Stacey and her class read Francesco D'Adamo's *Iqbal* together before moving into literature circle novels. In chapter 6, Mehjabeen and Krista began with the accessible, shared novel, *Fish* by Laura S. Matthews, to introduce key concepts and target key thinking strategies with their classes. Alongside this shared text, they introduced literature circle texts that included novels at various reading levels that explored the same theme. While reading their literature circle novels, students applied the thinking strategies that they had practised with *Fish*. The groups were fluid. As students completed a novel, they moved on to another literature circle group. Students then applied thinking skills—questioning and making connections—to explore and compare how the theme of survival was developed by different authors.

In chapters 6, 10, and 12, you will see how students choose their own books, read at their own pace, engage in conversations about what they are reading, and keep journals about what they are learning through readings and conversation. Literature circles allow students to read at their own pace, apply strategies that have been introduced previously, and develop enduring understandings about big ideas through conversations about the texts they choose to read.

Information circles involve taking the literature circle structure and applying it to information texts, including textbooks. Students have discussions about the text they have chosen to read in small, peer-led discussion groups. Information circles offer students a choice of text in the Social Studies classroom. They help teachers gradually release the use of particular thinking strategies and allow a deeper investigation of key concepts first explored as a whole class. Of course, the power of talking together helps to enhance student understanding. All students get a chance to share ideas and develop meaning together without deferring to the teacher. Like literature circles, information circles have several key components:

- Students choose the reading materials from texts that the teacher has introduced.
- An information circle is a group of students who have chosen to read the same article, chapter, or book.
- Students keep notes to guide both their reading and discussion (e.g., a journal entry, a graphic organizer, sticky notes, annotations in the text).
- Groups meet regularly to discuss their reading.
- Discussion points and questions come from the students, not from the teachers or the textbooks.
- Personal responses, observations, and questions are the starting point of discussion.
- The teacher acts as a facilitator and observer.
- When information circles finish a cycle, groups may share highlights of the reading with classmates through presentations, discussions, dramatizations, or other media.
- New groups form around their new reading choices, and a new cycle begins.

In chapter 9, you will read how Kathy chose a variety of information texts about China. She introduced the articles and asked students to each select one to read. Students coded their thinking to share with others reading the same article. As in literature circles, students share their thinking in their small groups. Discussion helps the students prepare to write a response to the article. Over time, Kathy, like the teachers in this book who use literature circles, asks students to help create criteria to define what goes into an effective discussion and response.

6. Inquiry

The inquiry approach is another framework that engages and supports all learners. Inquiry provides a planning structure to help students develop thinking strategies that lead to deeper understandings about concepts. Inquiry can also help us match our teaching to our students' learning. When working with an open-ended question over the course of either several lessons or a full unit of study, students collect, compare, and synthesize information over time. Embedded within an inquiry are several thinking skills. In chapters 5 through 12, you can see how thinking skills can be introduced and used to explore big ideas in relation to an overarching question or to student questioning within the unit of study. Krista and Mehjabeen focus on questioning in their opening unit (chapter 6), so that students can call upon this core strategy throughout the year.

The teachers you will meet in the following chapters use open-ended inquiry questions that set a purpose for learning. Students read, write, explore, make meaningful connections, and apply what they are learning to new texts and situations. Dave and Julie Anne use inquiry to help students examine current and historical perspectives around Aboriginal Peoples of Canada. Kathy uses inquiry to help transport her students to an ancient civilization where they seek information and work to synthesize and apply what they are learning —as opposed to expecting students to learn the "right answers." Terry poses two or three questions per novel for students to reflect upon and respond to in their online posts, thus starting a conversation with an online peer. Catriona links inquiry to critical thinking, and Joanne injects inquiry into the writing process, where authors ask themselves about the choices they are making.

Conclusion

Together with our colleagues, the teachers you will meet in the next eight chapters, we are committed to working and learning together. Teaching in ways that support thinking and learning in all of our students continues to fuel our own process of inquiry. Along the way, we have discovered and tailored frameworks and approaches that support the diverse learners of our classrooms. We embrace the diversity in our classrooms. We want to help all students develop and use their strengths and interests while also developing common thinking strategies. We invite you to adapt these ideas for the grades and units that you teach. Make them your own. The frameworks and approaches introduced here are not grade-specific or topic-specific. They can easily be used in several grades, whether in Social Studies, in English

Language Arts, or in Humanities classrooms. Turn to the chapter that interests you most and think about how you might adapt the approaches described—assessment for learning, open-ended strategies, gradual release of responsibility, cooperative learning, literature circles, information circles, inquiry—for your students.

Chapter 5

Starting the Year with Significance

Grade 9—Humanities

Co-Teaching

- Classroom teacher and resource teacher plan, teach, and reflect together

Assessment FOR Learning

- Who am I? Profile
- Performance-based reading assessment
- Co-creating criteria for field book entries
- Descriptive feedback
- Self-assessment and goal-setting

Differentiation

- Open-ended strategies
- Common learning outcomes, varying degrees of support
- Descriptive feedback and follow-up instruction

Gradual Release of Responsibility

- Modelling
- Guided practice and feedback
- Independent practice

Assessment OF Learning

- Choice of field book entry for assessment

The Collaboration

Linda Watson and Leyton Schnellert have been working together for the last four years to develop Linda's Humanities 9 program. Linda teaches Humanities classes and Theatre classes at MacNeill Secondary School. They have taught and co-taught English 9 and Social Studies 9 as separate courses and as integrated courses over the years—in middle, junior high, and high schools. In addition to their experience teaching Humanities, they share strengths in Fine Arts and literacy. Leyton began to work with Linda as part of his role as a district resource teacher. In this district "helping-teacher" role, he made co-planning and co-teaching with colleagues a priority for his time—helping them make learning more accessible for all students within inclusive classrooms. Planning and teaching together has helped them discover the difference that collaboration makes, not just for students but also for professionals. Together we are better!

The Context

In this unit, Linda and Leyton set the stage for the kinds of teaching and learning their students will encounter over the course of the year. The goals for the first two weeks of class are to build relationships and understand the learning needs of the students. They begin with familiar content before diving into historical content; by moving from the known to the unknown, they scaffold students' active learning and their capacity for meaning-making.

Linda and Leyton take key thinking skills for Social Studies and the strategies to use when reading for information and link them with their students' own interests and histories. In Humanities courses, which combine Social Studies and English Language Arts, the teachers present both content areas as an integrated unit; by addressing multiple learning outcomes from each field, they develop their students' abilities to reflect and make connections.

In this unit, as students explore personal artifacts and family experiences, they learn to record their thoughts in field books. As they gain experience in analyzing, making connections, and reflecting on artifacts, they develop skills that they will apply over the school year. In later units, students identify and reflect on artifacts and events from particular eras. Starting with personal artifacts, students learn to use evidence that supports their thinking, a critical learning outcome in the curricula of both disciplines.

Essential Questions

How can we explore and explain the significance of events? Who are you as a person and a learner? What is the significance of an artifact? What do artifacts tell us? How does our personal history relate to the present?

Key structures

Co-teaching

- Students see different teachers' approaches to the same idea or thinking skill.
- The teachers reflect on how things are going and what their next steps might be in the lessons or in the adaptations they make.
- Because a resource teacher is not in the class every day, the time for co-teaching is allotted on a priority basis to the lessons in which new approaches are introduced.

Integrated planning

- Learning outcomes common to both subjects are addressed within the unit.
- The big ideas and key skills are reinforced within the integrated unit.

Assessment for learning

- Co-creating criteria are given, for field book entries.
- Descriptive feedback is given, related to the criteria.
- Questions—an invitation to explore and make meaning.
- Ownership—focusing on involvement, self-awareness, and making choices.
- Self-assessment—students reflect on and set goals for their learning.
- Who am I? Profile helps identify students' learning styles and preferences for teachers to use in tailoring instruction, activities, and performance tasks.
- Performance-based reading assessment (see chapter 3, pages 29–33) is used to develop a class profile, identifying class and individual strengths, stretches, interests and goals.
- Teachers communicate to students that they come with strengths and abilities; all students need to know that their prior experiences, abilities, and knowledge will be honoured.

Differentiation

- Using open-ended strategies (see pages 9 and 48–50), all students observe the teachers modelling a particular thinking strategy and then are given opportunities to apply that strategy themselves.
- All students work toward the common learning outcomes, but some students may require more practice, more support, or more time, in order to achieve the outcomes.
- When individual students are at different stages in their skill development and learning journey, descriptive feedback enables individual development toward the class's shared criteria.

Learning sequences
- Strategies organized by purpose:
  - **Connecting**—with background knowledge and with others
  - **Processing**—new material
  - **Transforming and Personalizing**—what you know and are learning
- Learning sequences may take more than one class period

Assessment of learning
- Students choose their best field book entry and identify which criteria it meets.
- The teacher scores them against the class-developed criteria.

Lesson 1—Rationale

Formative assessment is a vital first step in getting to know the students as individual learners. Tuning in to the dynamics of the group informs the instructional decisions that teachers make—ways to use their students' strengths, ways to stretch their reach. The teachers begin by discussing with students the notion that everyone has strengths and challenges, everyone has abilities in some areas, stretches in other areas. Students need to be reassured that their prior experiences, abilities, and knowledge will be honoured. When they have opportunities to use what they already know and what they already can do, they are more eager to engage in a new unit of study, more likely to take risks in their learning. To develop independent and confident learners, we must build on the strengths and extend the abilities of each student. When students feel welcome and have opportunities to make connections between their prior knowledge and new course content, they can more easily share what they know about topics, issues, ideas, and themselves as learners.

Connecting—The Who Am I? Profile

- Ask the class, "What do you need to know this year about me/us that will help you learn?"
- Be prepared to field all kinds of responses, including questions about teaching styles and what students have heard from others about the class. Make it an interactive conversation that allows students to see teachers modelling how their interests and passions relate to how they teach and learn. This also sets up a key instructional approach—modelling.

Processing—Building learning profiles

- Display the organizer Who am I? Profile (Figure 5.1) using the overhead projector. Model responding in the first two boxes (*Words that describe me; My favourite books/stories*) as students listen and watch. Give a lot of explanations as you work.
- Provide students with their own copy of Figure 5.1. Explain to the students that this is an opportunity to learn about them and will guide teacher decisions about how to plan and teach in ways that will help them learn best.
- After you fill out the first two boxes of the organizer, have the students fill out theirs, jotting down all the ideas that come to mind. Continue the turn-taking (teacher modelling/student responding) routine throughout the other boxes on the organizer.
- When they have completed the organizer, have them turn over the page and ask students to share any fears or worries they have about the course and school. Model this using the frame "*Sh–h–h–h, I'm afraid of.../that....*" Invite students to respond about the class, about their learning, about success in school, or about their life hopes. The more sensitive we are to our students and their profiles the more willing they are to engage and take risks in their learning.

Transforming/Personalizing—Sharing and personal fieldwork

- Ask students to pick one important idea from their organizer to share with a partner. This is the first time in class that you have asked them to evaluate by determining the importance of one idea over another and to justify their choice.
- Provide a break for students to think about and choose what they will share.
- Ask students to share with the class.
- Collect your students' Who am I? profiles and look for patterns to support your planning and teaching.

Preparing for next class—Personal artifacts

Share one of your own artifacts—a symbol of some accomplishment, a place enjoyed, one particular interest, a connection to personal history—and model the presentation of this personal artifact to the class.

- Ask students to bring an item for next class that represents and connects to them. It is most important to emphasize that the item should be personal. Brainstorm with them what such an artifact might be.
- Ask students to bring a notebook for next day that they can use like a journal but will be called a "field book." Discuss with your students how many social scientists, like anthropologists, collect artifacts and jot down field notes in a field book.

Figure 5.1 Who am I? Profile

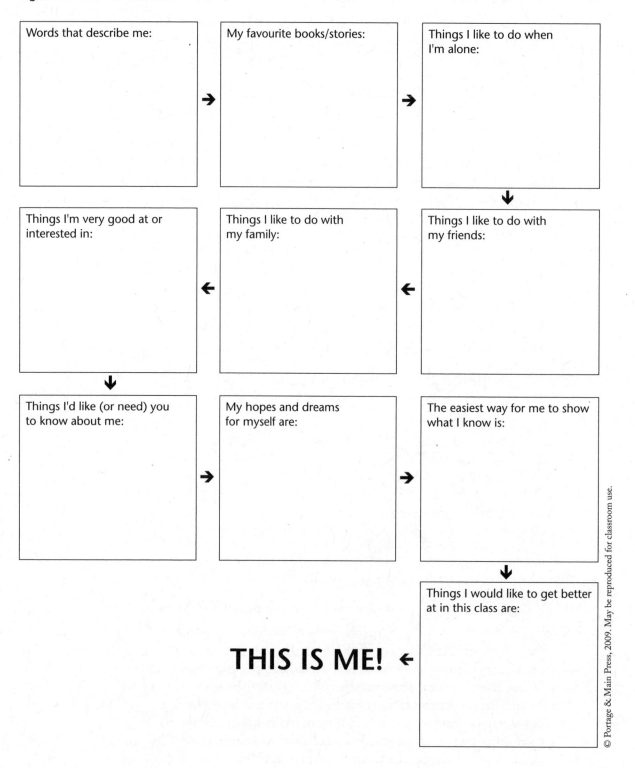

Words that describe me:

My favourite books/stories:

Things I like to do when I'm alone:

Things I'm very good at or interested in:

Things I like to do with my family:

Things I like to do with my friends:

Things I'd like (or need) you to know about me:

My hopes and dreams for myself are:

The easiest way for me to show what I know is:

Things I would like to get better at in this class are:

THIS IS ME! ←

Lesson 2—Rationale

This second lesson continues to work with the Who am I? Profile, and focuses on developing the social health of the class, building a sense of community among the students. We use oral language strategies to help students communicate and develop their thinking.

Connecting—Mining and sharing ideas

- Give students their Who am I? Profile sheets from the previous day; ask them to find a different partner from the one they worked with in the previous class and ask them to choose one item from their sheet.
- Then, invite students one by one to share with the whole class. Offer no comment or judgment about what each student says, just say thank you. However, notice the level of risk-taking as you continue to model a non-judgmental approach. The goal is to develop the ability to be self-reflective and to move beyond a search for one right answer. Move on to discuss the item they brought to class, modelling how to talk about their chosen artifact. For students who have not brought an artifact, have them choose something on their person, for example, from their pencil case, book bag, pocket, or purse.

Processing—Reciprocal learning

- Explain to students the key skills that they will learn about today:
  - describing significance
  - explaining the logic of their thinking
  - determining importance
  - active listening
- Write these four learning intentions on the board so that everyone can refer to them.
- Begin with "A/B talk."[1] Two co-teachers should model this process, or possibly the teacher and a volunteer student. Decide who will be partner A and who will be partner B. Explain why you made the decision; for example, A is older, taller, woke up first today. Explain that you want students to provide a reason for their choices, describing the logic behind their choice. This activity leads you and your students back to the thinking skill of making a decision and explaining the reason for the decision.
  - Provide all students with a piece of paper, their "thinking paper" (a place to jot down one's thinking for later use or reference) with the question Who am I as a person and learner? at the top.
  - Partner A explains the meaning of their artifact and its significance, how it relates to who she/he is, to their personal history, and possibly to information in their profile. Partner B listens very carefully

---

1. Thanks to Susan Close for introducing us to this A/B partnership structure.

because he or she will have to share three important words they
heard Partner A use to describe A's artifact. Emphasize the idea of
picking words they hear that seem important. Partner B shares the
words that stood out, and Partner A records those words on his or
her thinking paper along with any other ideas that come to mind.
At this point, you are introducing the idea of "holding your thinking."
• Then repeat this whole process for Partner B.

Transforming—Creating records

- When anthropologists study either ancient or contemporary cultures,
  they look for artifacts from that culture and take notes in their field
  books to describe what they notice and their thinking about the
  significance of what they have found. Anthropologists always date
  their notes as well to capture their thinking at the time.
- As a class, we want to develop this kind of careful thinking through
  the study of our own personal artifacts and field notes.
- Model the steps of recording your artifacts in your field book; ask your
  students to do the same. Say, "Write today's date; record information
  about your artifact; note the year or period in your life that it was
  created or acquired. Include the three most significant words your
  partner identified as you shared and any other information."
- Ask the students to brainstorm, as partners, the criteria for
  distinguishing the qualities of a good personal artifact. Then, jot down
  their key ideas on the board or on an overhead.
- Ask the students to bring another artifact to the next class—one that
  meets some of the criteria that they have discussed.

Lesson 3—Rationale

These opening lessons are a time for teachers to get to know their students and
to develop an environment that encourages the students as you ask them to
share and to take risks with their learning. It's also the time to introduce key
oral language and writing strategies that help students become deliberate and
critical thinkers. The language you model for them to use and the interaction
processes you introduce also help create a learning community.

Connecting—Oral rehearsal focusing on significance

- Model partner talk around a second artifact.
- Ask the students to listen closely for key information shared during the
  explanation of the item. Try to include a few key details about yourself
  and explain how they reveal something about a personality trait.
- Ask students to share their own observations of the talk.

- Partners A/B then share with each other (after deciding who will be A and who will be B and explaining why). Have students write at the top of their thinking paper the questions What is the significance of an artifact? What do artifacts tell us about ourselves and others?
- Partner A explains the significance of his or her artifact as Partner B listens for and jots down at least two significant phrases on their thinking page. Partner B then shares what he or she noticed.
- Repeat after the partners trade roles.

Processing—Recording your thinking

Demonstrate the process of adding notes on, or a sketch of, the artifact in your field book. With the criteria describing what makes a good artifact (from yesterday's class) on the board or the screen, model the process of recording field notes by jotting down your reflections. If there are two teachers, one might write directly in the field book while the other writes on the overhead so that students may see a sample entry. During the writing process, share how the artifact relates to you or represents something about you. The entry in the field book might include the phrases your partner shared along with further explanations.

Some students may need to start by just getting the phrases down on paper; they may then be able to build, in future field notes, toward recording more of their thinking.

Before asking the students to write, give them three basic guidelines:

1. Describe your artifact.
2. Explain why it is important.
3. Do not censor yourself; this is draft writing.

Transforming

- Give five to 10 minutes for writing. Build the length of engagement in writing over several lessons and, eventually, over weeks.
- Have students share their writing with another partner, alternately taking A or B roles.
- Invite students to share with the whole class, asking first for volunteers and not requiring that everyone share. Make no judgments; just thank volunteers for sharing.
- Ask students, What have you learned about field books today? Write their responses on an overhead. With two teachers, one might interpret responses with drawings and symbols while the other lists their ideas in words. Try to model and reinforce multiple ways of expressing thoughts on paper.
- Remind the students to select or collect more artifacts; each will need another one in a few days.

Lesson 4—Rationale

Writers use language and structure their text to engage and interact with their expected audience. In this lesson, we link our students' prior knowledge of Social Studies to the textbook selected for our course. We will use other texts or textbooks over the year, but the course textbook is an excellent tool for this lesson.

We want to help students develop the habit of using a fresh thinking paper each class. This is the beginning of helping students develop their skills in note-making. This process is parallel to the field-book process we have introduced, but these notes go in the students' course binders. On their thinking page, ask students to write notes following the sequence of the lesson by writing, connecting, processing, and transforming or personalizing before each section. The teacher does the same when using the whiteboard or the overhead.

Connecting—Making and showing links on thinking paper

- Ask students to jot down the question of the day at the top of their thinking paper: How can texts help us to learn about others?
- Ask students what topics or themes they recall from Social Studies 8, then share with a partner. Ask them to jot down their ideas under the heading Connecting on their thinking paper.
- Ask students to open up their textbook so that they can see the front and the back of the cover at the same time (sometimes the cover image wraps around from front to back). Student partners tell each other what they see and record the information on their thinking paper.
- Probe students' thinking by asking them to speculate about the title and images on the textbook cover, how they relate to what they already know, and what it might mean to their studies this year. What prior knowledge can they use to make sense of the cover?

Processing—Using a text to help us infer and make meaning

- After they have practised with the cover, ask students to use a few key pages at the front of the text to see what they can determine about the author(s), their history and training, the point of view that they might have taken in writing the text, whose point of view might be missing, and what might be learned from the text. With these prompts written on the board or overhead, ask them to draw a chart to show their thinking.
- While the students generate responses and provide evidence to support their thinking, they are drawing on their work with artifacts. To support their responses, they need to use text features, bibliographic information, and quotations.

Transforming — The Grand Debrief

- Debrief the students as a class about what they are finding. Jot down the groups' ideas on the overhead or whiteboard. This is The Grand Debrief. Call on each group to add their thinking; as each group shares information, invite the rest of the class to add additional information that they think relevant to their charts — we call this getting inspiration from others. Bring the discussion to an end by asking the students how their text might be helpful and what questions they have about it.
- Invite students to share any questions they have formulated based on the activity. You do not need to answer any of these questions, but rather you should honour the formulation of them.
- Request that students bring a third artifact for next class, something that is directly related to their personal history.
- Students brainstorm with their partners what they might bring.

Lesson 5 — Rationale

We want students to have experiences in which they can develop their ability to reflect and think critically. When students have a chance to brainstorm the criteria for tasks, they can "get inside" a process and others' perspectives, which helps them to think like social scientists. Engaging students this way covers both Social Studies and English Language Arts outcomes.

Prepare for this lesson by looking at the students' field book entries. Collect a range of samples that have different strengths. Ask these students ahead of time for permission to share their draft field book entries with the class (or another class if you have more than one) to get better at writing field book entries. Let them know that only the strengths of their writing will be discussed.

Connecting

The focus of this lesson is moving students into developing criteria for field book entries that will become the criteria for formative and summative assessment. The same field book processes will be used over the year and, now that they have experienced the process a couple of times, they are able to build some criteria that describe the qualities of an effective field book entry. Individual students and social scientists have their own styles; we all work to meet the same criteria, we just work in different ways so the field books will look different from each other.

- Hand out the graphic organizer (Figure 5.2) and let the students know that the criteria will be built by examining student samples for strengths.
- Pose the question What are the qualities of an effective field book entry? With this question in mind, put a student sample on the overhead (see Figure 5.3). Examine several other student samples.

Figure 5.2 The graphic organizer: What are the qualities of an effective field book entry?

Private brainstorm:

Our group's 4 criteria:

The top 4 criteria of the class:

One criterion I met:

Quote:

- Students privately brainstorm at least two strengths from each sample.
- After each sample, you might have partners turn and share what they noticed; based on this conversation, the students might revise what they have.
- After looking at three or four samples, move students into groups of four and have them discuss and select their top four criteria. Students record these in their graphic organizers.
- Circulate around the class to help as needed.
- As the groups share their list with the others, record the criteria on an overhead, encouraging the students to link their ideas to other ideas. The class might come up with four or six criteria in all, or quite a long list. Regardless of the number, accept what is shared and, if needed, narrow the focus for the day to those criteria that are truly central. Students generally will mention:
  - that an artifact or its representation must be in the field book, labelled and dated
  - why the object/symbol/event is or might be important
  - what memories the artifact brings to mind

Figure 5.3 Student sample of a field book entry

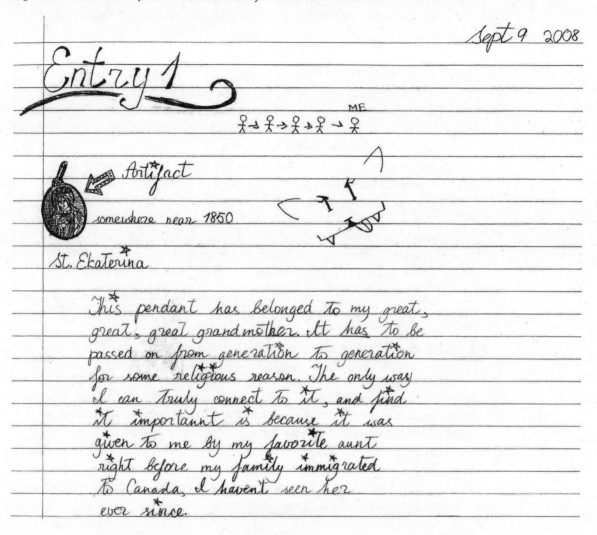

- If the students do not come up with such ideas, add your own or look for more samples with these qualities and examine them over the next few lessons.

Processing

- Have students take out the artifacts that they brought for today's class. Then have them represent (sketch) their partner's artifact in their field book.
- Ask students to jot down notes, trying first to be descriptive about what they see; then have them write about why it might be significant to that person.

- Then the owner of the artifact shares how significant it is in their life/personal history. Students add this information to their field book entry, using quotation marks.

Transforming/Personalizing

- Ask students to write in the fieldbook about how their own thinking was the same or different after the owner explained the artifact's significance.
- Invite students to share how their understanding of the artifact and its significance is now different.
- Before handing in their field book for their first teacher feedback, have students check them against the criteria. In the last section of the graphic organizer, ask them to jot down which criteria they believe they have met. If possible, have them provide a quote from their entry that demonstrates these criteria or provide an explanation.
- Teachers collect the field books and write descriptive feedback (referenced to the criteria) on sticky notes placed on the students' work.
- Use feedback stems like: I am noticing that…, I like how you…, I wonder if…, How might you…, In your next entry…, You effectively….

Lesson 6—Rationale

We learn about ourselves, about others, and about the world through speaking, listening, reading, and writing. In this lesson, students create and participate in an "artifact gallery walk." We all can learn in a number of ways, and we want all students to have at least some experiences that suit the ways they learn best. Of course, this means that at some point students will be working in modalities that are less comfortable. Try to expose students to a range of thinking and learning approaches so that they can identify and, eventually, advocate for what works best for them.

Connecting

- Ask students to place their artifacts and a blank paper on their desks, then create a title for their artifact, and write it on the paper.
- After setting up their artifact and before leaving their desks to view at least six other artifacts, model a few questions that they might use with each other's artifacts, questions that cannot be answered by a simple yes or no but that require deeper thinking.
- Ask questions that prompt students to look at the artifact's age, consider who might have used it, how it might have been used, its possible meaning or significance to the owner, and what activities it might relate to.
- Canvas the class about what they notice about your questions. Jot their responses on the board.
- Students study the first artifact they visit, posing a question on the thinking paper next to the artifact.

- Have volunteers share their questions; invite the rest of the students to identify what is effective about the questions shared.
- Add to the criteria already generated in response to your questions.
- As students move to their second artifact (one person per artifact so that everyone gets the same number of questions), encourage students to use the criteria, the title, and any other evidence in order to form a powerful question.

Processing

- Students continue to move around the room.
- Facilitate by keeping traffic flowing, and by encouraging and pointing out thoughtful questions. As fits the flow of the activity, stop to ask students to share questions, assessing them against the criteria and refocusing their efforts as needed.

Transforming/Personalizing

- When students return to their desks and their own artifact, ask them to transfer the artifact (or a representation of the artifact) into their field book.
- Invite them to select the three most interesting questions their peers asked about their artifact. If the questions do not meet the quality set out in the criteria, students can formulate their own questions, by themselves or with a partner.
- After revisiting the field book criteria from the last lesson, ask students to respond to the three powerful questions.
- Circulate around the room, engaging with students where needed and providing support. Wherever possible, rather than telling students what to do, ask them to rephrase the task and identify what they plan to do next.
- The plan for the next class requires the students to bring another artifact of personal significance—this time, a photo of themselves and family members, perhaps, or something related to a celebration or accomplishment.

Lesson 7—Rationale

As we have moved through this introductory mini-unit, we have introduced thinking strategies and approaches that help students think carefully about what they notice in personal artifacts. These activities involved students describing what they see and telling the story of why an artifact is significant. Objects/artifacts have personal and cultural significance. Over the course of Humanities 9, students have opportunities to examine events and representations of artifacts related to several events in Europe and North America.

Descriptive and analytical thinking skills are important in all Social Science disciplines and in English Language Arts. In today's world, historians, anthropologists, archaeologists, and geographers draw on techniques used by each other's discipline. In this lesson, we borrow and adapt the notion of *backstory* from literary analysis to help students think about two things: (1) the key events that lead up to an individual's or a group's current identity, and (2) how our stories can change, depending on our audience.

Connecting

- Ask students specific questions about the backstory of a familiar character from a story—Harry Potter, for instance, or Bella from *Twilight* (2005). A backstory cannot be changed to suit an audience. Usually in fiction, a backstory can be traced and analyzed based on the evidence provided by the author.
- Share with students that in non-fiction a backstory can differ depending on how it is told and who it is told to.
- Share your artifact (e.g., a family picture) with the class, telling specific details about why it is important to you, and what it reveals about how you and your family live (e.g., how neatly you all like to dress, how important it is to all be together for dinner, how happy you all are to have this photo).
- Tell your story, including locations and key events, but make sure that your story is specific to a single, personal point of view and that the details shared are suitable for a classroom audience (selective/bias).
- Then, ask students to share their artifact with their partner and describe how it is part of their backstory. Have the partners take notes about each other's story.

Processing

- Invite another teacher into the class and role play being in the staff room with coffee mugs and tell the story behind the artifact very differently. Tell the story of the same picture but emphasize or share new information (e.g., "The only time my family wears these outfits is for special events," "I can't remember the last time we were all together for dinner"). You have now told your story two different ways, each story relevant to your audience and purpose.
- Students draw a Venn diagram on their thinking paper and label circle A: Version One and label circle B: Version Two. Then, they complete their diagram, jotting down the information that was the same or different.
- Circulate through the class to assist students in this process. To complete the diagram, ensure that students look at each circle to determine the parts of the stories that overlap and should be included in the middle section of the Venn—that is, in both circles where they

overlap. This graphic representation provides another way for students to clarify the similarities and differences between the two versions of the story. One story or version might be recognized as "true or factual" but, depending on the teller and the audience, the story may be noticeably different, having been adapted for different audiences and purposes. This observation is true also for how many artifacts and events are understood and described.

Transforming/Personalizing—Bias and perspective taking

- Ask students to tell their partner a story related to their photo. They must use details from it to help tell their partner what a remarkable individual they are.
- Each partner takes a turn telling their story and, while being the listener, writing down three important points and two clarifying questions.
- Students enter in their field book a description of their artifact (suggest that they draw or represent a photo if that item is too valuable to the family). They make three columns underneath and, in the first column, they jot down their partners' observations and questions (see Figure 5.4 as one example).
- Students retell their story but, this time, pretend that their partner is a teacher who needs to give them more time or help because of the activity or situation in the photo. Encourage them to be very convincing. Each takes a turn telling their story and the listening partner writes down new important points and two clarifying questions. In the second column, students then jot down their partners' observations and questions.
- In the third column, ask them to reflect on what they noticed about how audience and purpose filtered what was said. Their reflections introduce them to the concepts of *bias* and *perspective*.
- For the next lesson, ask students to bring a personal artifact that tells something about how they have contributed, or will contribute in the future, to their family or to another group. Students might bring something related to a hobby, a cultural celebration, a certificate for an achievement, or pictures of themselves with family members.

Figure 5.4 Student sample of a three-column entry in a field book (bias and perspective taking)

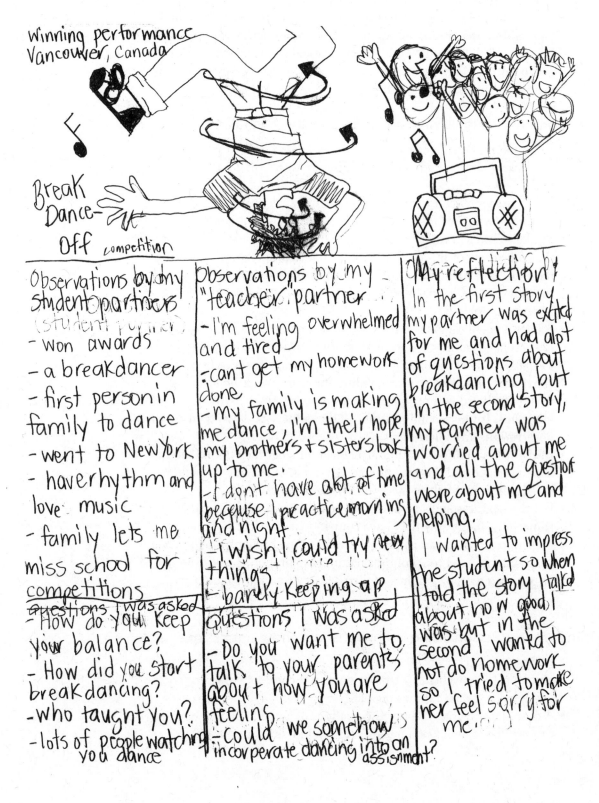

winning performance
Vancouver, Canada

Break
Dance-
Off competition

Observations by my student partners (student partner)	Observations by my "teacher" partner	My reflection
- won awards	- I'm feeling overwhelmed and tired	In the first story my partner was excited for me and had alot of questions about breakdancing but in the second story, my partner was worried about me and all the questions were about me and helping.
- a breakdancer	- can't get my homework done	
- first person in family to dance	- my family is making me dance, I'm their hope, my brothers + sisters look up to me.	
- went to NewYork	- I don't have alot of time because I practice morning and night	
- have rhythm and love music	- I wish I could try new things	
- family lets me miss school for competitions	- barely keeping up	I wanted to impress the student so when I told the story I talked about how good I was but in the second I wanted to not do homework so I tried to make her feel sorry for me.
questions I was asked	**questions I was asked**	
- How do you keep your balance?	- Do you want me to talk to your parents about how you are feeling?	
- How did you start breakdancing?		
- who taught you?	- could we somehow incorperate dancing into an assignment?	
- lots of people watching you dance		

Lesson 8—Rationale

Artifacts are clues to a culture's values and practices. Social scientists look for these clues, ask questions, and document specific information in a field book to help them better understand what is significant to a group. This mini-unit helps students look at personal artifacts to see what is significant to them. The following sequence often takes two or three lessons, linking artifacts, reflection and synthesis through the use of epitaphs. It consolidates the concepts of the last several lessons (e.g. how key details determine the role and impact of artifacts). This epitaph/gravestone enactment strategy reinforces students' understanding of artifacts and their significance through another modality—that is, representing and speaking instead of writing.

Connecting—Sharing artifacts

- Students have brought to class a significant artifact that relates to their own personal history.
- Students talk to their partner about how this artifact can be used to convince others about why they should be remembered for having a positive impact on others. They practice explaining the artifact's significance and how it relates to them.
- Partners listen for words or phrases that highlight the impact or potential impact of the student on others.
- Each talks and exchanges words and phrases.
- Students put the artifact (or a representation of the artifact) in their field book and date it accordingly, along with words and phrases from their partner. Students may sketch their artifacts because some items may be too valuable to the family or are not easy to glue or tape into a field book.

Processing—Using criteria to write field book entries

- Review the guidelines for writing field book entries before students begin to write about their artifact's significance.
- Tell students that they will be sharing a portion, or all, of their entry. Students now set out to complete their field book entry about their artifact and how they can use it to support their story about its impact on others. Allow them time to write their entry.

Transforming/Personalizing—Epitaphs that show significance

- Introduce the concept of an epitaph. Offer students several examples of epitaphs. (The website <http://www.alsirat.com/epitaphs/> offers the epitaphs of several famous people.)
- Ask students to think about the qualities of a good epitaph, how it captures the essence of a person's legacy and draws the reader in.

- Students share their artifact with a partner, while their partner jots down any powerful words or phrases they happen to hear that would work as part of an effective epitaph. Give students time to work with their partner to come up with epitaphs for each of them, keeping in mind the examples.
- Have students imagine themselves in the role of a headstone in a graveyard. Model this yourself, standing still like a cold stone statue. Have students position themselves around the classroom. Establish the role by having them freeze in position, then shake off a couple of times to really get the giggles out and focus.
- Inform the students/headstones that their role is to be a marker for a life lived. Have them imagine themselves as dormant and inactive in a graveyard until someone passes by to look at and notice them. Walk by one student/tombstone and have them share the epitaph. Have students circulate around the "graveyard," passing by all the headstones so that all have an opportunity to recite their epitaph.
- Prepare the students to talk beyond their written epitaph, to perhaps describe the story of how they reached this graveyard or how they feel about being there. Give them a short time to think about what they will say.
- Have the student's headstone turn to a partner and share their story. Pass by certain headstones, inviting them to speak to the graveyard.
- Students return to their field books and expand their entry to include some reflection on the activity—for example, what they noticed about their legacy; how their artifact connects to it; why their epitaph is appropriate; how it could be more effective.

Lesson 9—Rationale

Introducing the final assignment (summative assessment preparation)

We want the students to demonstrate the thinking skills that we have been exploring over the previous eight lessons.

Connecting—Sharing artifacts
- Review the criteria for What are the qualities of an effective field book entry?
- Provide exemplars of what an entry might look like at each of the four levels: Good start; You are getting there; You did it; and Wow!
- Explain that these criteria are common in the learning outcomes of both the Social Studies and Language Arts curricula.
- Now that students have practiced these skills, it is time to revise and submit a piece.

Processing
- Students find their best entry to date in their field book, and identify which criterion it meets.

- Have students, in groups of three, share these best entries; ask them to give each other ideas and feedback about how to revise their entries to make them even better.
- Students make a plan to revise their selected field book entry. They write their plan on a separate piece of paper so that it can also be referred to and handed in.

Transforming/Personalizing

- Students revise their entry (with the criterion in mind) on a separate piece of paper so that they can continue to use their field book.
- Collect entries and assess them, using the criteria (see Figure 5.5).

Figure 5.5 Sample rubric of criteria for entry in field book

Criteria for Field Books	4: WOW!	3: You did it!	2: You are getting there	1: Good start
Description	Artifact is described using multiple senses and refers to concrete, observable details. Explains where it comes from.	Artifact is described using sensory information. Good use of details.	Includes an artifact or representation that is labelled and dated. More description would be helpful.	Try to include more details in describing or representing your artifact.
Importance	Explains why object/symbol/event is or might be important to self and others and gives examples.	Explains why object/symbol/event is or might be important to self or others and gives examples.	Explains why object/symbol/event is or might be important. Could be developed further.	Try to explain why your artifact is important to you and/or others.
Analysis	Explanations and questions suggest more than one possible interpretation of artifact's importance. Recognizes others' perspectives.	Explanations and questions relate personal experiences and interpretations. Be careful about making assumptions.	Explanations and questions are logical but may need further development.	Try to explain your ideas more.

Reflections

We have spent the last four years working with and revising this process. It differs a little (or a lot) each year, depending on the changing needs of our students and what parts of our lesson sequences need to be re-visited and re-taught. Together with our colleagues Catriona Misfeldt and Eve Minuk, we have reworked and developed our sequences and, over time, Catriona and Eve took over for Leyton, providing Linda with new perspectives and talents to draw from. While Leyton and Linda share a drama background, Catriona brings a passion for visual arts, and Eve has provided deep insights into the ways that students with significant needs can be supported.

Although we have designed these sequences so that all students can take part regardless of their strengths and challenges, we still have to make some adaptations and modifications for particular individuals. We develop key thinking skills together through modelling and guided practice, and thus can better meet the needs of these students from the outset. Students feel invested in the process because they play a role in identifying what skills and strategies are needed in using the field book, by carrying out related activities, and together developing the criteria for these skills. Collecting artifacts, examining and explaining their significance, engages the students in the heart of the disciplines. After this introductory sequence of lessons, we learned a lot about our students and witnessed their engagement and ownership in our classrooms. They have become ready and able to use the lens of artifacts to make sense of the Social Studies curriculum. We see that marrying Social Studies to English Language Arts provides a powerful way to develop and reinforce higher-level thinking across the curriculum.

Chapter 6

Inquiry and Thematic Teaching

Grade 8—English

Assessment FOR Learning	• Co-creating criteria for journals • Co-creating criteria for group discussion skills • Self-assessment • Descriptive feedback
Diverse Texts	• Literature Circle novels
Open-Ended Strategies	• Quick-Write • Open-ended questions • Say Something • Three-Way Interview
Gradual Release of Responsibility	• Shared text to multiple texts • Modelled thinking strategies
Assessment OF Learning	• Reading Journal • Character Survival Kit
Essential Question	• How are hope, knowledge, and friendship necessary for the survival of the human spirit?

The Collaboration

Leyton, Krista, and Mehjabeen have collaborated for several years. Krista Ediger teaches English and Writing 12 at McRoberts Secondary, a grade 8 to 12 school; Mehjabeen Datoo teaches English, Humanities, and Social Studies at McMath Secondary School. Krista and Mehjabeen taught at the same school one year early in their careers and found that together they were able to give meaningful feedback to one another about their teaching. Unfortunately, though, like many new teachers, Mehjabeen had to move to a new school as part of the spring staffing process. Seeing the exciting work Krista and Mehjabeen were doing, Leyton Schnellert, a district helping teacher at the time, was looking for classroom teachers to learn with. Krista and Mehjabeen so valued their collaboration that they, along with Leyton, decided to get together regularly to share ideas and plan. Even though they work in different schools, they continue to find their collaboration invaluable. Together they build text sets, redesign lessons to develop students' thinking skills, devise new assessment practices, and plan theme-based lessons. They are convinced that their combined ideas, resources, experiences, and passions enable them to more fully meet the needs of their diverse students.

The Context

In this unit, Krista, Mehjabeen, and Leyton combined thematic teaching with an inquiry approach to use as an overarching framework for planning units of study. Early in the unit, they introduce open-ended questions related to the theme. At the end of the unit, students demonstrate their learning by addressing these questions. In addition, the teachers use inquiry to explicitly develop their students' ability to both devise and respond to questions—an important thinking skill of inquiry. They find that their approach helps students develop the tools and knowledge they need to discuss an abstract concept, in this case *survival*, with more depth and breadth. The classes are full-inclusion classes with high numbers of English-language learners. Grade 8 is the students' first year of secondary school.

Essential Question

How are hope, knowledge, and friendship necessary for the survival of the human spirit?

Key Structures

Assessment for Learning

- Students co-create criteria for journal entries with the core thinking skill of questioning in mind.
- Students co-create criteria for small-group discussion skills.
- Students are given multiple opportunities to practise, self-assess, and receive explicit feedback in order to improve their work.

Gradual Release of Responsibility

- Teachers model, with a shared text (novel, short story, picture book, newspaper article), how to look for evidence of an author's representation of an abstract concept (survival).
- Students use thinking strategies modelled first by the teachers, then practise using them in their small-group discussions to discern how and when the theme of survival is developed in a text.

Diverse Texts

- A conceptually rich, accessible, shared text is used to introduce the concepts and strategies.
- Students choose and read novels in a literature circle. The text set for the circles (see page 98) includes novels at various reading levels but on the same theme.
- As the students explore and compare their novels, they apply specific thinking strategies to help them understand how the authors develop the theme of survival.

Assessment of Learning

Reading Journal

- Over the course of the unit, students learn how to develop questions for discussion. In their journals, each selects one question they have developed in class and writes a response to it. They receive feedback from other students and the teacher based on the criteria they have developed. At the end of the unit, each student selects three responses to be assessed by the teacher against these criteria, and the teacher grades those responses selected.

The Character Survival Kit

- As a final assessment, the students create the Character Survival Kit, which requires that they demonstrate the skills and strategies introduced and taught throughout the unit.

Targeted Thinking Skills

- Accessing prior knowledge
- Questioning as you read
- Examining an abstract concept through questioning
- Making inferences
- Applying abstract concepts to personal reading

Targeted Writing Skills

- Impromptu writing
- Response writing

Lesson 1—Rationale

The year's plan is to work with an inquiry approach to learning. Since this is the beginning of the course, questioning is the thinking skill targeted for this unit. The goal is for students to get to know one another while learning how to develop and phrase effective questions. During this process, they will consider what makes an effective question (generate criteria) and revise their questions accordingly (use their criteria to focus their learning).

Figure 6.1 provides an overview of the teachers' collective planning process. The left column contains teaching aspects considered in the planning. The right column gives examples of how these are addressed.

Twenty questions

- Hide an object in a box. Students may ask up to 20 questions to guess what the object is.
- Record students' questions on the board.
- After they have asked a few questions, stop the questioning and have the students examine the questions recorded on the board. Ask them to consider which questions have been the most effective and why.
- Point out to students that analyzing which questions elicited the most effective answers helps us to think about our thinking. It is important not only to apply thinking strategies and activities but also to involve the students in thinking and talking about how they learn. This process enables them to gain more insight and personal control over the thinking strategies.
- Continue the question-answer process until the students have discovered what the object is or until they have asked the allotted 20 questions.

Three-way interview

- Students work in triads to develop three interview questions that will help them get to know another person in the class.
- Have students, in their triads, choose their most effective question, one that provides both insight and interest.
- The triads share their questions with the class while the teacher records them on the board.
- Have the students work as a class to critique the questions, considering which gave them the best information and why.

Lesson 2—Rationale

Engagement in learning counts. Beginning with personal experience and recognizing what you know and can do helps students connect with new content. Writing is used to make connections with background knowledge and personal experience and to generate new ideas.

Figure 6.1 Sample of teachers' planning for unit of study

Unit Theme: Survival	
Thematic questions	How are hope, knowledge and friendship necessary for the survival of the human spirit? In the novel you read, is hope, knowledge, or friendship most important for the survival of the character's spirit?
Shared text	Model text: *Fish* by L.S. Matthews
Literature circle text set	See titles and authors in the text set on page 97.
Writing genre/types	Impromptu writing (quick-writes, response journals) The beginnings of literary analysis
Writing/Representing strategies	Coherence (staying on topic) Using quotes and specific evidence and explanations to support thinking Representing ideas graphically
Reading strategies	Activating prior knowledge Questioning
Teaching strategies	Quick-Write Think-Aloud Say Something Three-Way Interview Twenty Questions
Assessment for Learning	Learning intentions—end goals Descriptive feedback Criteria-building Self-assessment and peer-assessment Ownership
Assessment of Learning	Reading journal Summative assignment that tracks thinking and deals with the essential question(s) related to survival: Character Survival Kit

Quick-Write

- Model, using the word *bread* as a prompt, how to brainstorm all the possible ways you might write about this topic.
- Choose one of the ways and write about it in front of the students, modelling the decisions you are making as you write.
- Give the students the prompt *fish*.
- Have students brainstorm, independently, all the possible ways they might write about this topic.
- Using one of the ideas they have brainstormed, have students do a quick-write about *fish*, allowing 10 minutes. This activity serves as an introduction to the upcoming shared text, the novel *Fish* by L.S. Matthews.
- Have students share what they wrote about and why, rather than reading aloud their actual writing. This encourages more students to share their thoughts, and it is less anxiety-inducing for them than having to read their draft writing so early in the school year.
- Encourage everyone to share and to notice how varied their voices can be.

Lesson 3—Rationale

Using a common text gives all learners a shared experience and allows them to work together to understand what is valued and targeted in the class. Think-alouds demonstrate that reading involves thinking and helps students to further develop questioning as a strategic reading skill. After first listening to the self-questioning being modelled, then trying it themselves in guided practice, they should be ready to work independently on fine-tuning their questioning and self-questioning. The novel is used to introduce students to the main inquiry: "How are hope, knowledge, and friendship necessary for the survival of the human spirit?"

Figure 6.2 Question types for inquiry approach

Question Types	Description
1. Right There	**factual questions**—that is, students can locate an answer to these questions by pointing and saying, "right there."
2. Think and Search	**interpretive questions**—that is, students have to search for details in the text, then link them together to shape an answer.
3. Author and Me	**personal input questions**—that is, students have to search for information in the text and fill in their knowledge gaps using personal background knowledge from outside the text.
4. On My Own	**evaluative or appreciative questions**—that is, questions for ongoing inquiry that can be applied to many texts or situations; students search outside sources for information to support their position.

Think-Aloud

- Begin to read the text aloud, stopping occasionally to share your thoughts about the text, especially the questions that occur to you as you read.
- Have the students record in their journals their questions about the part of the text that has been read.
- Invite students to share their questions and write them on the board. Categorize them, with the students, using the four question types in Figure 6.2.
- Provide time for the students to practise asking questions of each type (see Figure 6.3).

Questioning the abstract concept of *survival*

- Use the word *survival* as a prompt.
- Have students develop questions on the topic of *survival*.
- Record these questions and post them in the classroom, making a list to which students can return throughout the unit.
- If student interest warrants extending the discussion about survival, bring in various texts to support further exploration of the theme.

Examples of effective choices:

- a mini-lesson on Maslow's hierarchy of needs (<http://en.wikipedia. org/wiki/Maslow's_hierarchy_of_needs>)
- an excerpt from *Into Thin Air* by Jon Krakauer (1997) about the 1996 storm that claimed five lives on Mount Everest.

Figure 6.3 Student sample of questions in categories

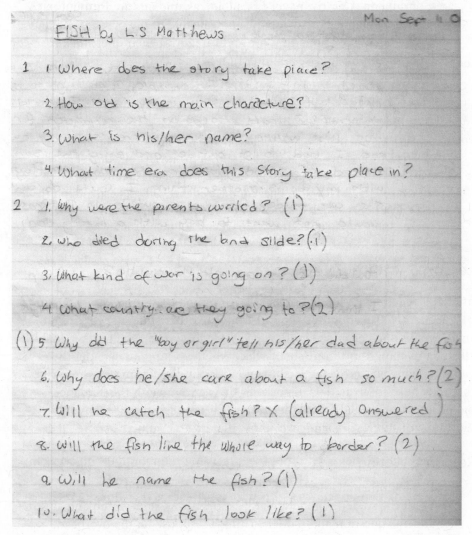

Lesson 4—Rationale

Students benefit from guided practice with the key concepts and strategies that are being studied. In this unit, quick-writes, questioning, and response-writing are modelled and gradually released by the teacher. These three open-ended strategies are used many times, with less and less teacher support, so that students gain more independence as they become more familiar with using them.

Quick-Write

- Have students think of an object that is precious to them.
- Have students prepare a quick-write to describe the object and why it is important to them.

Read-Aloud, Response-Writing

- Continue reading the novel *Fish* aloud, as students are introduced to the fish, which is both symbolic and valuable to the protagonist, and have students continue to write and categorize their questions.
- Choose a think-and-search question from the students' list of questions; model the writing of a response, talking as you write about the decisions you are making as a writer.

  A sample think-aloud with writing:

  I think I will use the question Why were the parents so worried? I am going to try and use specific evidence from the novel as I write. They have left most of their possessions behind. They are taking only what they can carry.... Now that I have some evidence, I think I can interpret it. I think they must be in danger or they would have taken more time, packed more carefully. I certainly do when I am going somewhere.

Lesson 5 — Rationale

Students benefit from guided practice with response-writing before writing independently. Collaborative support from the other students working in small groups and continued guidance and feedback from the teacher enable all students to perform more successfully when working independently.

Students have more ownership and more understanding of criteria that they have co-created. Categorizing their criteria with the guidance of performance standards includes an outside voice, ensuring that your indicators of success are similar to those of a greater group.

Response-Writing

- Read another chapter of *Fish*.
- With the students, generate at least one think-and-search and author-and-me question and model writing a response on the overhead, thinking aloud. Invite the students to coach you as you write, making suggestions about details to include, about why these would be helpful, and about how effectively you are explaining your thinking. Make adjustments to your responses using their ideas and feedback.
- Have students in small groups select one question to respond to, and write a group response on an overhead transparency.

Co-constructing Criteria

- Share these small-group responses with the class, having students identify strengths from each.
- Compile these strengths on the board to create a list of which criteria make a good response.
- Sort the criteria using your local curriculum and standards for reading as a reference. (We use the *BC Performance Standards* (2002) <http://www.bced.gov.bc.ca/perf_stands/reading.htm>.)
- Make these criteria into a rubric. Some teachers develop these rubrics with their students, but, at this time of year, after having spent a lot of time co-constructing criteria, many prefer to develop various levels of the criteria within the rubric.

Lesson 6—Rationale

Students are now ready to write a reading response to a question independently, to receive descriptive feedback from the teacher, and to self-assess using the rubric co-created with the class criteria. When the feedback is descriptive, it acts as a tool for conversation about powerful responses. Numbers at the top of the scale give students a sense of how these criteria might later translate into marks (9 or 7 out of 10). Do not grade student work at this point in the year—this is practice time. The summative assessment, with a marking scheme, takes place after the students have had a great deal of practise with descriptive feedback, with using criteria, and with continued instruction.

Reading response with criteria

- Read another chapter of *Fish*.
- Practise using the rubric (Figure 6.4) by assessing your written response to that chapter. This practice helps prepare students to self-assess their responses.
- Have students write an individual response to *Fish*, accept your descriptive feedback, then self-assess using the rubric. Give students the option of revising their response or write a new response based on the feedback they have received and on their self-assessment.

Figure 6.4 Rubric developed by teacher with class for evaluating students' journal entries

Reading Journal	1–4	5–6	7–8	9–10
Thinking ideas, opinions, depth, questions, connections	• very little thinking is evident, may not make sense or seem "random"	• thinking is simple and makes sense • points may be very obvious	• thinking is clear and logical, may have some depth • straightforward points	• thinking is logical, thought-out and "deep" (insightful) • may have some unusual points but used in a thoughtful way
Support & Detail examples (including from book), amount of detail	• few or no examples • little or no detail	• some examples • some detail	• points have reasons/examples • points are developed with detail	• points have logical reasons and examples • points are developed with good, specific detail • may also have variety in detail/examples

Lesson 7—Rationale

Students need to read diverse texts, and a literature circle text set allows for choice. All the texts that have been chosen for the literature circles collection have strong characters and have survival themes. Moving to diverse novels allows students to apply more independently the thinking skills and comprehension skills that have been introduced with the common novel.

Literature Circles

Character Survival Kit—Introducing the Novels
- Introduce the literature circle novels by sharing scenarios from each one—interesting facts without the names of characters. The task for the students is to make a survival kit for the character introduced in this novel scenario, based on the inferences they have made after reading the scenario.
- Give each group a scene from one of the novels, for example, the scenario for the novel *Speak* by Laurie Halse Anderson (1999):

  You've been traumatized. You can't bring yourself to tell anyone, so no one knows why you've withdrawn yourself completely. Everyone hates you at school. No one talks to you.

  and for *Tomorrow, When the War Began*:

  You come back from a camping trip with friends and your families are gone—you don't know where. Soon, you realize a country has invaded yours and everyone has been captured except you and your camping friends.

- Each group lists (or draws) the items for their survival kit, then shares with the class.
- Connect each novel with its corresponding scenario before allowing students time to browse and choose their books. Students approach the novel choices filled with curiosity and questions.

Homework

Students begin to read the novels and to ask questions as they read, recording these on sticky notes to be used in their journal responses next class.

Lesson 8 — Rationale

Students need support in applying abstract concepts to their reading. The survival inkshed and three corners debate strategies help students recognize what they know and believe as they hear and see the thinking of others and begin to develop new understandings around abstract concepts, in this case survival, knowledge, hope, and friendship.

Survival Inkshed

- Write each of the words *knowledge*, *hope*, and *friendship* on large sheets of paper, one word per page. Place the sheets around the room.
- Have students write their thoughts as they move from word to word.
- Once completed, discuss with the class the thinking revealed in the responses.

Three Corners Debate

- Pose the question What is most essential to survival—hope, knowledge, or friendship?
- Have students move to the corner of the room that represents their choice so they can talk with like-minded students.
- Students then listen to the viewpoints from the other corners. If a larger number of students converge on one of the corners, divide them into two groups for a total of four corners.

Lesson 9 — Rationale

When students meet in small groups and talk about the book they have been reading, their thinking about the book grows and their understanding of the book deepens. The ultimate goal of these small-group discussions is that students meet independently and discuss in such a natural and spontaneous way that all voices are included and that the thinking of all group members is changed as a result of being in the discussion. The say-something strategy is a step toward independence.

Say-Something Strategy

- Ask for volunteers to meet in a fishbowl literature circle. These students sit together in the fishbowl and, together with the teacher, they talk about the chapter in *Fish*, the read-aloud novel, that was last read in the class. Using this text to model the discussion strategy is a good idea because all the students have become familiar with it.
- All the other students sit outside the fishbowl and record the techniques that they notice being used that move the discussion forward.
- Introduce the students to the say-something strategy. In this strategy, each student in turn shares a comment or a question connected with the chapter, or a quote from the chapter, or a response to the previous speaker's comments. A strategy like this avoids the situations where one student's comments are met with silence. It is the responsibility of each student to continue the conversation. No student may speak a second time until each student has had an opportunity to speak at least once. Students can say whatever comes to mind about a topic or quote, add to the previous speaker's point, or try extending the conversation with a question.
- Once the discussion is complete (usually 15 minutes), collect the ideas that the observers have noticed—techniques that moved the conversation forward. Invite discussion participants to add their ideas to this list.
- Use the list to develop criteria for small-group discussion (Figure 6.5 is a polished version, developed with students). Using the criteria, students can self-assess their participation and set goals for future discussions (see stems in Figure 6.5). The more explicit teachers are when building expectations with students, the easier it is for most students to achieve these expectations.
- After the students have seen the literature discussion modelled and they have developed the criteria for effective discussions, they can meet in small-group discussions, each group formed by the common book—that is, those reading *Speak* meet together, those reading *Tomorrow, When the War Began* (Marsden 1993) meet together, and so on. Students will continue to meet and discuss in small groups, following the same structure but moving on to focus on questions.
- Once a week, we ask students to use reflection and goal-setting prompts (see Figure 6.5) to help develop the capacities identified by the criteria.

Figure 6.5

Name _____

Small-Group Discussion Criteria

Preparation
Come prepared for the discussion. Do your reading. Have your book, journal, and pen with you. Bring your ideas and questions.

Participation
Participate fully and respectfully. Say what's on your mind. Don't be afraid to share. Make eye contact with the other members of your group. Stay focused. Respond to other people's ideas. Listen to one another. Encourage quieter members to speak—everyone should participate.

Comprehension and Response
Challenge yourself to offer good ideas. Provide specific details to support your ideas and to elaborate on another's ideas. Make connections to personal experience, to past and current events. Ask insightful questions (e.g., suggest inferences, extend others' ideas, require the group to relate events to important themes).

Individual Reflection on Small-Group Discussion

Preparation

What have you been doing well?	What do you need to work on?

Participation

What have you been doing well?	What do you need to work on?

Comprehension and Response

What have you been doing well?	What do you need to work on?

Lesson 10—Rationale

At this point, students will have the opportunity to weave together the separate elements they have had modelled: themes, questioning, small-group discussion. They begin with the support of using questions from the shared novel, then move on to work within their literature circle group with questions that their group has created on their own. This gradual release of responsibility enables more students to succeed.

Figure 6.6 Sample of questions used, related to knowledge and *Fish*

Fish—Read-Aloud Activity: Knowledge

In the novel *Fish*, the guide is very knowledgeable. Below are four questions about knowledge. Each of the questions is one of the question types that you have been looking for in your novels. Answer the questions below as you listen to the reading of *Fish*.

Right There—What are some ways that the guide uses his knowledge to help the others?	**Think and Search**—Is the guide's knowledge *unique* or *special* in some way?
Author and Me—In our society, or in your experience, do you know of people who have knowledge like the guide? Or, think of people who are knowledgeable. How are they similar to or different from the guide?	**On My Own**—Is knowledge the same thing as wisdom?

Using question types

- Prepare four questions (see Figure 6.6) on the novel *Fish* based on the three overarching themes for the unit: *knowledge, hope,* and *friendship.* Share these questions with the students.
- Read another chapter of *Fish*.
- Have students meet in small groups to discuss these questions. These four questions, which correspond to the four types of questions already discussed, act as models for students' own questions, which they will generate in response to the novel selected for their own literature circle. It is helpful if they can focus on one theme at a time—*hope*, then *knowledge*, then *friendship*. Model your questions with each key idea, if necessary.
- Students develop four questions, following the chart (see Figure 6.7), on their novel. These form the basis of the discussion in their literature circle groups. Students who need more support are able to adapt the questions from *Fish* to their novel. Others develop new ones, perhaps using those they have recorded during their reading the night before.

- Students meet in their literature circle groups and discuss answers to their questions.
- Move from group to group, coaching and providing descriptive feedback on students' questions and group discussion skills as they work through these structured discussions.

Figure 6.7 Suggested layout of discussion organizer

Right There	Think and Search
Author and Me	On My Own

Continuing the Literature Circle discussions

- Have students continue to meet in their literature circles and discuss their novels, using the graphic organizer for questions. Introduce Figure 6.8. This is a chart that helps students focus on the theme of *survival* and the thinking that is required of them in their final assessment of learning. Following each discussion, students track and find evidence to support their thinking by filling in the chart. Notice that the summative evidence is being set up early in the learning and that students are practising the thinking required in this assessment throughout the unit.

- Explain to the students in each of your novels, *hope, knowledge,* and *friendship* contribute to the survival of your characters. In your group, fill out the table in the handout (Figure 6.8) by finding quotes in the novel that you are reading. You must come up with five quotes about hope, knowledge, and friendship.

- Have students continue to meet in their literature circle groups. Some students may finish their novel and move on to another literature circle group and a different novel. This leads to richer discussion, as these students find patterns and ideas across books and groups.

Figure 6.8 A chart to help students find evidence to relate *survival* to key ideas

Literature Circles——Discussion Organizer

Quote or example (include page number):	How are hope, knowledge, or friendship helping the characters to survive ?	Does this connect to the other two factors, hope, knowledge or friendship ? Explain how.

- Have students continue to develop the four kinds of questions in relation to the theme of survival as they read their novels.

- Every second class, ask students to respond to one of their own questions, with the shared criteria in mind.

- Continue to provide students with formative descriptive feedback. This helps students become more independent in writing their responses and provides them with opportunities to expand their thinking. Students' responses will improve because of the descriptive feedback provided in relation to the criteria they established. Figures 6.9 and 6.10 are student samples. This prepares them for the summative assessment, which uses the same criteria for the essential question "How are hope, knowledge, and friendship necessary for the survival of the human spirit?"

Figure 6.9 Student response to question based on novel *Speak* by Laurie Halse Anderson

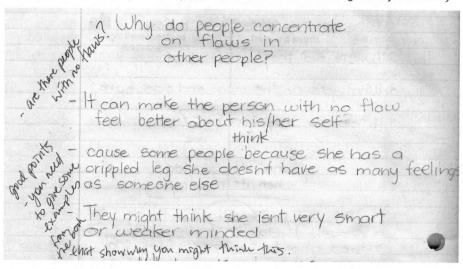

Figure 6.10 Student response to question based on novel *Gathering Blue* by Lois Lowry

Lesson 11—Summative Assessment

Summative assessments should assess what has been taught. Students need opportunities to practise the targeted skill areas throughout the unit, then to apply their learning during a summative assessment. There should be no surprises.

Assessment of Learning 1: Student Journals

- Students choose three journal entries to be assessed summatively. After an extended period of writing responses, getting descriptive feedback and practising skills such as questioning, supporting thinking with evidence, and looking for patterns relating to the big ideas for survival (i.e., friendship, hope, knowledge) with shared criteria in mind, students are ready for a summative assessment, a measurement of their learning. Teachers assess students' questioning skills as well as their written response and their thematic connections to the big idea of survival (friendship, hope, or knowledge) because these have been the focus areas.
- Students may choose to rework the responses on which they have previously received feedback. We want students to do well—when they are deciding on and practising what is most important, they feel that they have control. This is an example of self-regulated learning. The gradual release of responsibility for using and working with criteria involves students taking ownership of—and using—both the thinking skills and the criteria.

Assessment of Learning 2: Character Survival Kit

- Students are asked to respond to the question What helps your character survive? The tasks in the assessment allow students to show how hope, knowledge, and friendship play a role in the survival of the characters in their novels. The tasks match the skills and understandings that have been developed. For example, this assessment requires students to support their thinking with evidence from the text. The summative assessment, therefore, assesses students' ability to support and communicate their ideas (Figure 6.11).
- To support students in completing their final assessment, provide the model organizer What helps your character survive? As with any other learning strategy or activity, first model with the students, using the shared text *Fish* (see excerpt in Figure 6.12).
- Students then complete their Character Survival Kit Organizer (Figure 6.11), based on and using their literature circle novels and with reference to the rubric on the second page.

- Provide the summative assessment rubric so students know how they will be judged. The criteria have been adapted from the journal response criteria. Thus, the thinking skills that are assessed in this final assignment are the same as those they have worked on throughout the unit.
- Have students initially work as partners or in small groups to record their thoughts. Working with a partner or small group helps students to clarify task expectations and share different ways to approach the task.
- Several times during this process, ask students to explain what they have done so far, how this relates to the criteria, and what their next steps are.
- Move from group to group, addressing questions that come up and monitoring students' understanding.

A Character Survival Kit

In each of the novels you read, the qualities of hope, knowledge, and friendship contribute to the survival of one or more characters. In your group, fill out the table below by finding quotes from your novel that relate to any one of those qualities. You must come up with five quotes that relate to the ideas of hope, knowledge, and/or friendship).

Your name: _____ Novel title: _____

Character name and short description:

_____

What helps your character to survive?

Abstract idea	What is the role of hope, knowledge, and friendship in the survival of your character? What form do the qualities of hope, knowledge, and friendship take? Give an example of how hope, knowledge, or friendship helps your character survive. Explain.	Write quotes and other evidence from the novel that support your idea. Include the page number. Explain how the quote supports your idea.
Hope		
Knowledge		
Friendship		
Quick-thinking		
Luck		

Pay attention to dialogue among characters, events that take place in the book, objects from the story that seem important, as well as the thoughts of your character.

- Once you have completed your chart (your planning and thinking), write your character's name and/or draw a picture of your character in the middle of your page.
- Record your four answers to the question What helps your character survive? around this centre piece. Each answer should include the abstract idea, an explanation, and a quote to support the explanation.
- Create a title or write the question in a logical place on your page.
- Choose a way to show which of the four abstract ideas (big ideas) has the most impact on your character.
- On the back, in about 150 words, explain why either hope, knowledge, or friendship is most important to the survival of your character.
- (Optional.) To extend your thinking, consider this question: What is most important to the survival of the human spirit—hope, knowledge or friendship? Answer in a second paragraph of about 150 words.

Figure 6.11 Summative Assessment Rubric

Criteria	You can do it. Spend some extra time with the criteria and ask for help.	Good start. Your engine is revving.	You did it.	Wow. This would knock anybody's socks off.
Explanation of how each abstract idea (hope, knowledge, or friendship) helps your character to survive and the paragraph response (which is most important)	Not a lot of thinking is evident; may be illogical in places	Straightforward thinking; may be simple and obvious, but is logical	Thinking is clear and logical; some insight	Thinking is logical and insightful; some complexity
Reasons and quotes to support the above explanations	Little or no support (few details or examples)	Some examples and some detail	Reasons and examples support all opinions and are developed with detail	Specific, relevant detail; variety of well-developed examples
Overall (presentation, conventions, organization, identification of most significant idea)	Lack of effort in terms of presentation or conventions	Satisfactory work; may be concerns about presentation or conventions	Very good effort; completed with care	Outstanding effort; completed with extra care

Asking questions helps to focus your attention on what you're reading and helps you to think more carefully about the ideas that are discussed in whatever you might be reading. List the best question you developed while reading this novel. What makes it powerful?

Did you enjoy this novel? Why or why not?

If you read more than one novel in this unit, list the other titles you read:

Which one was your favourite? Why?

Figure 6.12 Excerpt from summative assessment based on the novel *Fish*

What helps your character survive?

Hope	Hope takes the form of a fish. When you have something else to think about, you don't have time to feel sorry for yourself or to get lost in your own fear. The fish always seems to survive the least likely of situations. Surely if the fish could survive, Tyger could, too. Not surviving isn't an option.	p. 112/3: "Creatures are so tough," said Mum, "it's amazing what they'll put up with. Poor Fish was still trying to breathe in the mud puddle, wasn't he, when you pulled him out. Maybe thinking, It's worth it, more rain might come and fill this pond again—who can tell?" p. 146/7: "Suddenly I remembered Fish. I had rescued him from mud like this—what must it have seemed like to him to be sinking into it again? Then I remembered that the lid of his bottle would be screwed on tight, and that he was still breathing easy in his own element. The mud would be too thick to squeeze through those tiny pinprick holes. He would have coped much better than I. He would be fine, if I could just get out of this." This is most important in the scene with the mud. The fish is taken from a mud puddle earlier in the book. In the first quote, the fish is an example of something that can survive in the worst circumstances. When Tyger finds him/herself in a mud puddle (the second quote), he/she is able to survive, too. By thinking about the fish, Tyger is reminded of that example and also provides Tyger with motivation to survive. The fish gives him/her hope and strength.
Knowledge		
Friendship		
Quick-thinking	Jumping into the mud.	
Luck	The two men don't see Tyger when he or she crawls out of the mud.	

Reflections: Leyton, Krista, and Mehjabeen

At the end of the first few weeks of school, we feel that we are beginning to really know our students, and we have become aware of their strengths and their challenges. They, in turn, have learned what we value: deep thinking, personal responsibility, explicit expectations, and engaged, thoughtful learning. We find that practice over time with key thinking skills makes a significant difference in ensuring that all students can achieve success. We accept all ideas from students and then support them in relating their ideas to the criteria.

Our collaborative process makes the task of developing units more manageable and enjoyable. Our different tastes and interests help us collect a broader range of text sets that better match and extend the interests of our students. Throughout the school year, we teach four thematic units, each of which has a text set of novels at its core. Therefore, by the end of the year, each of our students has read, analyzed, and discussed at least five novels and has had over 30 novels to choose from. Many students read three or four novels from each text set. In each unit, we focus on a few key thinking, reading, and writing skills. This is how we develop thoughtful readers and writers who choose to read and write beyond our classroom.

Text Set for Students

- *Gathering Blue* by Lois Lowry
- *Speak* by Laurie Halse Anderson
- *Tomorrow, When the War Began* by John Marsden
- *House of the Scorpion* by Nancy Farmer
- *Max the Mighty* by Rodman Philbrick
- *Stuck in Neutral* by Terry Trueman
- *Julie of the Wolves* by Perdita Finn
- *Deathwatch* by Robb White
- *Invitation to the Game* by Monica Hughes
- *Night* by Elie Wiesel
- *The Wreckers* by Iain Lawrence
- *The Tunnel King* by Barbara Hehner
- *The Wind Singer* by William Nicholson
- *Parvana's Journey* by Deborah Ellis
- *Forbidden City* by William Bell
- *Mud City* by Deborah Ellis
- *The Garbage King* by Elizabeth Laird
- *Theories of Relativity* by Barbara Haworth-Attard

Chapter 7

Memoir Writing

Grade 8–10—English

Assessment FOR Learning	• Descriptive feedback • Self-assessment • Ownership • Rubrics
Gradual Release of Responsibility	• Modelling • Guided practice in small groups with feedback • Individual application
Differentiation	• Student choice of topic • Students receive varying amounts of support, depending on need • Open-ended assignment, experience-based
Assessment OF Learning	• Memoir • Self-assessment reflection
Essential Questions	• What makes a memoir good? • What does it mean to tell the truth? • Is it okay to lie? When? To what extent?

The Collaboration

Joanne Panas teaches English Language Arts in a school for grades 8 through 12; she has taught English for 15 years. She is a passionate reader of adolescent fiction and shares her own creative writing process with her students. Over the years, Joanne has co-planned and co-taught with colleagues, including Krista, Leyton, and Mehjabeen, whose work appears in other chapters. Collaboration can take many forms—for example, drawing ideas from professional books as Joanne has done with Nancie Atwell's *Lessons That Change Writers* (2002). When she first began teaching the memoir, she followed Nancie's lessons almost exactly. Over the years, she has revised what she does based on her students' needs, on provincial expectations for writing (using the *BC Performance Standards for Reading and Writing* 2002), on conversations with colleagues also teaching the memoir, and on a desire to have students experience a process for creating powerful pieces of writing. She continues to return to Nancie's words to reflect on and guide her practice while she transforms and personalizes how she teaches the memoir. Joanne finds that, as her practice grows and changes, she gains new insights from each rereading of Nancie Atwell's book.

The Context

Joanne's class includes students from a wide variety of cultural backgrounds—many of them immigrants, some still in the process of learning English, some from the French Immersion program, and several receiving a block of class time (each block is 75 minutes) for support and extra assistance. Joanne's instruction time and her task (the memoir) for assessing her students' learning requires eight to 10 blocks of class time. After this, students are allowed time to revise and edit their memoirs at home before Joanne collects them. In this chapter, Joanne integrates backward design, gradual release of responsibility, and formative assessment for a summative task within a larger unit. This series of lessons helps students work with big ideas, build background knowledge, take ownership of assessment criteria, and become reflective writers.

Joanne's students are involved in an inquiry unit on truth and lies. The summative assessment for this unit is to write a memoir, an assignment that links to four enduring understandings that are the focus of the students' work during the unit:

1. Effective communicators use a variety of skills and strategies to share, construct, and clarify meaning.
2. Authors make revisions in order to clarify meaning.
3. People "draw the line" between truth and lies at different places, for different reasons.
4. We need to decide for ourselves where to draw our line between truth and lies.

Specific to memoir writing, Joanne asks the students: "What would make a memoir good?"

Key Structures

Assessment for Learning

- Students practise using rubrics in small groups before applying them to their own work.
- Students work toward the clearly stated expectations.
- Students assess their own progress and reflect on their work as they progress.
- Students receive descriptive feedback while they are working.

Gradual Release of Responsibility

- Expectations are modelled before students practise in small groups.
- Teacher monitors and supports individuals to help them achieve expectations.

Differentiation

- Students choose their own topics.
- Students receive varying amounts of support, depending on what each requires.
- The writing assignment is open-ended so students can build from their own experience—everyone can participate.

Essential Questions

- What makes a memoir good?
- What does it mean to tell the truth?
- Is it okay to lie? When? To what extent?

Lesson 1—Rationale

Building background knowledge

Before students can write a memoir, they need some background information on making connections between ideas and applying their thinking to different situations. Use several different scenarios to build an understanding of truth and lies.

Class discussion to reach "official" definition

- Pose a series of questions to students that have no clear right or wrong answer, such as:
  - What should you say to a friend who asks you if she looks okay in her outfit when you think the outfit is not flattering?
  - What should you say if a friend asks if you think he should invite a certain girl to a party—the same girl that you were thinking of asking out?
  - What do you say to a friend who wasn't chosen for the soccer team and who says that the process was unfair? You have been chosen for the team.
- Discuss with the students what it means to tell a lie. Are there different categories of lies? Are some kinds of lies okay?
  - Create a class definition of an "official" lie.
  - List situations in which a typical teenager might tell an "official" lie.
  - Brainstorm different ways of lying—for example, with words or actions, by doing or saying nothing, by telling only part of the truth.

Joanne's class created the following definition of an "official" lie:
- A lie that is deliberate and results in someone getting hurt.

Moving beyond personal experience

- Read "The Dare" (Ellis 1995), a short story about a teen facing an ethical dilemma: Does he say nothing and allow another boy—a troublemaker and bully—to take the blame for his actions? Or, does he speak up, saving the other boy from being punished for something he didn't do?
- Talk with the students, as a class, about the story.
- After discussion, present students with two other ethical dilemmas (Figure 7.1) focusing on three questions:
  - What are the possible outcomes if this person tells the truth?
  - What are the possible outcomes if this person lies?
  - What should this person do?
- Students work in small groups to discuss these questions.

- Return to a class discussion and share responses to the questions. Encourage students to see that there are many perspectives on these situations, and much conflicting advice.
- Have students do a quick-write explaining how they decided what advice to give the people in the dilemmas.
- Summarize this information and share it with the class.

Figure 7.1 Two dilemmas

Dilemma #1

Donna has been invited to a party—a very cool party, and a guy she likes very much will be there. Donna's best friend Krista has not been invited and Donna knows it, and she knows that Krista is currently not speaking to the girl who is throwing the party because they had a fight last month.

The day before the party, Krista texts Donna: "Hrd abt Marias prty. UR NOT going R U?" Donna *is* going to the party; she and Maria are friends (that is, Donna is not mad at Maria, Krista is), and she wants to spend time with the guy she likes as well as have some fun. But Krista has been her best friend for a long time, and she doesn't want to hurt her feelings. Donna texts back...

- What are the possible outcomes for Donna if she lies to Krista?
- What are the possible outcomes for Donna if she tells Krista the truth?
- What do you think Donna should do? How did you come to that decision?

Dilemma #2

Frank is in grade 12 and wants to be accepted into a good university. He is doing well in all his classes, except one, History 12, in which he has received a C+. The universities will soon ask him to submit his current marks, and Frank is worried that unless he has all As and Bs he will not be accepted or will not be eligible for any scholarships; on top of that, his mom and dad won't be happy.

Ms. Morgan, his history teacher, has given him the chance to bring up his mark in History 12 with a major essay. However, Frank is busy and overwhelmed. In desperation, he buys an essay off the Internet and hands it in. However, Ms. Morgan is suspicious. After class, she asks to see his drafts as proof of his work. The penalty for plagiarism is a zero on the paper, a phone call home, and a note in his disciplinary record, all of which could ruin his chances of a scholarship, maybe even admission. Frank is known as a good student and has never done anything like this before. He could claim to have erased the drafts and thrown out his notes. Frank takes a deep breath...

- What are the possible outcomes for Frank if he lies about his paper?
- What are the possible outcomes for Frank if he tells the truth about it?
- What do you think Frank should do? How did you come to that decision?

Lesson 2—Rationale

Developing students' writing ideas

Memoirs, especially short ones, are personal stories about the impact of significant events or situations in our lives. Because they are based on personal memories and perspectives, there is more wiggle room for interpretation of events than in writing a biography which should be well-documented. Biographies, while also personal and reflective in nature, usually tell more of a life story than a short memoir. Students need to clearly understand what a memoir is, and need the time to build their thinking toward choosing their topic.

Choosing a topic

- Review what memoirs are, comparing and contrasting them with biographies and novels.
- Give four topics for students to choose from as a memoir:
  - a time I lied
  - a time I told the truth
  - a time someone lied to me
  - a time someone told me the truth
- Share a few of your own ideas for each topic.
- Have students brainstorm at least two possible ideas for each.
- Remind students that the audience for this writing is their peers. They will share their memoirs with their group at the end of the unit.
- We will track the development of two students—Katherine and Jordan.

> *I told my mom I'm busier than I actually am.*—Katherine
>
> *Telling the truth about a friend's project.*—Jordan

Lesson 3—Rationale

Establishing criteria helps students clearly understand your expectations of them. Clarity of purpose gives all students the opportunity to succeed. Building the criteria with your students gives them ownership of the criteria and increases their understanding of their purpose. Because the criteria have been developed from their own words and experiences, they cannot then say, "I didn't know I had to do THAT" or "What all am I supposed to do here anyway?"

Consider the question What would make a memoir good? Because you have discussed with your students the connections and differences between memoirs and stories, they should be able to develop some good descriptors.

Going deeper with the topic

- Show students a first draft of a memoir you have created that is deliberately poor in quality. Ask them to discuss in their groups whether the memoir is good or not. Have them explain the reasoning behind their choice of good or not.

- Discuss with your students what would improve your memoir, focusing on Atwell's idea—students read a section of your memoir, then ask the question So What?
  - Okay, you stole a candy and lied and got caught—so what?
- Use Figure 7.2, the Memoir Graphic Organizer, to get the So What? into a memoir.

Figure 7.2 Memoir Graphic Organizer

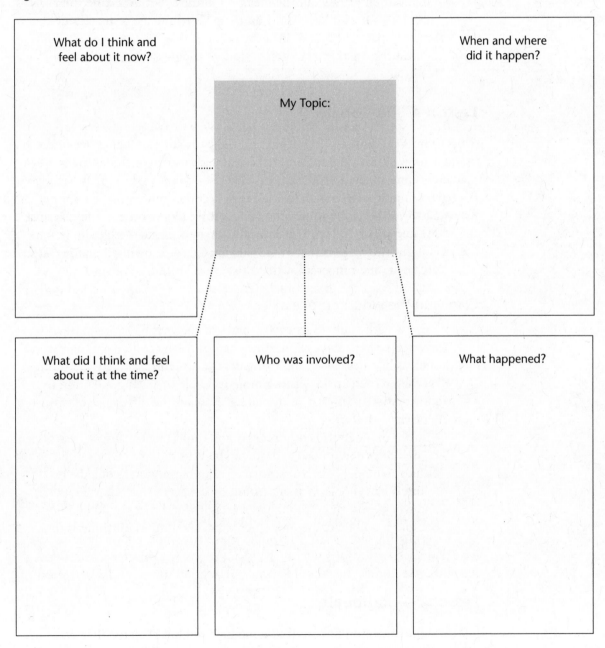

- Model how to complete the organizer using your own ideas, explaining that the "So what?" can be answered through details about your thoughts and feelings, especially as you look back on the event from your current perspective.
- Have students complete the organizer, following your lead. Working through this organizer helps students realize the necessary depth of thought and feeling required for an event chosen to be a memoir.
- Help students draw out the meaning in the event by asking themselves questions such as: Why did I do that? Why did she or he tell me that? What impact did that event have on me?
- Collect the organizers to assess student progress and give descriptive feedback.

Lesson 4—Rationale

Most writers need to put their ideas and their thinking on paper or on screen in order to work with them. The writing process usually includes many edits, many revisions, many drafts. Students also need to understand that writing is a recursive process in which the wording becomes more exact over time. Knowing this is helpful both for the reluctant writers (who get stuck because they don't know how to begin) and for the anxious-about-perfection writers (because it gives them permission to make mistakes, knowing that you can work with them and return it for them to revise later).

Clarifying the writing process

- Review with your students the stages of the writing process. Revision is when writers make significant changes to the content of their work, such as big ideas and supporting details, structure, and style. Editing is when writers make writing more readable by paying attention to punctuation, grammar, and spelling. Explain the difference between *revising* and *editing*.
- Explain that a draft is often messy and imperfect because it hasn't been revised or edited; in fact, a draft can be very rough in terms of being clear or telling a coherent story. For example, a writer could begin by telling a bare-bones factual account of the event—who, what, when and where—with no thoughts or feelings, and that would be fine, because it will be revised together later. The important thing is to get thinking down on paper that can be revised.
- Have students write the first draft of their memoir.

Lesson 5—Rationale

Clearly defined assignments and expectations are a roadmap for students. The rubric is based on the criteria that students first developed, but has been created by the teacher. Although Joanne often builds the rubric with her students, in this case, she already had a good rubric for memoirs and was reluctant to take several classes to work on a new one—there was an excitement and momentum about the memoirs that she didn't want to disrupt. Whether you choose to develop the rubric with the students or give the rubric to students, they need support in becoming familiar with the rubric and its meaning.

Building understanding and ownership of assessment

Prepare a two-sided handout of the memoir assignment (Figure 7.3) for students with the rubric (Figure 7.4) of the criteria developed for the memoir on the back side.

- To develop a deeper understanding of the rubric, review the Fully Meeting Expectations and Exceeding Expectations columns, pointing out key words and explaining the differences between the columns.
- Give students a sample memoir that they can evaluate in their groups, using the rubric. Students must quote from the sample to support their evaluation.
- Students then use the rubric to evaluate their own first drafts, focusing on what they have done well.

When I was 12 years old and in grade 7, I was at home, with my mom, who was trying to get me to study my math with her. —Katherine

I thought about it then. —Jordan

Lesson 6—Rationale

Using a rubric: Guided practice

- Using a rubric does not directly improve student performance. Most students require more coaching or guided practice to really understand how using the rubric can help their writing.
- Teach students how to use this rubric throughout their writing. Demonstrate each aspect using the sample memoir.
- To revise for meaning, students read through their memoirs and draw a box around every word or phrase that describes a feeling.
- Students read through their memoirs again and draw a circle around every word or phrase that describes a thought. If a student's draft lacks thoughts or feelings, they are to make a note of it.
- Students will reread their drafts multiple times, marking text, labelling, and making notes, as outlined in Figure 7.5. They are actively engaged in understanding what has to be present in their memoirs in order to create meaning in their writing. This is revision.

Figure 7.3 Memoir assignment

Inquiry Unit: What does it mean to tell the truth?

Assignment #1: Memoir and Self-Evaluation

Part 1: Memoir
- Your memoir will be evaluated using the rubric on the back of this page. (Total=20 marks)
- Final checklist for handing in your memoir—**in order, from top to bottom.**
  - ☐ This sheet, rubric-side-up, with your name and class on it, highlighted/underlined according to the Self-Evaluation instructions (see below).
  - ☐ Final copy of the memoir must be at least 500 words long (about 1 to 1¼ pages typed, double-spaced, 2 cm margins, 12 point Times New Roman font); typed or handwritten in dark blue or black ink.
  - ☐ Brainstorming web(s) from class.
  - ☐ 2+ drafts showing revision and editing on them (labelled Draft 1, Draft 2).
  - ☐ Self-Evaluation Questions & Answers (see below).
- If you have problems printing out your final copy, **hand in all the other parts** and email the final copy to < _____ >
  Do not email it to me if you can print it out.

Part 2: Self-Evaluation
- When you have finished the final copy of your memoir, take a few minutes to reread it. Then, using a highlighter or an HB pencil, highlight or underline the phrases on the rubric (turn over this sheet) that you think best describe your memoir.
- Next, answer the 3 questions below on a separate sheet of paper. Write 3 to 5 sentences for each question. You will be evaluated using the rubric at the bottom of this page.
  1. What are you most proud of in your memoir? Why?
  2. What do you think is your "weakest link" in it? Why?
  3. What might you do differently if you had a similar assignment again? Why?

Aspect	Not Yet Meeting (1)	Minimally Meeting (2)	Fully Meeting (3)
Content • Questions • Thought • Details	• 2 or 3 questions are not addressed, are minimal in length, or are off topic. • Response is on the "surface"; shows little thought. • There are few details in any answer.	• 1 question is not addressed, is minimal in length, or is off topic. • Response is thoughtful in parts. • 2 answers have good details.	• All 3 answers are of satisfactory length and stay on topic. • Response is thoughtful and reflects on learning. • Each answer has good details.
Writing/Format • Clarity • Organization • Conventions (spelling, sentences, and punctuation)	• Writing is generally unclear and hard to understand. • Response is disorganized. • Errors are frequent and/or repeated.	• Writing is generally clear, but sometimes hard to understand. • Response is somewhat organized. • Errors are noticeable but not too distracting.	• Writing is clear and easy to understand. • Response is well-organized. • Any errors are minor and do not distract the reader.

Figure 7.4 Rubric showing criteria for the memoir

Memoir Criteria

Total marks: /20

Criteria	Does Not Meet Expectations (0/1)	Minimally Meets Expectations (2)	Fully Meets Expectations (3)	Exceeds Expectations (4)
Meaning *What you say* • So what? • Thoughts and Feelings • Details **Score x 2**	The writing does not seem to have a point. It may just tell what happened. It has few or no thoughts and feelings; few or no details, examples, explanations, or sensory descriptions. There are too many unrelated details.	The writing has a point or message, but it isn't always clear or on topic. It shows some of your thoughts and feelings. It has a few details, examples, explanations, or sensory descriptions, but they may not all be related to the point.	The writer has a good point or message. Text shows writer's thoughts and feelings, and has good details, examples, explanations, background information, or sensory descriptions that get across the meaning in an interesting way.	The writer develops an insightful point or message. Text clearly shows writer's thoughts and feelings. Text has engaging details, examples, explanations, background information, or sensory descriptions that clearly show the meaning.
Style *How you say it* • Vocabulary • Sentences • Literary Devices • Effect	General, basic vocabulary; sentences tend to be simple and short. Writer does not use any literary devices. Text is difficult to follow. It may not always make sense, or is boring or repetitive.	Occasionally interesting vocabulary and sentence variety. Writer tries to use literary devices, but they may be awkward or unclear. Writing is conversational and fairly easy to follow.	Good choice and use of vocabulary. Writer varies length of sentences; uses some literary devices, but these may not be effective. Text is clear and understandable. Some parts are interesting to read.	Chooses vocabulary for effect. Varies sentence length and type for effect. Uses literary devices correctly and effectively. Text is engaging and interesting to read.
Form *How you organize it* • Introduction, middle, and conclusion • Organization • Transitions	Introduction gives the facts; middle and conclusion are weak. Organization is illogical; may be one paragraph only. Writer shifts abruptly from idea to idea with few or incorrect transitions.	Introduction tries to grab reader's attention; may list background info; middle and conclusion mostly but not always clear and/or logical; broken into paragraphs; uses some transitions effectively.	Introduction gets reader's attention; progresses with logical but predictable sequence and conclusion; good flow from beginning to end. Text is broken into logical paragraphs, variety of transitions helps it flow.	Reader is drawn into the writing (engaged). Interesting sequence. May use flashback well. Conclusion has impact. Paragraphs are effective. Varied transitions make text flow smoothly.
Conventions *Helping readers read it correctly* • Mechanics • Sentences • Editing	Frequent, repeated, basic errors make it difficult to understand. Writer shows little to no control over sentences. There are many run-on sentences or sentence fragments. Writer made few or no corrections in drafts.	Errors are noticeable and sometimes distracting, but meaning is still clear. Errors are somewhat basic. Text may have several run-on sentences or sentence fragments. Shows some evidence of editing/drafts.	Some errors are present, but they don't distract from meaning. Errors tend not to be basic or repeated. Text has few run-on sentences or sentence fragments. Text has been edited over several drafts.	Few to no errors—any errors present tend to be complex or the result of risk-taking. Any run-on sentences or sentence fragments are used purposefully. Many drafts and well-edited.

Figure 7.5

Whole-Class Revision Process: Meaning

- Put a box around every word and phrase **that conveys a feeling or emotion.**
  - Are the feelings specific, or did you just "feel good or bad"? What other words can you use?
  - What other ways can you show your feelings—physical symptoms, comparisons?
- Put a circle around every **thought** you express about what happened (words and phrases).
  - Are your thoughts and feelings given throughout the memoir or all in one place? Why did you make that choice? Is it effective?
- Every time you describe a **sense** (what you see, hear, touch, smell, taste) or an action you do, underline it and put an "S" above it.
- Every time you give a **detail** other than a sense or action (e.g., example, explanation, background information, or description), underline it and put a "D" above it.
  - Where are your senses, actions, and details? Are they throughout the memoir or all in one place? Do you describe them specifically? Are they effective?
- At the end of your draft, write down the point, message, or "So what?" that you are trying to get across. Below that, write the sentences from your draft that help get it across, or write new sentences to put into your next draft.

- At the end of the first class of revision, instruct students to go back over the notes they made on the draft and make those changes.
- During the next two classes, revise for "Style and Form" (Figure 7.6.) and for "Conventions" (Figure 7.7) using the same process.
- Students select aspects of the criteria on which they want feedback.
- Collect all drafts to give descriptive feedback on specific aspects of the criteria as requested by each student.

> *Once, when I was 12 years old and in grade 7, I was at home, finishing up my homework, when my mom started to try making me study math with her.* —Katherine
>
> *I thought about what the consequences would be to tell him the truth and tell him it was bad.* —Jordan

Lesson 7—Rationale

Creating reflective writers

As students work through the writing process, teachers work toward the goal of students taking personal control of their writing by having the students continue to apply aspects of the rubric to their writing and choose which aspect they would like feedback on. This practice not only lessens the teacher's marking, but also makes it more effective because the feedback given is directly on topic—dealing with the specific place where the student wants feedback. Small-group lessons can arise in response to the collective need that the teacher notices while giving the descriptive feedback. This is responsive teaching.

- Read through the memoirs, *revising* (asking questions, suggesting changes, noting confusing spots), and *editing* (making corrections for errors too challenging for the student, noting problems that the student was capable of correcting).
- Note the significant changes many students have already made from draft to draft in details, sequence, and leads, in order to share this with the class.
- Make notes of the most common problems and create a handout that details not only the problems but also ways to fix them, often with examples adapted from student work.
- Teach to these handouts; do not just give them to the students. Figure 7.8. is a sample created by Joanne for this particular class. This lets students know that they aren't alone in having some challenges, and that there are specific things they can do to improve.
- Make a list of students to conference with next day. Examples of student requests on 3rd drafts:

> *Can you check for literary devices?* —Kathleen
>
> *Can you check for organization and detail?* —Jordan

Figure 7.6

Whole-Class Revision Process: Style and Form

- Highlight or underline with a squiggly line every **interesting or specific word** you use.
- Label each sentence as short, medium, or long.
  - Short: usually up to 8 to 10 words long
  - Medium: 1 to 2 lines of type, or about 2 to 3 lines handwritten
  - Long: more than 2 lines of type, or more than 4 lines handwritten
- Figure out what percentage of each sentence length you have written.
  - Short: about 10% to 25%
  - Medium: about 60% to 75% of your sentences
  - Long: about 5% to 15% of your sentences
- In the margins, label each **literary device** (e.g., imagery, metaphor, simile, personification) you have used, and say whether it is effective.
- Put a star in front of each **transition** word you have used.
- Put brackets around the sentences in your **introduction**. In the margin, make notes on whether it engages a reader or how it could be more engaging.
- Put brackets around the sentences of your **conclusion**. In the margin, make notes on the impact it might have on your reader, or on how your conclusion could have greater impact.

Figure 7.7

Whole-Class Revision Process: Editing Conventions

• **Editing sentences** Begin at the end of your writing and read each sentence to yourself quietly.
  • Does it make sense? If not, why not? Do you need to read the previous sentence to understand it?
  • Is the sentence complete (that is, can it stand alone)?
  • Is it a sentence fragment that should be completed?
  • Are there actually several sentences joined with commas or *and… and…* that run on and on? Can you change them to complete sentences or join them with semicolons?

• **Editing punctuation** As you read each sentence out loud, does the punctuation tell you how to read it?
  • Use semicolons to join together 2 *complete* sentences — don't use semicolons as if they are commas.
  • Use commas to separate words, phrases, or clauses in a series or a list.
  • Use commas also after the introductory words, phrases, or clauses that make transitions between sentences.

• **Editing spelling** Begin checking from the end of your writing.
  • Read every word, tapping it with the tip of your pencil to slow you down.
  • Circle every word you are not 100% sure is correct.
  • Look these words up, or ask someone, or use spell-check.

• **Verb tenses** Make sure you used the verbs in a past tense when you wrote about the past, and that you used a present tense to write about your current thoughts and feelings.

• **Audience** Remember you are writing for your peers.

Figure 7.8. Memoir feedback created in response to the needs of a specific class

Challenges	Suggestions
Using paragraphs effectively.	• Break up your writing into paragraphs. • Remember to indent each paragraph about 2 cm or one tab; don't leave blank lines between them. • Remember the paragraph rules for dialogue (see below).

Adding more dialogue.	• Use dialogue whenever possible—it's much more interesting to read. Notice the difference in these two examples:
	
	TELLING dialogue (bor-ing):
	• My mom said that I had to get off the phone. When I asked her why, she said it was time for us to leave, so I hung up.
	
	SHOWING dialogue (better!):
	
	• Mom called from downstairs, interrupting my phone call. "Dale, get off the phone."
	    "Hang on," I said to my friend, and put my hand over the phone. "Why do I have to get off the phone?" I yelled down the stairs, the irritation clear in my voice.
	    "We're leaving in two minutes," she said impatiently. "Hurry up."
	I took my hand off the phone. "Gotta go," I said. "Talk to you later." We both hung up.
	
	• When you use dialogue, you need a new paragraph every time you have a new speaker or switch speakers (see example).
	
	• To show internal thoughts (vs. actual speech), use italics: "What's for dinner?" I asked. *It better not be meatloaf,* I thought. *I can't stand Dad's meatloaf.*

Using literary devices that don't connect to your feelings or the situation.	• Literary devices are really good at helping show feelings, but they need to clearly connect to your feelings and to the situation. • If you were grounded for stealing, "I was like a soldier shot by the enemy" doesn't work because the soldier isn't being punished for doing something wrong, like you are. "I was like a soldier about to be executed for treason" fits the situation.
Thinking carefully about where you want to put the most and the best details.	• Start the memoir with action, dialogue, or reaction to an event. A long description of who-what-when-where can distract from your purpose. What's essential to get your memoir going and grab our attention? Jump right into the story or hint at what's to come. • Be careful not to give away the main event right at the beginning. • Slow down key events by adding in details, thoughts, feelings, literary devices—but think about what events are key events. Don't add details to everything (notice where other authors add details). • It's okay to use details that are not 100% factual, as long as they are in the spirit of what you are trying to tell and/or help fill in any gaps in your memory. (Hint: Don't tell when you aren't sure of details.)

- Review the feedback with the class, noting both their overall growth as well as their collective challenges.
- Return the memoirs for final revisions and editing.
- Give the students a few minutes to read over their memoirs and your comments.
- Have students determine which of the problems on the feedback sheet were in their own work and highlight them on the sheet for reference.
- As students work, meet briefly with those whose writing has significant or multiple areas of weakness.
- Students continue to work over the next few classes, clear on how they are being evaluated and how to meet or exceed the expectations for their memoirs.

Once when I was 12 years old and in grade 7, I was at home, in my junk-littered room, finishing up the last of my homework, when my mom suddenly materialized behind me, wearing her usual pink pyjamas. As usual, she asked, "Katherine, are you ready to study math yet?"
—Katherine

... I thought about what the consequences would be to tell him the truth and to tell him it was bad. My mind was asking me questions. Will he still be your friend? Will he get mad? I also thought about the fact that Cam isn't the type of guy that could care if I didn't praise his work. But then a thought hit me. Was friendship all about making your friends happy? No. Are friends just there to make you happy? No. A real friend always tells the truth. —Jordan

---

Lesson 8—Rationale

Metacognition

Our goal as educators is to help students become more self-regulated learners, learners who cannot only plan for their learning but also can monitor and adjust their learning while in the process of learning, and can assess when their learning goals have been achieved.

- Ask students to highlight the phrases on the rubric that best describe their final work (Figure 7.3, page 108).

- Students answer three questions in short paragraphs. Joanne's students were familiar with this rubric, so she did not need to spend as much time helping students learn how to use it. If this is a rubric new to your students, follow the same steps as in introducing the memoir rubric—model and practise in groups with a shared sample, before personally applying the rubric to students' own writing.

The students' reflections showed the depth of their learning, learning about the task of writing a memoir, and learning more about themselves and the intent of writing a memoir.

> *After writing the memoir, I find that I am proudest of how I used literacy devices throughout the entire memoir. I usually don't use many similes, metaphors or anything of that sort in my other pieces of work. I spent lots of time trying to think of a perfect literacy device that fits perfectly with the sentence and the meaning.*
>
> *My 'weakest link' is my time management. I did manage to get everything but the self-evaluation handed in on time. However, at home, I always leave everything to the last minute, right before the day it is due. It usually puts a lot of panic into me, and that way, my writing isn't nearly as good as it would've been if I managed my time well.*
>
> *Next time I have an assignment similar to the memoir, instead of leaving all the work and thoughts/feelings to the last draft, I would probably try adding some into the first draft, then slowly edit my way up. Possibly that way, my essay/assignment would be better edited, and in the end, better written.* —Katherine
>
> *The thing that I'm most proud of that was put into my memoir were my thoughts, feelings and details. For instance, I tried to put pictures in peoples minds about the topic. For example, I said, "Some spots were darker than others, kind of like a checker board. As for thoughts and feelings, I pretty much had a full paragraph that was all about them.*
>
> *The weakest link to my memoir was the use of literary devices. I think that they were my weakest link because I didn't use a lot of them. When I did use them they were not effective. The one that was used for effect was to show a feeling.*
>
> *If I had a similar assignment I would change everything about how I say it. I would do this for more effect and impact. I think that I will put in more short sentences.* —Jordan

Lesson 9—Rationale

Sharing memoirs—a real audience

Writing deserves an audience. These students are writing their memoirs for a real audience of their group members. This is helpful in two ways: first, having an audience of peers in mind, students consider the effect of their writing choices; second, it gives students a chance to practise some oral language skills.

- Set up the reading session with clear instructions.
  - Writers focus on reading with expression and clarity.
  - Writers read with a pencil in hand to note any final errors (and fix them afterward).

- Listeners quietly focus on the readers and listen carefully.
- Listeners give specific, positive feedback at the end of each memoir.
- Working in their groups, students read their memoirs out loud.
- Circulate and listen in on each group. This is a celebration of work. It is not assessed.

Joanne's Reflection: The Assessment Experience

Evaluating these memoirs was an enjoyable experience. First, because of all the work leading up to their final drafts, my students' writing was better than usual; in addition, the pieces were longer and more fully developed than I have typically seen. I was not a frustrated reader, but rather an appreciative audience. I was focused not on errors but on what worked in their writing—leads, literary devices, details, meaning, transitions, and conclusions—all of which I noted with checkmarks and comments. Determining grades was a process of highlighting the rubric descriptors, calculating a grade from that, and adding a few suggestions or questions.

The students' metacognitive reflections were often illuminating, and several students made thoughtful and insightful comments on their work.

> **Juvan** noted: "I think my weakest link is grammar. I had a few difficulties while writing my memoir. There were some bits, that didn't make sense at all; which got me very frustrated. This is a big problem because grammar is what makes the reader understand the story."
>
> **Callie** reflected on how engaging her lead was: "After [the teacher] checked it and gave it back…when I read it, even I, myself, the one who wrote the memoir, want to know more about what is happening."
>
> After reading his work aloud, **Lucky** wrote, "I noticed…that I didn't have as many descriptive areas in my writing and my dialogues were a bit bland and not very exciting."

Each of these students learned something new about their writing and about themselves as learners and writers.

Chapter 8

Inquiry: Aboriginal Peoples of Canada

Grade 9—Social Studies

Assessment FOR Learning
- Know-Wonder-Learn chart
- Performance-based assessment in reading
- Co-creating criteria
- Peer-assessment and self-assessment
- Descriptive feedback
- Student reflection

Diverse Texts
- Google Earth
- Articles and class textbook
- Photographs
- Primary sources
- Websites

Differentiation
- Pyramid of learning outcomes
- Collaborative strategies
- Multiple modes of textual materials

Gradual Release of Responsibility
- Teacher modelling
- Paired practice
- Individual demonstrations

Critical Thinking
- Weighing evidence
- Interpreting
- Drawing conclusions
- Posing *Why?* questions

Assessment OF Learning
- Photo analysis
- Mind map
- Project
- Map

Essential Questions
- What do Aboriginal peoples value? How are their values evident in their lives?
- How does where we live affect how we live?

The Collaboration

Julie Anne Mainville and Dave Giesbrecht teach Social Studies in a grade 8 to 12 secondary school. Dave teaches Social Studies 8 and 11, Law 12, and Communications 12. Julie Anne teaches junior and senior Social Studies courses in French as part of the French Immersion Program, and she also teaches History 12 in English. Prior to co-planning this unit, Julie Anne and Dave had each been exploring the approaches of Backward Design and learning through inquiry. They decided that they might learn more by collaborating with others. They created the preliminary version of this unit of study in collaboration with several teachers who were new to teaching Social Studies 9, and they have modified and reworked it over the past three years.

Julie Anne and Dave believe that their ongoing teacher dialogue makes their planning, teaching, and learning work well for them. Their collaboration includes debriefing with one another on how lessons are going, brainstorming what they might do differently for individual classes, and reminding one another that questioning and adapting what they do leads to teaching that is more responsive to their students. As well, they find that their dialogue with and feedback from their students are equally powerful in making their classroom practice more effective. They decided that they might learn more by collaborating with others. They created the preliminary version of this unit of study in collaboration with a district based Aboriginal education specialist Lynn Wainwright and a number of other teachers and have revised and modified it over the past three years.

The Context

Julie Anne teaches grade 9 Social Studies in French, Dave in English. Engaging their students in more powerful learning opportunities is their motivator. They want their students to see history as a focused discovery of who people are by examining how they live, and to see that history is not just a collection of events and places. Julie Anne and Dave want to take the study of the past in a new direction, more in line with what historians do—to start with a question and then explore various forms of information in search of answers.

Because Dave and Julie Anne want to increase their students' engagement in their discipline, they incorporate open-ended strategies like Know-Wonder-Learn (K-W-L), and they have developed opportunities for students to use different ways (visual, kinesthetic, conversation) to engage with the key ideas prevalent in the social sciences. Combining open-ended strategies with the approaches of backward design and inquiry helps Julie Anne and Dave engage their students more deeply in their learning.

Essential Questions

- Who are Canada's Aboriginal peoples?
- What do First Nations and Inuit value, and how are their values evident in how they live?
- What would a First Nation school look like?

- How does where we live affect how we live?
- How do historians use evidence to support their understanding?
- What does a good paragraph look like?

Enduring Understandings

- Values affect our actions and the way we live.
- Identity is shaped by our values and geography.
- Canada is a nation defined by its geography.
- The information we access and use affects our understanding and our perspective.
- Evidence is needed to make an effective argument and to write a good paragraph.

Key Structures
Assessment for Learning

- A k-w-l chart to see what students already understand about First Nations and what they are interested in learning more about.
- A performance-based assessment (pba) to see what strengths students have in reading comprehension, vocabulary, note-making, and meaning-making and where they have to stretch.
- Peer-assessment and self-assessment of mind maps.
- Co-creating criteria for maps.
- Descriptive feedback and pre-test on individual photo analysis; e.g., observing detail, making inferences, and checking understanding.
- Descriptive feedback on note-making and mind-mapping; interpretation of regional geographic photos; interpretation of historical and current sources of information.
- Co-creating criteria for good paragraphs, including using evidence to support understanding.
- Survey on reflections about the unit is posted for all students to see.

Gradual Release of Responsibility

- Teachers model effective reading strategies for handling new text; marking up text to differentiate between what is interesting and what is important.
- Teachers model strategies for note-taking—sticky notes and mind maps.
- Teachers model photo analysis to address geography outcomes—show how photo analysis and related inferences are checked against the descriptors of a region.
- Teachers model how to use a historian's thinking skills—looking for patterns of behaviour and symbolism; analyzing a source for the values embedded in diverse texts.
- Teachers follow up modelling by having students practise in pairs while they give descriptive feedback. They encourage students to reflect on what they have discussed or read, and then to give individual demonstrations.

Diverse Texts
- Google Earth, various photos, maps, tactile objects that reflect regional attributes
- *Crossroads, BC First Nations Studies, Aboriginal Peoples: Building for the Future, Canada: A People's History:* "First Contact," "Native American Elders Speak," "Voyage of Rediscovery," "The Vision Seeker"
- Photos and other primary sources such as guest speakers and items related to their cultural practices (e.g., a medicine wheel, a smudge bowl, masks).

Critical Historical Thinking
- Weighing evidence and offering interpretations require students to consider what interpretations might be plausibly made from the evidence provided, and how adequately the evidence (e.g., stories, videos, historical accounts) justifies the interpretations offered.
- Exploring First Nations and Inuit cultures involves considering how particular human and environmental factors and events influence what they value and how they live (e.g., Why did some people live in villages while others were nomadic? Which First Nations create totem poles? Why?).
- Searching for and using multiple sources of information in order to understand and draw conclusions can move students to think whether enough information is available to provide the evidence for a clear picture of the past.

Differentiation
- Using Backwards Design and inquiry allows students to engage in learning with a focus on the essential questions. The learning outcomes are organized in a pyramid of "All, Most, Some"—that is, what is essential for "all" students to understand and do; what are "most" students able to understand and do; what are "some" students able to understand and do beyond expectations.
- Multiple modes of text provide the students with entry points and choice, and they also provide reinforcement of key understandings. Activities that help students process information are targeted at different learning styles such as visual, auditory, kinesthetic.
- Collaborative strategies for processing information include think, pair, share, partner reading, discussion circles.

Assessment of Learning
- Photo analysis of geographic regions
- Mind map on a specific First Nation
- First Nations school project
- Post-contact map

Lesson 1—Rationale

When beginning a new unit of study, it is important to determine what the students know already and what they are interested in learning more about. The k-w-l chart does this. It both accesses background knowledge and develops interest in the topic. Teachers encourage and model open-ended questions. Building a totem pole also helps build background knowledge by using visual and kinesthetic thinking, thus supporting different learners in the class. It also is a great format for getting to know more about your students.

Connecting—K-W-L

- Give students a k-w-l chart titled Who are the First Nations of Canada?
- Have students answer the question What do you know about the First Nations? in the Know column.
- In the Wonder column, have students write five questions about First Nations to which they want to find answers. Encourage thoughtful questions rather than "recall" questions by moving among them and helping them pose more open-ended questions to be considered throughout the unit. (See Figures 8.1a and 8.1b.)

Figure 8.1a These students' charts (k-w-l) illustrate the range of background knowledge in the class

YASMIN

Oct. 9th 2007

Block E

FIRST NATIONS

KNOW	WONDER	LEARN

- totem poles - lacrosse
- Haida   - one with nature.
- traders - used whole animal must skin
  - animal skins = hunting fishing. bow and
- no taxes   - dream catchers arrow
- First people in Canada - buffalo
- Ice Age - chief (head dress)
     "red skins"
- cree   - fire -fought with europeans for
- Ojibwa - worship spirits   land
- shuswap - paints horses. self.
- Okanagan - sports teams
     - made western saddle
- Villages / tribes. - popcorn
- mohawks - only took what was needed
- teepees - skin - different Mohicans
     - bread of horse "Paint"
- iquolis
     - cowboys and Indians
- Inuit - igloos - north - dances with wolves
- Huron - naming ceremony.
- leather skins - THANKS GIVING!
- some nomadic
- Nuu-chuu
   nulth
- coast salsh
	① If the Beringia theory is true how would these people survive in the cold times of the Ice Age. What adaptations would they make?
	
	② Why didn't the first nations stay in Beringia, weren't they happy there?
	
	③ What were some of the conflicts the First Nations had with europeans if any, what were they about?
	
	④ What kind of a government system did they go by? (eg. every-one for themselves)
	
	⑤ What types of unfriendly encounters would First Nations people have with other tribes? How were disagreements settled?	

Figure 8.1b

First Nations

BlOCKE Chos

KNOW	WONDER	LEARN
First settlers totem poles cheif peace pipes mohawk nation fishing hunting (somewhere nomatic teepees	5 questions 1 Were there indians (first Nations) in other parts of the world? 2 Was there a system like today (school, rich, poor, smart, dumb)? 3 How did they live? 4 was it tough to survive 5. were sources at limitations	

Connecting—Building personal totem pole

- Build background knowledge and interest by having students build totem poles. Use the Spirit Guide (Figure 8.2) to provide students with a list of names of animals and what they represent to First Nations.
- Model how to make a four-animal totem pole, choosing animal spirits that match your personality. You could use clip art for the animals.
- Then have students select four animals, thinking about how they will explain and justify their choice, to create a personal totem pole.
- Model for students how to justify their choice. For example, "I chose the beaver because it is creative" is not as powerful as "I chose the beaver because I am very artistic. I love to draw and do crafts. My favourite class is art and I also take painting lessons privately."
- Have students hand in their totem poles for your feedback on how they interpreted the task and how well they explained their choices using evidence from their life.

Figure 8.2 A First Nation Spirit Guide

Spirit Guide

Many animals have been used as symbols of the characteristics valued by the Aboriginal peoples who carved them on totem poles to represent the mythical ancestry of their clan or family.

BADGER: capable of reaching a desired goal; industrious

BEAVER: creative, artistic, determined

BEAR: strength, learned humility, motherhood, teaching

COYOTE: ability to laugh at oneself; humour

DOGFISH: persistence, strength, a born leader

DOVE: love, gentleness, kindness

DRAGON FLY: ever-changing life

EAGLE: great strength, leadership, prestige

FROG: spring, new life, communicator, stability

FOX: camouflage, protection, stealthy, intuitive, resourceful

HALIBUT: life protector, strength, stability

HAWK: strength, far-sighted

HERON: patience, graceful, easy-going

HUMMINGBIRD: love, beauty, intelligence, spirit messenger

KILLER WHALE: traveler, guardian, symbol of good

KINGFISHER: luck, patience, speed and agility

LOON: peace, tranquility, generous giving nature

MOON: protector and guardian of the Earth by night

MOUNTAIN LION: leadership, resourcefulness

OTTER: trusting, inquisitive, and bright, loyal friendship

OWL: wisdom

RAM: perseverance, agility, loyalty

RAVEN: creation, knowledge, bringer of the light

SALMON: dependability, renewal, a provider

SEAL: bright, inquisitive, organized

SNAKE: life, death, rebirth; friend of dreams

SUN: healing energy, guardian of the Earth by day

THUNDERBIRD: powerful, mystical, a leader

TURTLE: long, meaningful life

WOLF: intelligence, leadership, strong sense of family

Families or clans carved one or more totem poles to express their origins and the ideals they represent.

Create your own totem pole:
- Choose four animal symbols, plus one of your own creation with a secret meaning known only to you.
- The symbols from bottom to top represent your story.
- Be sure to use colour.
- Mount your totem on the sheet of paper provided.
- You and your fellow students will comment on each other's work, trying also to guess the meaning of each other's secret animal.
- The class as a whole will share their stories.

Lesson 2—Rationale

Storytelling is a strong tradition in many Aboriginal cultures. Model story-telling that gives students the experience of recognizing how quickly a story changes in the retelling. Reading and reflecting on their interpretations of historical documents helps students better understand the challenge of reading "stories," that is, history long past.

Connecting—Creation myths and oral tradition

- Read aloud a creation myth like one from the Iroquois Nation, introducing the concept of the Creator Kitchi-Manitou from Turtle Island, *Canada Revisited* (Clark and McKay 1992). Ask for four student volunteers. Ask one to stay in front of the class while the other three move out into the hall to wait, thus not hearing the story.
- Read the myth to the remaining members of the class. This activity may be challenging for the French Immersion and ESL students, so be prepared to read the myth twice or to read chunks and stop to allow the student audience to talk about what they have heard.
- Ask one of the students outside to return to the class, and have the student who was at the front (and heard the story) retell the myth to the new arrival. Continue this process, inviting in the next student from the outside and the most recent student retelling what he or she has heard until all four students have recounted the story, the last one retelling it to the rest of the class. By the time the last student tells the story, much of the information may have been lost or altered.
- Work, with the help of the class, to retell the story as originally written. Help the students see how stories often change in the retelling. This is one of the challenges faced in documenting the history of the First Nations who follow the oral tradition. Some information does get lost or changed through the retelling over time. Currently, many First Nations are working to document their oral stories and traditions in order to ensure these "histories" survive through time.

Processing—Notes on origins of First Nations

Students need to learn how to structure their own notes instead of just copying from the overhead. The writing process also helps them develop their individual understanding. With support, they can build their own notes, over time, from many different sources. These notes will show geography influencing settlement, activity, and the development of civilization.

- Prepare background information on different explanations of the origins of the First Nations, such as the Kitchi-Manitou myth and the Beringia Theory.

- Have students make a two-column page (Main Idea, Details) for their note-taking: first, on the Kitchi-Manitou myth, the creator who put the First Nations in Canada; second, on the Beringia Theory, the scientific and anthropological explanation.
- Display on the overhead the page of your own notes on these two explanations. As you talk about this page, ask students to add additional information to their own 2-column notes.
- Use wall maps to explain what scientists had to say. Note that good historians work with different sources of information (myths, history books, artifacts, oral histories) and include different perspectives (cultural, scientific, and others) in order to make a point. If time permits, ask and discuss the question How do these perspectives fit together and why? Encourage students to represent their thinking at the end of their notes page. They can use any combination of pictures, words, charts, and images.

Connecting—Making connections among artifacts

- Put a series of concrete objects that represent Canada's climate, resources and physiography (ski boot, umbrella, can of salmon, a nickel, a box of cereal, sunglasses, a pencil, sea shells, toque, ice scraper, etc.) on the floor in the middle of the classroom.
- Ask students, working in groups, to look at the objects together, then move into smaller groups and define categories to which the objects belong. Ask them to think of one category, that is, a main idea that includes all objects. For example, the ski boot can represent a mountain; paired with the toque and the ice scraper, it can refer to a northern climate zone. Figure 8.3 is an organizer for this activity.
- Write students' ideas for names of categories on the chalkboard, and ask students to explain the connection between all the objects. All objects must fit into the main idea; if some object cannot be connected, then the idea must be eliminated as a possibility.
- Have student groups redefine their answers and share their new suggestions until the class has clearly identified and explained the main idea.
- From this main idea, formulate your next inquiry question, How does our environment affect how we live?

Lesson 3—Rationale

This performance-based reading assessment gives a snapshot of your students' strengths and stretches in reading for understanding. The earlier in the year you conduct this assessment, the more useful the information can be in planning subsequent lessons and guiding your subsequent teaching of skills.

How do these things connect?

Look at all the objects laid out on the floor and try to figure out what the big idea is that connects them all. Some of the objects could go in more than one category and some you may have to think about for a while to understand where they fit, but try to come up with the big idea and place it at the top of the chart below. Then, create the category names and place them in the three columns below the main idea. Finally, place all the items in one of the three columns. Work together; talk it out; you'll get it.

Main Idea

Category	Category	Category

Items	Items	Items

- Use a section of your text for a performance-based reading assessment for learning (as explained in chapter 3). Dave and Julie Anne used a text on a different topic (climate change and global warming) with the goal of learning how their students use a text independently to make meaning.
- Analyze the results of this assessment to establish overall class strengths and stretches when reading for understanding. Dave and Julie Anne noticed their students needed support in finding and supporting main ideas as they read and in making inferences from the information.

Lesson 4—Rationale

After looking at the students' performance-based assessments, finding the main idea and relevant details often becomes a target area for students in Humanities and Social Studies classrooms. This was true for Dave and Julie Anne. When teaching note-making strategies, the teacher models using the gradual release of responsibility-first modelling, then having students work in pairs, then independently, and providing more support, feedback, and instruction to students, as needed.

Processing—Main ideas and note-taking

- In front of the students, talk about the different ways you can group topics and supporting details—webs, flow charts, two columns, diagrams. Explain which one works best for you and, using headings that match your text, create a structure for note-taking on the overhead project or white/chalkboard.

Figure 8.4 Kate's sticky notes

- Model the reading about one First Nation while using sticky notes. Find the main idea (what's important) in each section. Explain your thinking as you read aloud, choose key ideas, and transfer the information onto the overhead or white/chalkboard. You might make subheadings as you do this.
- Have students choose a First Nation they would like to study. Students complete the organizer by following the same process, alone or in partners, using a note-making format (their own or one that was modelled). Invite them to use the strategy of writing on sticky notes to collect key information while reading (Figure 8.4).
- When done, discuss what they determined to be the most important ideas. Work with the students to ensure the information is complete because they will use it to write a geography test later.

Figure 8.5 Kate's note-taking

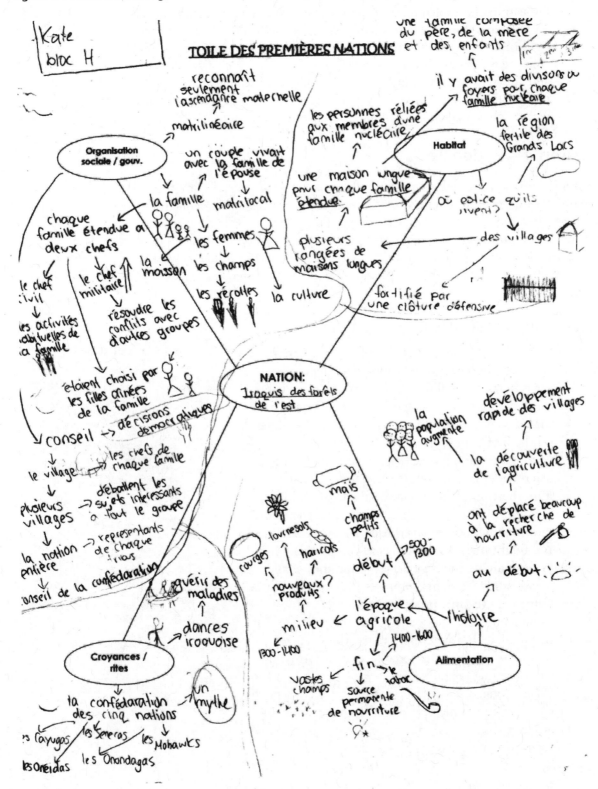

- After students hand in their notes for feedback, give them an opportunity to revise their notes. Figure 8.5 shows Kate's second attempt as she redid her notes after receiving descriptive feedback. Figure 8.6 shows the rubric on which her work is assessed.

Figure 8.6 The rubric used to provide feedback to Kate on her note-making

ÉVALUATION DE LA LECTURE: IDÉE PRINCIPALE ET LA PRISE DE NOTES   *Kate*   2 nd attempt   SCHUM9

Aspect	(1) Ne satisfait pas encore aux attentes	(2) Satisfait aux attentes de façon minimale	(3) Satisfait entièrement aux attentes	(4) Dépasse les attentes
Compréhension • Idées principales • Détails • Prise de notes	• Reconnaît quelques idées principales • Dégage quelques informations particulières • Utilise parfois des catégories logiques pour prendre des notes simples; omet ou interprète mal plusieurs informations • Est incapable de résumer ou d'interpréter des informations simples; semble incapable de comprendre le texte	• Dégage avec exactitude la plupart des idées principales • Dégage des informations particulières, mais omet parfois des détails importants • Utilise des catégories logiques pour prendre des notes; se sert souvent des en-têtes du texte; omet parfois des informations clés ou certains rapports	• Dégage les idées principales de manière concise; peut les reformuler avec précision • Dégage des détails particuliers pertinents • Prend des notes exactes et détaillées et se sert de catégories logiques; suit la structure du texte	• Dégage les idées principales de manière concise; fait une synthèse approfondie des informations complexes et en donne une excellente interprétation • Dégage des détails particuliers pertinents; cite le texte de manière efficace • Met au point une structure logique en vue de consigner des notes exactes et détaillées; réunit souvent des informations extraites de diverses parties du texte

Lesson 5—Rationale

Mapping skills are part of the learning outcomes for Social Studies 9. Teachers need to help students develop these geographical skills in the same way we help them read articles or write summaries.

Processing: Building mapping skills

- With students in groups of three or four, ask them to brainstorm what should be included on a pre-contact map of Canada.
- Give students the rules of map-making (Figure 8.7). Examine them together—ask students where their ideas fit and what is different.
- Ask groups to share their ideas and, as they share, write down their ideas, grouping them under relevant headings such as physiography, climate, waterways, and historical sites. Figure 8.8 on page 133 is a rubric for assessment of the map.

Figure 8.7 Criteria for pre-contact map

The Geography of Canada Map

You are now going to look at the physiography of Canada from a historical pre-and early contact perspective and chart them on a map. This assignment will challenge your map-making skills, your ability to create and use symbols and legends, and your map-reading skills. Use the *Canadian Oxford School Atlas* (8th ed.), the *Hosford Study Atlas, Crossroads*, and your own resources to complete this task.

How do the physical aspects of Geography affect how and where we live?

Mapping Skills

1. Neatness, spelling and capitalization matter.
2. Do a draft in pencil and then outline in a black felt pen.
3. Print words clearly and in one direction only.
4. Make a legend for all symbols and colours used.

Information that must be included on the map:

1. Bodies of Water—Pacific Ocean, Mackenzie River, Fraser River, Thompson River, Great Bear Lake, Great Slave Lake, Peace River, Lake Athabasca, Saskatchewan River, Lake Winnipeg, Red River, Churchill River, Hudson Bay, James Bay, Lake Superior, Lake Michigan, Lake Huron, Lake Ontario, Lake Erie, Ottawa River, St Lawrence River, Atlantic Ocean, Arctic Ocean.
2. Landforms—Outline and then shade, in different colours, the major Landforms that are present in Canada. Write the name of each landform in the legend.
3. People Groups—Place the following First Nations groups in the correct area on the map—Beothuk, Huron, Iroquois, Mohawk Nations, Cree, Ojibwa, Okanagon, Shuswap, Haida, Nuu-chah-nulth, Coast Salish.
4. Political—You must add the following major centres: Fort Langley, Fort Edmonton, Fort McMurray, Fort Saskatoon, Fort Garry (Winnipeg), Fort Thompson, Fort William (Thunder Bay), Fort York (Toronto), Huronia (Orillia), Fort Albany, Hochelaga (Montreal), Stadacona (Quebec City), Iqaluit, Acadia (Halifax to Fredericton), Louisbourg.

Once you have all the information down in pencil, check with me to see if it is accurate and meets the criteria before you begin to use ink. Finally, check the chart that has been provided on the different regions of Canada and what physiography, resources, and climate they each have.

Due:_____

Figure 8.8 Rubric to be used for self-assessment, peer-assessment, or teacher assessment

Exploration of the World Map

Name: _____   Score: _____

	Not Yet Meeting Expectations	Minimally Meets Expectations	Fully meets Expectations	Exceeds Expectations
Neatness and clarity of map	The words are hard to read and rules for maps are not followed at all	Most items are clear and easy to follow	All elements are clearly written and conventions are followed exactly	Extra effort has made the information much clearer and focused
Complete and accurate	Quite a few items are misplaced or missing	Some items are misplaced or missing	One or two errors may occur	Contains no errors
Symbols and legends	Legend and symbols confuse understanding	Legend and symbols provide a very basic understanding	Legend and symbols provide a lot of detail and information	Legend and symbols show creative insight to add meaning

- Ask groups to focus on the physiography part of the rubric. Ask groups to describe how they would compare the differences in physical environments. Invite them to create a Top Five List of things to look at when comparing different physiographical zones. Then have groups share what they believe is most important.
- To prepare for the next lesson, students create a physiography chart. They create their own chart, a chart using their Top Five List to help them create headings. Invite them to use diagrams, pictures, and/or icons to help identify and explain a range of physical qualities they locate for each category.
- Additionally, they need to add regional information—what they might see in the Arctic as opposed to the Canadian Shield. Suggest that their chart will need at least three columns. Ask students to use their texts, the rubric for mapping, and other reference materials in order to create this chart. Encourage them to find additional information and keep working on their charts for next class. Each student in the group will need a copy of the chart.
- Ask groups to make a plan to finish the activity so that all get copies of the map (photocopy or email or each draw their own) for next class.

Lesson 6—Rationale

Students have to acquire the skill of physiographical analysis along with the skill of using evidence to support and communicate their understanding. When examining visual texts like maps or photos, students are practising their ability to make inferences, supporting these inferences with details.

- You will need photos featuring distinct geographical features of various regions of Canada for the next class. You can collect a few of these yourself and then at the end of the next lesson assign groups a physiographical region and ask them to conduct a search on the Internet to find pictures from that region to bring to class.

Processing—Photo analysis, modelling, gradual release

- Show students different pictures representing different parts of Canada. With each picture, students use their physiography chart and their textbook to determine which region is in the photo and to justify their response.
- Ask one or two groups to share how they have used the skills of observation. Prompt them to explicitly connect the details in the picture to information in their notes.
- Model how to use inferential thinking in photo analysis. You might say at first, "I see mountains with pointy peaks… I see big coniferous trees… I see water… It looks sunny" and then explain that it is important to link detail to the region they think the photo comes from. "Pointy mountains mean they are young and young mountains are found in the Western Cordillera. Big trees are also found on the West Coast because the climate is milder and that helps the trees grow." Point out to students that details help support inferential thinking.

Transforming and personalizing—Physiography observations and inferences

- Ask students to work with a partner to complete Canada's Physiography chart (Figure 8.9). Encourage them to use their details both to identify the correct physiographical zone and to explain how it cannot be another region; for example, if it is a picture of the Arctic, ask students to explain why it is not the valley of the St. Lawrence and Great Lakes. Again, students use the details in their picture to make the inference.
- Explain that for each region, there is a series of pictures that will together help you identify a region. Make sure that you note what you see in each of the pictures, and then begin to draw your conclusions. After you have looked at all the pictures, explain which region it is and support your answer with at least two determining characteristics.

Figure 8.9 Canada's Physiography (a sample graphic organizer for use by students)

Region #1

What I see...	Inferences, conclusions, what regions it can't be...

This is the _____ region because...

- Offer students an example. You could write this on the board or overhead. A student might say, "There is no vegetation in this picture and the valley is full of trees and plants, especially for farming. There are big glaciers and the water is frozen which means it is cold. The valley has a continental climate which is warm in the summer to encourage plant growth."
- Have students practise with four different pictures.

Guided practice—Photo analysis with criteria

- Show students three photos and ask them to:
  - identify the region
  - justify with specific evidence why you think it is that region.
  - explain why it is not _____.
- Give students the criteria for a response that fully meets expectations.
- Assess several student samples using the criteria.
- Work with students to ensure they can use this practice to improve their own photo analysis response.
- Depending on students' comfort and success, you might want to add an additional class where students are assigned a physiographical region and ask them to conduct a search on the Internet to find a picture of that region and bring it back to class. Then have students use the same criteria to quiz one another.

Summative assessment

- Students have access to their pre-contact map, their physiography charts, their samples of powerful responses, and the classroom posters with pictures of the various regions to refer to while completing their geography test (Figure 8.10).
- The skills and understandings to be assessed have already been taught and practised. The summative assessment is an application of their learning, judged on the co-created criteria.

Figure 8.10 Photo Analysis Summative Assessment

Name _____

Date _____

Canada's Physiography

For each image identify the region and list reasons to support your answer. Answer in complete sentences. Each image is worth 5 marks.

Image #1

1. Region: _____

2. List 2 attributes that you notice which support your answer.

_____

_____

3. List 2 regions it cannot be and why it cannot be those regions.

_____

_____

Image #2

1. Region: _____

2. List 2 attributes that you notice which support your answer.

_____

_____

3. List 2 regions it cannot be and why it cannot be those regions.

_____

_____

Image #3

1. Region: _____

2. List 2 attributes that you notice which support your answer.

_____

_____

3. List 2 regions it cannot be and why it cannot be those regions.

_____

_____

Lesson 7—Rationale
Transforming—Building criteria, practising mapping skills

- Have students examine their map of Pre-Contact Canada and decide on which items are important to include on a map. Negotiate these as a class. Figure 8.11 is the list generated by one class. Figure 8.12 is the finalized list and the rubric for assigning a grade. Figure 8.13 is one student's reflection on his assessment.
- Distribute copies of a map of Canada and have students complete a modern map of Canada.
- Collect these maps for summative assessment of mapping skills.

Figure 8.11 One class's list of important items to include on a map

- Provincial Borders (territories, provinces)   - terrain
- Farmlands   - First Nation's lands
- Forests   - Arenas / sports facilities
- Major cities   - Capitals
- Economic activites   - mountain ranges
- Lakes & rivers   - islands
- elevation
- population
- U.S border
- oceans
- seasons
- airports
- schools

Physical Features	Economic Activities	Optional	Political
- waterways	- fishing	- schools	- prov. borders
- forests	- farming	- arenas	- U.S borders
- elevation	- mining	- airports	- capitals
- mountain ranges	- forestry		- Major cities

People groups
- population
- First Nation's Lands

Figure 8.12 Reference list of information to include and rubric for evaluating work

Canada Now Map

To help us see how Canada is today and how it might be different if Aboriginal peoples had been left to develop on their own, you will be asked to generate another map.

Information to be included

Political. Show the 10 provinces and three territories together with their capitals. As well, show five additional major cities and on the back of your map explain why you added these cities (they show culture, economy, etc.).

Physical. Label the following physical features: Coastal Mountains, Fraser River, Rocky Mountains, Peace River, Lake Athabasca, Great Bear Lake, Great Slave Lake, Mackenzie River, N/S Saskatchewan River, Lake Winnipeg, The Great Lakes, Hudson Bay, James Bay, St. Lawrence River, Gulf of St. Lawrence, Labrador Sea.

Economic. Show the major economic activities for each region of Canada. Be selective. You do not need to include all activities, but focus on what is significant for that area. Include mining, forestry, fishing, farming, business, etc. (Hint: this may influence which cities you add in section 1.)

People. Use symbols or shading to show where Canada's population resides. You will also want to show where First Nations people form significant populations.

How you will be assessed

	Back to the Drawing Board (1-2)	Mapping Apprentice (3-4)	Expert Cartographer (5-6)
Content	Incomplete or missing significant parts of the required elements. May have numerous errors in placement or omit key economic activities.	Accurate, complete placement of required elements. May have a few minor errors in placement, or miss a key economic activity.	Accurate and detailed. May have included relevant information beyond the required elements.
Legend	Too many or too few symbols are used and the legend is hard to follow. Does not have a legend.	Legend is accurately employed to produce clear information. The symbols or colour chosen make the meaning stand out.	A sophisticated use of symbols, colour and legend to make a clear map. Thoughtful use of the legend is obvious.
Appearance	The information is hard to read and may be too cluttered to make the map useful.	The information is easily read and presented in a clear format. There is no cluttering or misspelling.	A high quality product that is attractive and informative. Extra effort is evident.

Figure 8.13 One student's reflection on the map of Canada

Effective	Needs work
-colourful	- too much time colouring
↳ helps to organize	- pin-point where cities are
-eye catching	- too much writing clumped in one place
-uses #'s instead of words	- erase the pencil
to avoid crunching together	- legend too crowded
↳ letters and symbols	- make colours clear in the legend
- labeled neatly → clarity, all	- make sure names clearly connect w/
writing in one direction	rivers, city, etc.
- made rivers distinct → used blue	- organize the legend
- complete and accurate info.	

What is important to First Nations People?

- traditions
- animals (creation of Earth)
- myths

- Ask the students to work with a partner to brainstorm how the population and economy of Canada might have developed differently if European traders had not come. Encourage them to compare the two maps to do this.

Lesson 8—Rationale

By beginning with their own experiences, students will come to understand the abstract concept of a core value by trying to define what values they took from their experiences, then moving to connect their learning to the experiences and the values of Aboriginal peoples.

Processing—Defining core values

- Have students in small groups brainstorm definitions of a core value. Share the groups' brainstormed lists.
- Then have students brainstorm what they would do if given $1,000.
- After the brainstorming session, model the use of a chart like the following, using at least three of their responses.

What would you do with $1,000?	Value
Save $500 for school/university Spend $300 on new clothes and shoes Spend $200 on gifts for my family	Education Materialism, nice things… Family, charity

- Have students complete the chart from their own lists.
- Have students brainstorm a list of activities they do outside of school.
- Have students now fill in a similar values chart, identifying the core value that each activity reflects.
- Using all three lists, help students understand that values determine or influence our choices and our activities. Link this personal information to how these values might influence a community's development, settlement, and activities.
- Have students complete a mind map of their own core values, then compare this to their totem poles. Do they reflect the same values?

Lesson 9—Rationale

Processing/Transforming—Main ideas and core values

- Use a creation myth or story. Dave and Julie Anne use the Ojibwas of Kitchi-Manitou. Divide the class into small groups of students.
- Have each group of students read the story and find what they consider the most important lines of the text. Have students draw what is important on a piece of chart paper and add their quote.
- Display the chart paper around the room and have each group of students add another line as a way to tell the whole story to the class.
- Choose a second story or article. Use sticky notes to find actions that reveal core values. Model this strategy before asking students to complete the assignment independently; for example, from the second story, Julie Anne wrote, "Il y a très longtemps, les hommes, les animaux et les oiseaux étaient tous de la même espèce, seule leur apparence était différente." The core value revealed was expressed as "equality among all living things."
- Have students complete a chart, with headings as in Figure 8.14, using information gleaned from their two stories.

Figure 8.14 Identifying values according to evidence

Value	Evidence from stories
Nature	The first things that Kitchi-Manitou invented on Earth were the trees and the leaves.

- Have students turn their chart into a mind map to show what they think is the same or different between the two First Nations. Figure 8.15 is an example of a mind map where the student illustrates similarities and differences between the Iroquois and the Squamish values.

Figure 8.15 Examining and comparing the values of two First Nations

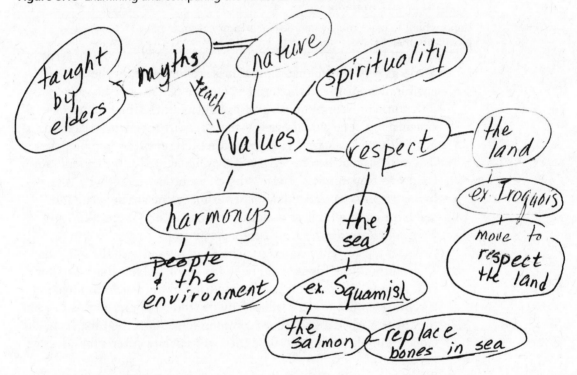

Lesson 10—Rationale

All Aboriginal peoples do not have the same practices, beliefs, or histories. Yet there is much that is similar as is, for example, the connection to and the valuing of nature. The purpose of this unit is not to over-generalize or smooth over the unique histories of Canada's Aboriginal peoples. Rather, it is an opportunity to learn about perspectives and world views that pre-date the arrival of European explorers and settlers in the vast regions of what is now Canada. While the Inuit do not identify as First Nations, they do have a close connection to the land, and like many First Nations, their world view is ecological.

Processing/Transforming—Connecting to current events, core values

- Choose a current event, like the Atlantic seal hunt. You may prefer to choose a more local article related to differences between local Aboriginal and non-Aboriginal perspectives.
- Have students read the article, identifying what is important to both the environmentalists and the seal hunters and what core value that represents, in a chart form (see below).

Figure 8.16

What's important to the seal hunters? (evidence from the text)	What core value does this represent?
Hunters hunt to make money in order to provide for their families	Family, responsibility

- Students may realize that some values are the same for the environmentalists and the hunters, but the reasons for the values are different. For example, both groups talk about the importance of sustainability. The hunters' view is that there are too many seals eating too many fish, and they need to be controlled. The environmentalists' view is that the seals may become extinct if they are hunted at the current rate. Lead your students to consider Who do we believe and why?
- Invite students to read a newspaper or magazine article related to seal hunting or a local issue (local newspapers or *Time for Kids* and *National Geographic for Kids* are good sources).
- Connect the current seal hunt to the Inuit people with the question "Do you think the Inuit would be in favour of seal hunting? Explain your answer, in a paragraph, referring back to the article and making specific reference to their values." Invite students to relate this to what they have learned about values common to some of the First Nations.
- Collect sample paragraphs. Use these to generate criteria for effective paragraphs.
- Students use the criteria to analyze their own paragraphs. They may revise and edit their paragraphs, using the criteria information.

Lesson 11—Rationale

A primary source of information is people themselves. Dave and Julie Anne invited Lynn Wainwright in to lead traditional activities that embody the oral traditions in order to help students gain perspective and knowledge of the importance of Aboriginal story telling. Revisiting and practising note-taking skills can help students understand how social scientists, like sociologists and historians, focus their listening and generate more thoughtful questions. Dave and Julie Anne often use a video recording as a source of information for students to develop note-taking skills and to analyze what they are hearing and seeing before and after an oral presentation or interview. The purpose of this analysis is to infer how the actions and values of individuals might demonstrate the values held by their First Nation.

Processing/Transforming—The importance of elders

- Have students jot down observations and quotes while watching a few clips from *Native Elders Speak* (<http://embedr.com/playlist/native-american-elders-speak>).
- Ask the students to share information with their partner, and to be descriptive. Then, together as a class, ask the groups to look for patterns in what they have seen and heard.
- Have students add this information to their mind map of values held by Aboriginal peoples.

Lesson 12—Rationale

Processing—The importance of community

- Invite a speaker from a First Nations band in or near your community to talk with your class.
- Have students work in groups of three or four, in advance of the speaker's arrival, to generate questions they may want to ask during and after the presentation.
- Ask the speaker to bring artifacts and stories to help students understand the importance of the community and the environment in the cultures of First Nations; for example, the use of the Talking Feather or the Smudge Ceremony (burning of sweet grass as a ritual cleansing). The experience is multi-sensory. Such a first-hand experience can be most engaging for the students, one that has the most powerful impact and creates a vivid memory.
- Have students jot down key points during the presentation.
- At the end of the class, students share information with their partner. Ask them to be descriptive. Then have the groups together look for patterns in what they have seen and read.
- Have students add this information to their mind map of the values shared by many Aboriginal peoples.

Lesson 13—Rationale

With the goal of continuing to learn about different nations within the First Nations, support students by providing a template and a strategy for note-making. Use "gradual release" to support a wider range of students. Model the strategy for the whole class, then give students a choice of one nation to study and create their own mind map. Teachers circulate and provide assistance, as needed, during class time.

Processing—Note-making with a mind map

- There are different tribes and bands within the First Nations of Canada.
- Choose one tribe to use as a model when you show the students how to take notes.
- Model using a template for the mind map with the following headings:
  - social organization/governing
  - habitat
  - beliefs and rituals
  - diet and lifestyle
- Give students sticky notes (four different colours, one for each heading) to use as they collect information. Model finding this information as you read a short section from an article or story. Write relevant information on the appropriately coloured sticky note.
- Then have small groups choose another First Nation to read about and make a mind map of their notes.
- While students read, have them look for information in each category to record on their coloured sticky notes, then transfer the information from their notes to a mind map. Figure 8.17 is an example of a mind map.
- Teachers might choose to use these mind maps for a summative assessment.

Figure 8.17 One student's mind map about the people of the Northwest Coast

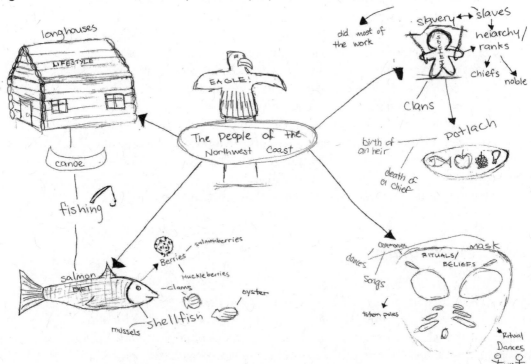

Lesson 14—Rationale

The Medicine Wheel is one way that many Aboriginal peoples represent a holistic or ecological perspective—four seasons, four directions, four stages of the life cycle, four elements. Using information that they have already gathered on their mind map, invite students to represent their information in a Medicine Wheel format and, in doing so, achieve a deeper understanding of their information.

Transforming and personalizing

- Have students return to their mind maps on common values of First Nations.
- Students transform this information into the organizer called a Medicine Wheel. Figure 8.18 is a student sample. Figure 8.19 is the handout of instructions to complete a medicine wheel.
- Completion of this activity provides a check-in, or "ticket," to begin the final project. It can be used as a formative assessment to identify any gaps in students' understanding that might be supported by a class discussion. The information contained here can also be used as part of the summative assessment for the unit.

Figure 8.18 A Medicine Wheel

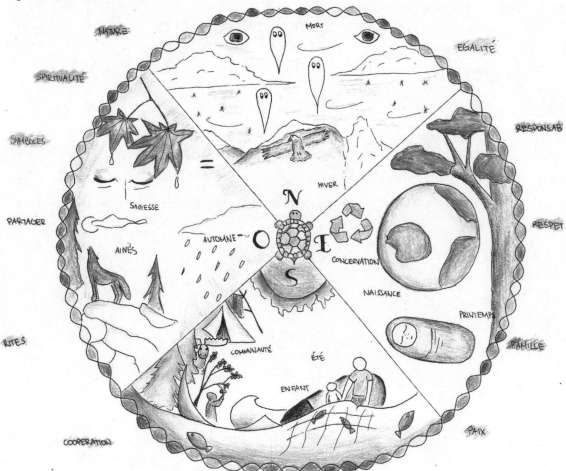

Figure 8.19

Medicine Wheel Graphic Organizer

The Medicine Wheel is used in some Aboriginal cultures as a way to symbolically organize their thinking. You must take the information that we have been looking at during this unit and create a Medicine Wheel that shows your understanding of the Aboriginal world view and some of the values demonstrated by them. You need to use a mix of symbols and key words to portray your thinking.

The must haves of this assignment are:

- A key symbol for the creator at the centre of the wheel
- A key symbol and/or organizing idea for each quadrant
- Key words or images for each value
- A short explanation of each quadrant

Criteria	Unclear/ Incorrect	Clear/ Basic	Clear/ Strong	Original/ Insightful
Values The wheel includes several central or important values.				
Understanding A clear comprehension of how values dictated how the people lived.				
Key words Well-chosen words that connect to values, rituals, beliefs, practices.				
Symbols Uses appropriate Aboriginal symbolism.				
Organization Ideas are grouped or connected accurately.				

The Medicine Wheel is due _____

NOTE: This must be completed prior to starting the First Nations School Project.

Lesson 15—Rationale

To consolidate and apply their understanding of the perspectives and values of Aboriginal peoples, students need to examine their own school environment, then redesign it to reflect the values of Canada's Aboriginal peoples. By applying what they have been learning to new situations, such as the Final Project described below, students have the chance to demonstrate what they understand.

Transforming and personalizing

- Discuss with the students how a school reflects what its teachers, students, and community value.
- Then, have students describe aspects of their own school to identify the values that they think are represented by the physical environment—the posters on the walls, the rules and guidelines presented in their school agenda, the organization of the classrooms, the design of the school building, the school grounds, and so on.
- Have students work in partners to suggest a redesign of these aspects of their school that would reflect the values of some of Canada's Aboriginal peoples. This is the final project explained in Figure 8.21 (pages 149–151), assessed with the rubric in Figure 8.22 (page 152).

Lesson 16—Rationale

Returning to the K-W-L page from the first class completes the circle of learning. As students re-examine what they thought they knew, they can see how their knowledge has grown, which of their questions were answered in the course of the unit of study, and which questions remain that they would still like to research independently. Reflecting on the content and processes of their learning also helps them grow as self-regulated learners.

Transforming and personalizing

- Revisit and complete the K-W-L with the students.
- Have students complete a content and process survey, such as provided in Figure 8.20, with two focus areas: What did you learn? How did the learning sequences support your learning?

Figure 8.20

Sample Student Survey

We are interested in your feedback in order to improve the way we teach this unit. Thank you for responding to these questions.

1. What was the purpose or goal of this unit of study?

2. Identify at least three things that you have learned during this unit—for example, content such as the values of Aboriginal peoples or skills such as note-taking.

3. What did you like most about this unit?

4. What did you like least?

5. What did you think about the final project? Did you like the options?

6. Have you any suggestions to help improve this unit to make it more interesting and relevant to you?

Figure 8.21

FINAL PROJECT
A First Nations' School

Purpose

You will apply the knowledge acquired about the First Nations in order to create a school that reflects the beliefs and values of one First Nation's culture.

What would a First Nation's school look like?

Think about:

- The values of the people
- What you would see
- What you would hear
- What you would feel emotionally

Your task

Now that we have finished our unit on the First Nations, you may begin to think that a school that reflects the values of a First Nations might be an interesting place to learn. Therefore, your job is to recommend to the Superintendant of Schools that our schools be transformed based on values held by one or more Aboriginal peoples. To do this, choose one of the projects below. You may choose to work alone or in a group with a maximum of three people. Three core beliefs (Nature, Elders, and Community) must be represented in your project. You must then choose from two to four other values that you would like to add to your school. Each group must complete a research plan of "Before—After" and this sheet must be handed in with the final project. Caution! If you work in a group, be sure to choose people you get along with and who will do their share of the work. The mark is for the group.

Option 1: Physical structure

Take a look at our current school. Create a model or a drawing of the school that shows the changes you have imagined. You must label all of the spaces in your school and justify your choices based on the beliefs and values of one or more Aboriginal people. The evidence should be written in a support document that will accompany your model. Here are a few questions to guide you:

- What is the structure of the school now? Are there any elements that already reflect values of one or more First Nations or Aboriginal peoples?
- What kind of materials would you recommend we use to build this school?
- What would the property look like?
- What changes do you recommend? Think about the organization of the school, the classrooms, the office.
- What are the needs of the learners? The teachers? Others?

Figure 8.21 (cont'd).

Option 2: Multimedia oral presentation

This project is similar to the first one but instead of building a model and writing down your recommendations and analysis, you are to prepare a multimedia and oral presentation to promote and explain the changes that you would like to make to our school. You have to try to sell your ideas to the superintendent. The presentation must show evidence of one or more of the First Nations and Aboriginal peoples' beliefs and values. Caution! This project is best for those who are comfortable speaking in front of the class. You will need to know how to use the software and technology to support the presentation (PowerPoint, iMovie, Comic Life). Here are some questions to help guide you:

- How is our school organized right now? What are your recommendations?
- What is the point of your presentation? Why should we consider a First Nations inspired school?
- What would there be in your school to help students learn?
- What do you need to do to make your oral presentation interesting? What about visuals? Sound? Special effects?

Option 3: Preamble to the agenda

Find references to the values of our school. Now imagine a school that reflects the values and beliefs of one or more First Nations and Aboriginal peoples. Create a new school philosophy and motto. Write a school vision statement as well as a code of conduct. Justify your recommendations. Here are some questions to help guide you:

- What does the vision and/or values look like now? What needs to change?
- What would be your new motto or vision statement? Why?
- What are the expectations of a First Nations-inspired school?
- What should appear in the code of conduct?
- What are the rules and regulations?
- Are there any awards? Why?

Each project will be evaluated on the following elements:

- A completed task that meets expectations
- Logical and thoughtful justifications for your choices (you must have an analysis with references!)
- The presentation
- Your communication skills

Figure 8.21 (cont'd).

Name: _____

BEFORE ➜ AFTER

Use the chart below to help you plan your project. Don't forget the three required beliefs that must be in your new school as well as two to four other values.

I/We have chosen to do: _____

_____

_____

BEFORE (What are the current values of our school? Evidence?)	AFTER (What parts should we keep, what should we change or add to the new school? Evidence?)

Date Due: _____

Figure 8.22 A rubric for assessing student's presentation

Common to all presentations	4	3	2	1
Analysis	Well illustrated/argued research plan. Support documents include a variety of evidence and references.	Evidence of logical thinking in research plan. Support documents include some evidence and references.	Some gaps in overall logic of plan. Evidence and references lack connection to task.	Plan needs more clarity. May be missing logical evidence and/or references.
Presentation	Presentation is interesting and convincing. Elements of senses including sight, sound, and feeling are explored and create engagement.	Presentation is engaging and some elements of senses are used to create interest. Audience can follow sequence and understand logic.	Information is presented logically and sequentially. Needs to be more connected to audience to create engagement.	Presentation may be difficult to follow and/or understand.
Communication	Current First Nations elements have been clearly identified and elaborated upon. Three core First Nations beliefs and 2–4 values have been explained and thoughtfully used as rationale. Recommendations for changes are clearly presented, logical, and justified. The needs of the learners and the teachers have effectively been taken into consideration.	Current First Nations elements have been clearly identified. Three core First Nations beliefs and 2–4 values have been used as rationale. Recommendations for changes are clearly justified. The needs of the learners and the teachers have been taken into consideration.	Current First Nations have been identified. Some core First Nations beliefs and values have been explained. Recommendations for changes identified but need more explanation for justification. Some needs of the learners and the teachers have been taken into consideration but need more elaboration to be connected.	First Nations ideas and elements may need more explanation to be understood and followed. Core beliefs and values may be disconnected to content and need to be used more to build rationale and justifications.

Specific to choice of presentation	4	3	2	1
Option 1: Physical Structure	Presentation includes a detailed model or drawing of changes with labels. Clear that choice of building materials, use of space, design of property, and organization of school have been thoughtfully taken into consideration.	Presentation includes a model or drawing of changes with labels. Some evidence of building materials, use of space, design of property, and organization of school have been taken into consideration.	Presentation includes a model or drawing. Some choices of building materials, use of space, design of property, and organization of school seem to have been taken into consideration. May need clearer labels.	Presentation includes pieces of a model or drawing. Choices of building materials, use of space, design of property, and organization of school need to be taken into consideration to communicate rationale.
Option 2: Multimedia	Engaging and clear voice supported by technology used in presentation. Technology relates to presentation, explains and reinforces content. Use of visuals, sound, and special effects are creatively used efficiently and effectively.	Voice is clear. Some technology relates to presentation, explains and reinforces content. Visuals, sound, and special effects are used to communicate rationale.	Voice may be unclear and/or difficult to hear. Technology relates to presentation but may have had difficulties in its use. Need more use of visual supports and/or special effects to successfully create engagement and communicate rationale.	Speaker may need more practice in speaking for an audience to feel more comfortable. Technology needs to be used more effectively to highlight features that would communicate task and content. Choice of effects may be disconnected to theme.
Option 3: Preamble to Agenda	School motto and philosophy is thoughtfully created with attention to expectations of school, clearly stated rules and regulations, consideration of awards, processes of code of conduct, and a logical and justified vision statement.	Logic of school motto and philosophy is evident with attention to expectations of school, rules and regulations, consideration of awards, code of conduct, and vision statement.	School motto and philosophy are somewhat connected to expectations of school, rules and regulations, consideration of awards, code of conduct, and vision statement.	More thoughtful attention to philosophy, expectations of school, rules and regulations, consideration of awards, code of conduct, and vision statement needs to be evident in order to clearly communicate rationale.

Reflections by Julie Anne and Dave

Our chapter is about a journey of discovery, the discovery of what better planning practice looks like, of how essential collaboration is to getting there. We have clarified our understanding of how Backward Design, in the context of collaboration, helps us not only get at the content of our courses but also uncover the deeper lasting connections that run underneath. Our discovery of student involvement in and ownership of assessments helped create our shift from a teacher-focused classroom to a learner-focused one. We have seen how thoughtful design and scaffolding of assessment and learning breeds more success for both students and teachers. We have seen that, when a teacher comes to class with purposeful planning, a willingness to see the students' learning as the essential element, and an ability to adapt and incorporate lesson plans throughout the process, students move from passive indifference to confident engagement. As the students generated and worked with the criteria, they were better able to understand and demonstrate the learning targets.

Since the first printing of our chapter, we have received a great deal of feedback from our readers. Many of our students are English language learners. We have few First Nations learners in our school. With this unit it was our intent to widen our students' horizons and to begin to build both their background knowledge and their curiosity about the importance of First Nations People in our development as a country. It was never our intent to present this unit as a thorough investigation of First Nations People.

We also wish to acknowledge the historic *Delgamuukw vs. British Columbia* [1997] 3 S.C.R. 1010, also known as *Delgamuukw vs. the Queen* case. The Supreme Court ruled that oral evidence carried as much weight as written evidence in determining historical truth. We now discuss this decision in Lesson 2 with our students, acknowledging both how stories tend to change in the retelling and the importance of knowing and using oral histories.

We are excited about the conversation around our chapter. Our collaboration has now grown outside the boundaries of our school and presented us, and our students, with continued opportunities to learn together.

Chapter 9

Inquiry and Oral Language

Grade 6/7 — Humanities

Assessment FOR Learning

- Co-creating criteria
- Peer-assessment and self-assessment
- Descriptive feedback
- Goal-setting

Diverse Texts

- Information articles
- Literature circle novels
- Choice of difficulty

Gradual Release of Responsibility

- Note-making
- Preparation for debate

Assessment OF Learning

- Literature circle responses
- Debate
- Literature circle conversations

Essential Question

- What is Ancient China's greatest legacy?

The Collaboration

Kathy Pantaleo has participated in the Strengthening Student Literacy Network (SSLN) for six years. SSLN is a study group in which teachers of grades 4 through 10 (intermediate years in BC) meet once a month to discuss their teaching and to share ideas (see Schnellert 2004). Each month, group members read a chapter or article in selected professional resources; they also bring examples of ideas they have been trying out in their classrooms and share them with the group. Each meeting includes discussion, sharing, problem-solving and planning. Being part of a study group like SSLN is a way to collaborate with colleagues and find support in your professional development. Over the years, SSLN has provided Kathy opportunities to collaborate and share teaching ideas with other intermediate teachers, and read and discuss professional resources together. One of those professional resources is Jeffrey Wilhelm's *Engaging Readers and Writers with Inquiry* (2007).

As a teacher of a combined grade 6/7 class in a K-to-7 school, Kathy has worked over the years to incorporate Writers' Workshop and Literature Circles in her classroom. Like other teachers in the group, she was looking for ways to deepen her students' learning in Social Studies. Using inquiry and information circles seemed like logical next steps. Kathy enlisted the support of her teacher-librarian, Janice Cramer, to join her in implementing discussion groups in literature and information circles.

The Context

In this Humanities unit, a study of China, the primary goal was to have students learn through the lens of inquiry, a shift in Kathy's practice inspired by the Jeffrey Wilhelm book. She formulated essential questions to direct the unit of study, in which the students work toward an explicit culminating project—in this case, a debate. This unit occured in January of the school year. By this time, she was well aware of her students' strengths and capacity for stretching their limits. Kathy integrated learning objectives from Social Studies, Language Arts, and Computer Studies. This integration of the curricula released time to help the students build the necessary background knowledge. After establishing some background knowledge, students begin literature circles. By the last week of January, they are working in the computer room researching China's Three Gorges Dam, and participating in literature circle discussion groups once a week.

Essential Questions

What is a legacy? What is my greatest legacy? What is Ancient China's greatest legacy?

Key Structures

Assessment for Learning

- Students co-create criteria for effective use of oral language in small-group discussions of each literature circle, then in debates.
- Teacher provides descriptive feedback to students on their performance in small-group discussions.
- Students self-assess and peer-assess their participation in small-group discussions, then set personal goals.
- Students take ownership of personal learning goals and take responsibility for monitoring their progress as they work toward them.

Diverse Texts

- Information articles about modern China
- Grade 7 *Outlooks* series; chapter about Ancient China
- Literature circle novels, chosen to offer a range of difficulty

Gradual Release of Responsibility

- Teacher models effective language and behaviour in small-group discussions, then observes students in small groups, providing guidance that helps them move on to independent group discussions.
- Teacher conducts large-group discussions about legacies in general, moving on to independent research about Ancient China's legacy.
- Teacher provides frequent opportunities for debate during drama class.

Assessment of Learning

- Students write bi-weekly responses about the novels they read and discuss in literature circles.
- Students debate Ancient China's greatest legacy and complete a self-evaluation of their participation in the debate.

Lesson 1—Rationale

This is a mid-year unit with lessons that focus on building background knowledge. Students need to build their content background and their skills background as they are introduced to new material. At this point, they are quite unfamiliar with China and with the concept of legacies. An overriding goal for the unit is asking and responding to open-ended questions. Based on the year's learning to date, students have begun to use thinking strategies to read and respond to informational texts and fiction in both written and oral form.

Students need opportunities to continue developing their skills in drawing information from a piece of text, in writing what they think about their reading, and in building on the ideas of others in group discussions. The knowledge objective in the Social Studies curriculum related to China's legacies provides the vehicle for developing students' thinking and oral language skills while learning the content. Students begin with their experiences and analyze them through the lens of an abstract concept. With this ultimate goal in mind, the teacher's lessons use the students' expanding content knowledge to focus on developing the following skills:

Thinking skills

- Determining importance
- Supporting an opinion with specific evidence
- Building on one another's ideas

Connecting—Legacy stars

- Begin with the questions What is a legacy? What would you like your legacy to be? Ask students to work in groups to brainstorm their responses to these questions.
- Kathy's school participates in the Effective Behaviour Support program where students model the STAR acronym—Safe, Thoughtful, Accepting, and Responsible—behaviour. To demonstrate their legacy, ask students to discuss how their legacy might be related to the four ideas behind the STAR acronym. Using this STAR metaphor, invite students to create two-dimensional or three-dimensional stars using pictures or words to represent their legacy. This may take up to three classes.

Lesson 2

Connecting—Carousel

- To begin thinking about China's Greatest Legacy, write the following questions on chart paper; have students write their thinking in a carousel.

- What is a legacy?
- What is China's legacy?
- What would you like to learn about China?
- How are China and Canada similar?
- How are China and Canada different?

- Place each question (one per page) on desks around the room. Students, in small groups, read the question, discuss it as a group, then add their thinking to the chart paper.
- After three or four minutes, have students move on to the next question. They read the question, read what the preceding group has written, and add their thinking.
- When the groups of students return to their first question, they summarize the thinking of all the groups and present it to the class.
- At the end of the lesson, tell the students that your plan for the culminating activity in this unit is a debate on the question What is China's greatest legacy? In preparation for this debate, the students will begin reading information articles to develop their background knowledge.

Lesson 3—Rationale

The think-aloud demonstrates to students how to read a particular form of text. By slowing your thinking down and talking about what you are doing in your head as you try to take meaning from the text, you show how a reader actually builds an understanding. By following your model, students find that reading for understanding becomes more accessible; this process clarifies the reader's task when assigned an informational text to read. The task is not just to reach the bottom of the page, but to think about and reason with the information they are reading *as* they read.

Processing—Think-Aloud with information text, modelling, Guided practice

- Model how to read the informational text. Choose a portion of text and put it on an overhead.
- Read it aloud, slowly, in smaller chunks.
- Write your thinking around the text as you read it, coding the text. You might write *I* beside an inference you make, *Q* beside a question you ask, and *C* beside a connection you make. With the teacher and the teacher-librarian working together, the students can witness two different think-alouds about the same piece of text, which illustrates, first, how two different readers construct meaning and, second, how the students can work together in their subsequent partnerships.
- Have the students pair up, and give each pair an enlarged 11" x 17" copy of the next portion of text in the article.

- While reading the text with their partner, students continue the process of writing around the article and perhaps coding their thinking.

Lesson 4
Processing—Independent Think-Aloud

- Choose a variety of information texts about China with a range of reading levels.
- Briefly describe each article, and the degree of difficulty.
- Invite students to skim-read the articles and select which one they would like to read.
- Place students in groups no larger than four, according to the article they are reading.
- Students read their article independently and code their thinking to share with their group on the following day.

Lesson 5—Rationale

Talking with others about what you understand from your reading helps build deeper, richer understanding. Students can use the information gained from their personal reading and their think-aloud/write-around as they participate in group discussions. These group discussions enable them to write their own, more informed, response to the article. Building criteria for the discussion clarifies for all students everyone's expectations of what is required of them to be an effective group member.

Processing—Small-group discussion, Information Circles, Creating Criteria

- Students arrive with their articles coded, and share their thinking in their small groups.
- Group discussions will range from students helping each other understand challenging words or sentences to raising questions that evoke deep thinking from each other.
- When the discussions are complete, write on the board, "What makes a good circle discussion?"
- Give students time to talk with their discussion groups.
- Have each group report back to the class their criteria.
- Use these criteria to create, alone or with them, the Information Circle reflection sheets.
- After generating the criteria, give time to begin writing a response to the article.

Lesson 6—Rationale

China's development has been influenced by its geographic isolation. Use a guiding question to focus students' reading of both text and map and assist them in more quickly and more ably gaining the required content knowledge.

Processing—Questioning, common text, summary

- Ask the question How does isolation impact the development of China's civilization?
- Using a text such as *Outlooks*, the Social Studies text for grade 7 (Toutant and Doyle 2000), have students examine a map of China and read the supporting article.
- Give students a copy of a map of China and have them highlight the geographic features that they think contribute to the isolation of a civilization.
- Have students summarize in a paragraph of no more than 30 words what they have read in the textual material and observed in the maps.

Lesson 7—Rationale

Students expand and internalize their content understanding by talking about it with others. They practise being an effective discussant both by observing and critiquing others and by being the actual discussant.

Processing—Inside/Outside Fishbowl discussion, peer-assessment feedback

- Students arrive with their paragraphs complete and ready to share their thinking about the impact of isolation on the development of China's civilization.
- Use the inside/outside fishbowl discussion format. Ask one group of four students to volunteer to sit inside a circle while another group of four is on the outside.
- While the inside group discusses, the outside group members each observe one person in the inside circle. The observer's job is to write down positive feedback for the participant.
- When the group is ready, switch roles, giving the outside group a chance to discuss the impact of isolation on the development of China's civilization, and giving the inside group a chance to observe and give feedback.
- When all members have had a chance to share, work with the class to generate criteria for participation in discussions. Figure 9.1 is a sample of the criteria created in Kathy's class, criteria of what is important when participating in a discussion.

Figure 9.1 Criteria for discussion

- Do your research so that you know what you are talking about.
- Pose questions to the other participants.
- Support what you are saying with examples.
- Use a clear voice when speaking.
- Show that you are listening to the speaker.

Teacher homework

Use the criteria generated in class to create a participation checklist (Figure 9.2), referenced to local performance standards and/or curriculum outcomes for oral language. Present this checklist to the students, and use it for the next debate. It can be used by the teacher, the teacher-librarian, or any other adult observing the small-group discussions.

Figure 9.2 Participation checklist (sample)

Name	Strategies		Exchanging Ideas	Listening + Speaking	
	Prepared notes with background knowledge	Asks questions that sustained and/or extended the conversation	Supports, providing reasons and examples	Listens to speaker	Uses a clear voice when speaking

- Create a reflection sheet for students to complete after each group discussion or debate.
- Students use this on a regular basis to help them reflect on their explicit use of the requisite expectations and to set personal goals. Figure 9.3 is an example of a student reflection sheet.

Figure 9.3 Sample of form on which students reflect and assess their participation

Before the discussion	I did my research so that I knew what I was talking about.	1 2 3 4 5
During the discussion	I asked questions of the other participants.	1 2 3 4 5
	I supported what I said with examples.	1 2 3 4 5
	I used a clear voice when I was speaking.	1 2 3 4 5

My goal for participating in our next discussion is: _____

I will work toward my goal by: _____

Comments from Mrs. P: _____

Lesson 8—Rationale

Using a shared text, students form an opinion and defend their opinion with evidence. They collect evidence on both sides of their opinion, a practice that will help them anticipate arguments when they are debating later.

Processing—Coding the text, supporting an opinion with evidence

- Continue to use the *Outlooks* text or another text.
- Ask students to read a photocopied text page from the article "The Three Gorges Dam," coding their thinking while they read. The Three Gorges Dam, which is built on the Yangtze River in China, is the largest hydroelectric power plant in the world. Completed on the north side in 2006, it caused the relocation of 1.24 million people, and the reservoir has flooded or will flood many archaeological and cultural sites.
- Provide students with a graphic organizer, identifying the pros and cons of building the Three Gorges Dam. A graphic organizer like the sample in Figure 9.4 will help the students prepare for their debate.

Figure 9.4 Organizer for debate on the Three Gorges Dam

Name:_____

Pros of building the dam

Supporting facts: _____

_____

_____

_____

_____

Cons of building the dam

Supporting facts: _____

_____

_____

_____

_____

_____

My position is:_____

_____

because _____

Lesson 9—Rationale

Reading historical fiction set in China helps build background knowledge about the country. The choices in the literature circle novels address diverse interests and reading levels. Students can read as quickly as they like, so no student is limited to keeping pace with others. The literature circle discussions and the students' response journals continue to provide support, feedback, and practice in the key thinking skills and oral language skills of determining importance, supporting opinions with evidence, and building on one another's ideas.

Processing—Literature Circles, book choices

Establish guidelines to help make literature circles successful. Figure 9.5 provides a sample of literature circle guidelines.

Figure 9.5 Literature Circle guidelines

- Come to class once a week ready to share something new about your novel.
- Read a maximum of one novel each week.
- Complete a weekly journal response.
- Complete one four-quadrant chart for each novel you read.
- When you have finished reading your novel, record the date and title in your reading log at the back of your reading key tab.
- Place your finished novel in the bin and select another one. If there are no novels in the bin that you would like to read, see Mrs. P.
- Don't give away the ending in your discussion group!

- Introduce each novel (eight choices) by reading a short captivating passage, giving a quick description, and recommending the type of audience who might enjoy reading this novel.
- Give students a chance to have a quick look at each novel, before they make their choices of the five class novels
- Have the class vote on the 5/8 novels they would like to read at this time.
- One class chose these novels (see Student Resources, page 249):
  - *Throwaway Daughter*, Ting-Xing Ye
  - *A Single Shard*, Linda Sue Park
  - *Tiger*, Jeff Stone (first novel of the five-book Ancestors Series)
  - *Year of Impossible Goodbyes*, Sook Nyul Choi
  - *So Far from the Bamboo Grove*, Yoko Kawashima Watkins
- Use a random draw of student names; invite students to choose their novel and begin reading.
- Before the end of the class, establish discussion groups. Students meet in discussion groups with others who are reading the same novel.
- Assign a morning for each discussion group. During the 15-minute discussion, the teacher will join the group while the other groups read.

Lesson 10—Rationale

The note-taking sheet with four quadrants can help guide students as they are reading. It helps them focus on key ideas (themes), questions, images, and quotations. This format also acknowledges different learning styles and supports students in the reading tasks of finding evidence (quotations) in the text, determining importance (themes), and interacting with the text by posing questions.

Processing—Literature Circle discussion groups, Four Quadrants, Response-Writing

- Students prepare a Four Quadrants chart in their reading key tabs.
- Each quadrant represents a way of responding to the text.

Figure 9.6 Four Quadrants chart

Questions requiring Deep Thinking	Powerful Images
Quotations or Passages	Themes

- Give students time to meet in their literature circle (novel groups) to help each other begin to gather ideas in their charts for their discussion groups the following week.
- Response-writing to literature was introduced in the first term. Much of the first term was spent examining examples of a good response, generating criteria as a class, and having an opportunity to write a response. Kathy provided feedback to each student in the form of a personal letter. As a result, by the time they begin to write responses in a literature circle, the students understand what a good response looks like, and they can choose what to include.
- Have students use sticky notes, while reading their novels, to write their questions and connections or to mark a powerful passage.

- To prepare for their discussion group, and organize their thinking for writing responses, students look at the collection of sticky notes in their novels and record their thinking in a Four Quadrants graphic organizer.
- Continue with the letter-writing format, and respond to student thinking, building upon their ideas, making positive comments and offering suggestions for improvement. Figure 9.7 provides an example of a student journal entry and the teacher's response.

Figure 9.7 Response to *So Far from the Bamboo Grove*

I can't imagine what it would be like to be Yoko. At the beginning of the book she is just an ordinary school girl, when she suddenly has to leave with her mother and older sister in the middle of the night and leave her father and brother behind. They sneak on the train and travel with the sick and wounded being transported to the hospital. This is when the harsh realities of war began to sink in. Yoko sees a baby die and get thrown off the train, and her character is changed forever. I was shocked and sad when I read that part and I wondered how I would react. It's on that train ride and the long walk afterwards where Yoko's strength and maturity in her character grows for her family to survive. She learns that she needs to do anything to survive, and seems to be able to overcome pain and hunger just to survive and not be like that woman jumping from the train. When she was hit by pieces of metal, and her ear was ringing and in pain, she continued on with her mom and sister without complaining until she got medical help. That's what makes Yoko an amazing character, and more amazing that her experience is based on a true story.

Thoughtfully written response! I liked it when you described Yoko's change in character starting from the shocking train ride. That's a great example of supporting your reactions with examples. For your next response, try to include a passage to support your thoughts and ideas. Well done!

Lesson 11—Rationale

Preparation for a debate should be thorough and supportive of all students. The students have had practice in collecting information to defend an opinion. They have practised considering both sides of an issue. They have been working on listening to each other and building on each other's ideas. They have been working with criteria to improve their performances. This debate is an opportunity for them to put into practice all that they have been learning. It is a final opportunity for teachers to provide descriptive feedback before marking students' performance on the final debate on China's greatest legacy. No student debates should be scheduled without providing several opportunities for them to rehearse their knowledge—through their note-taking, their work in the fishbowl, and their self-assessment according to established criteria. They are set up for success.

Transforming—Debating Three Gorges Dam, Inside/Outside Fishbowl, feedback

- Students should have already prepared their debate sheets for the Three Gorges Dam.
- Use the checklist (Figure 9.2, page 162) to quickly record whether students had their notes prepared by completing their sheet.
- Move students into pro and con groups.
- Give time for the students to review their notes and to help each other prepare supporting facts for their position.
- Move into the fishbowl discussion format as used earlier for the articles about China. In each fishbowl, have two inside circle students who are pro, and two who are con. The outside observers should also have some pro and some con. If there is an odd number of students, then some students can choose to be the lone debater, while others can choose to change their position.
- Review with students the established criteria for debating. Review with the observers how to record their observations.
- While the fishbowl debates are on, walk around the room and record your observations on the criteria sheet (Figure 9.2, page 162).
- When the debates are finished, both the teacher and the student observers should provide positive comments and observations noticed in the class.

Lesson 12—Rationale

The culminating activity flows directly from the content and the skills that were the focus of the unit. The students are preparing to engage in a debate about China's greatest legacy. This lesson returns students to the activity, that was introduced in lesson 2, at the beginning of this unit of study.

Transforming—Note-making, China's legacy

- By now, most of the students have chosen their topics and those who have not yet done so have a chart of sample suggestions from their classmates for reference. Be prepared for high energy, enthusiasm, and ownership.
- Give each student a planning sheet to help them outline their thinking in preparation for the debate, as in Figure 9.8.
- Ensure that students collect their information over several days before the actual debate begins.

Figure 9. 8

Name: _____

Planning for Debate

What is a legacy? _____

_____

_____

What is Ancient China's greatest legacy? _____

_____

_____

_____

_____

Supporting evidence 1. _____

_____

Supporting evidence 2. _____

_____

_____

Supporting evidence 3. _____

_____

_____

How has this legacy contributed to present-day cultures?

_____

_____

_____

_____

Meet with students who have similar points to prepare for the debate.

Lesson 13—Rationale

Two threads have been woven throughout this unit—the debate and the literature read in small-group literature circles. Both threads have involved the key thinking skills of determining importance and supporting an opinion with evidence. Both have required students to focus on building on one another's ideas during their discussions. At this point, students can build criteria for their discussions in literature circles—the criteria that they also use to guide their performance in small-group discussions. The expectations are very clear by now, and all students have been involved in co-creating these expectations.

Transforming—Developing criteria

- By this time, students have had a chance to participate in at least one literature circle discussion group with the teacher and have received descriptive feedback and coaching on their participation from the teacher.
- Pose the question *What makes a good literature circle discussion?* Have students develop criteria for good participation in a literature circle.
- Have students brainstorm their thoughts in small groups and report back to the class as a whole.
- From the criteria generated in class, create reflection sheets for each student to complete after the discussion group, as well as oral language rubrics for each grade based on local curriculum outcomes and/or performance standards. See figures 9.9 and 9.10A for samples.
- Photocopy one sheet per student, and keep them in your class binder. After each discussion group, write your comments and/or highlight the rubric (Figure 9.10B, page 174). Use the same page each time the student participates in the discussions so that by the end of the term, you can readily develop comments for report cards from the evidence highlighted on the rubric.
- After the discussion group, and using either Figure 9.9 or 9.10, have students circle or highlight how they think they participated, a goal for improvement, and their plan for working towards this goal.

Figure 9.9 Reflection on Literature Circle discussion

Name: _____ Novel: _____ Date: _____

	Not prepared!	Prepared to Share	Can't wait to share!
Before Discussion Group	• I don't have my book. • I didn't do my reading. • I didn't have my thinking prepared in my book.	• I have my book. • I read more since last week. • I had a powerful passage to share. • I was prepared to share thinking (e.g., had questions, connections, reactions) in key tab.	• I have my book filled with post-its of powerful passages. • I have deep-thinking questions and thought about possible answers. • I prepared connections with background research to share.
During Discussion Group	• I wasn't able to share.	• I shared with encouragement. • I asked questions or made connections. • Most of my thinking was at surface level.	• I extended our conversation. • I asked questions. • I tried to build on the ideas of others.

Figure 9.10A Oral Language Rubric

Grade 7 Speaking Criteria

Name:_____

	Not Yet Within	Meets	Fully Meets	Exceeds
Strategies				
makes logical connections to prior knowledge and beliefs	makes connections to prior knowledge and beliefs, with support	makes some connections to prior knowledge and beliefs	makes logical connections to prior knowledge and beliefs	makes insightful connections to prior knowledge and beliefs
asks questions to sustain and extend interactions	asks relevant questions, with support	asks some questions to sustain interactions	asks relevant questions to sustain and extend interactions	asks a variety of questions to sustain and extend interactions, and find out others' views
Exchanging Ideas/Information				
expresses views appropriately with relevant supporting reasons	expresses views	expresses views appropriately, with some reasons	expresses views appropriately with relevant supporting reasons	expresses views effectively, with some convincing reasons
evaluates solutions/options and explores implications	identifies solutions and options, with support	identifies and sometimes evaluates solutions and options	evaluates solutions/options and explores implications	systematically evaluates solutions/options and analyses and considers implications
includes technically accurate and relevant details	sometimes offers own views, without reasons	generally expresses own views appropriately; gives few reasons	includes technically accurate and relevant details	chooses effective and convincing detail; accurate, specific, relevant
speculates	limited speculation, with support	limited speculation	speculates	speculates reasonably and insightfully
Listening				
paraphrases opinions and views accurately	paraphrases opinions and views, with support	generates some relevant questions to make predictions	paraphrases opinions and views accurately	succinctly and effectively paraphrases opinions and views
Reflection				
contributes to and uses criteria to self-assess and set goals	assesses own behaviour; sets a simple goal, with support	assesses own behaviour; sets a simple goal	contributes to and uses criteria to self-assess and set goals	assesses own behaviour; shows insight; sets appropriate goals

Lessons 14 to16 — Rationale

The students have been reading for a month. All students have been exposed to teacher modelling and support from discussion groups. It is time for further gradual release of responsibility.

Transforming — Independent Literature Circles, discussions with assessment

- As the month of reading continues, take out novels that most students have read and add new titles as needed.
- Have students meet in their literature circle groups.
- Use the fishbowl discussion format for literature circles, with an adult observing on the outside of one or more discussions. Align your library block of class time so the librarian can also support the discussion group observations.
- Use the same Oral Language Rubric as before (Figure 9.10A, page 171) while the students use the same Reflection sheet as before (Figure 9.9, page 170), and observers use the same reflection sheet but photocopied on a different colour.
- Repeat this observing/feedback process over the course of several days, having students also be observers, giving feedback to others in the group.
- After the discussion group, ask students to circle or highlight how they thought their peer participated. Remind them to provide some positive feedback, perhaps a question or suggestion. Ask them to sign their name, and hand it in to the teacher.

Lesson 17 — Rationale

The final debate is the one that will be evaluated for marks. By this time, students are well-prepared to be judged on their learning.

Transforming — The debate

- Prepare the class for the debate, dividing into opposing teams. In Kathy's class, most students had chosen the Great Wall of China as the greatest legacy, so the debate became the Great Wall of China group vs. Everyone Else who had chosen gun powder, calligraphy, or paper as the greatest legacy. The Everyone Else group was smaller, but included a strong group of independent thinkers.
- As a class, develop the rules of the debate before beginning or, as you proceed, based on what students expect will be necessary. Most students will recognize a need to have a protocol for taking turns, for being recognized as a speaker (perhaps by standing), the number of times a person may speak, and so on. Alternatively, you

might introduce more formal debating rules, like the first speaker of the group in favour of the topic presents his/her statement, then the speaker of the opposition group follows, then they take turns defending their opinion, then rebutting the opposing opinion.

- Be prepared for a passionate debate, including all voices. For Kathy, it was by far the best debate she had ever experienced.

Assessment of Learning—Generating the marks

When it comes time to enter students' end-of-unit marks or to enter marks on their report cards, you can refer to the rubrics and annotated figures with highlights or notes that you have collected in your binder for each student throughout each unit.

- Some teachers give each student a number at the beginning of the year to organize their binder; others organize their records by student name.
- For this unit, you would want to keep a copy of the speaking criteria sheet (Figure 9.2, page 162) and a copy of their oral language rubric (Figure 9.10B) in each student's section. After you have observed each discussion group, highlight on the rubric or check off on the criteria sheet (Figure 9.11) the behaviours that have been observed.
- You might also use the same rubric following class debates, and looking for checked or highlighted items in the Exchanging Ideas/Information section of Figure 9.10B.
- When you collect your students' literature circle responses, check the self-reflection sheet, and highlight the reflection section of the same speaking criteria sheet.

Figure 9.10B Sample of scored Oral Language Rubric

Samples were collected over time.

Literature Circle Discussion Groups: Feb 20, Feb 27, March 5   Name: Sharon

Grade 7 Speaking Criteria

	Not Yet Within	Meets	Fully Meets	Exceeds
Strategies: ·makes logical connections to prior knowledge and beliefs ·asks questions to sustain and extend interactions	·makes connections to prior knowledge and beliefs, with support ·asks relevant questions, with support	·makes some connections to prior knowledge and beliefs ·asks some questions to sustain interactions	·makes logical connections to prior knowledge and beliefs *"To build on Sara's idea.."* ·asks relevant questions to sustain and extend interactions	·makes insightful connections to prior knowledge and beliefs ·asks a variety of questions to sustain and extend interactions, and find out others' views
Exchanging Ideas / Information ·expresses views appropriately with relevant supporting reasons	·expresses views	·expresses views appropriately, with some reasons	·expresses views appropriately with relevant supporting reasons	·expresses views *theme of peace* effectively, with some convincing reasons
·evaluates solutions/options and explores implications	·identifies solutions and options, with support	·identifies and sometimes evaluates solutions and options	·evaluates solutions/options and explores implications	·systematically evaluates solutions/options and analyses and considers implications
·includes technically accurate and relevant details	·sometimes offers own views, without reasons	·generally expresses own views appropriately; gives few reasons	·includes technically accurate and relevant details	·chooses effective and convincing detail; accurate, specific, relevant
·speculates	·limited speculation, with support	·limited speculation	·speculates	·speculates reasonable and insightfully
Listening ·paraphrases opinions and views accurately	·paraphrases opinions and views, with support	·generates some relevant questions to make predictions	·paraphrases opinions and views accurately	·succinctly and effectively paraphrases opinions and views
Reflection ·contributes to and uses criteria to self-assess and set goals	·assesses own behaviour; sets a simple goal, with support	·assesses own behaviour; sets a simple goal	·contributes to and uses criteria to self assess and set goals	·assesses own behaviour; shows insight; sets appropriate goals

seemed a little unsure at first to share, but read aloud a powerful passage to get discussion going. No goal set for next week in response book.

more enthusiasm and excited to share about the theme of persecution. Goal set to build on ideas of others.

Great to see her trying conversation strategies tried in class!

Figure 9.11 Sample scored literature circle response.

Grade 7 Reading Response Criteria   Name: Sharon

So Far From the Bamboo Grove

	1	3	5
Comprehension: • story elements	• identifies main characters events	•describes setting, main characters, events in own words	•describes story elements in detail; explains relationships
• predictions	•predictions and inferences are unsupported	• predictions and inferences are unsupported	• makes insightful predictions that are supported by specific evidence
•details	•offers inaccurate details in response	•identifies relevant details in response	•identifies precise details in response
• theme	• does not interpret theme	• interprets obvious themes	•interprets complex themes
Response and Analysis: •connections and experiences to other selections	•makes simple connections to self	•makes and supports logical connections (T-S, T-T, T-W)	•makes and supports logical connections (T-S, T-T, T-W), may risk a divergent response
•reactions	•reactions tend to be unsupported	•offers reactions and opinions with some support	•offers reactions and opinions with reasons and examples

Thoughtfully written response! I liked it when you described Yoko's change in character starting from the train ride. That's a great example of supporting your reactions with examples. For your next response, try to include a passage to support your thoughts and ideas. Well done!

4.5

Reflections by Kathy

Generating the oral language criteria together and providing opportunities for gradual release is what helped make my debates and literature circles so successful. The descriptive feedback and coaching along the way allowed all students to be successful. Their written responses and their small-group discussions, both in debating and in literature circle groups, improved remarkably over the time of the unit. The students did not want literature circles to stop—so they continued for the remainder of the year. They were disappointed to end the debate and *begged* to have more the following term. To respond, I changed my persuasive-essay-writing time to include opportunities for debate as well. Students had lively discussions about dress codes, blogging, and wearing helmets when riding their bikes. These debates helped them develop arguments and counter-arguments when writing their individual essays. It was a powerful and exciting way to end the school year!

Chapter 10

Engaging Critically with Text

Grade 5/6—English and French Language Arts

Assessment FOR Learning

- Learning intentions
- Co-creating criteria for small-group discussion
- Co-creating criteria for journal responses
- Descriptive feedback
- Peer assessment
- Goal-setting

Diverse Texts

- Literature circle novels, in English, thematically connected
- Literature circle novels, in French, not thematically connected

Gradual Release of Responsibility

- Read-aloud shared text, modelling three types of connections
- Applying strategies in text sets

Assessment OF Learning

- Small-group discussions
- Journal responses
- Dialogue journals
- Ideagram (English)
- Learning Journey (French)

The Collaboration

Lisa Chang and Stacey Wyatt have been teaching intermediate classes at the same dual-track elementary school for the past six years. Lisa teaches in the French Immersion Program while Stacey teaches in the English Program. Despite the difference in languages, they have been successfully collaborating to plan curriculum, to develop lessons, to build text sets, and to redesign their assessment strategies. Although they do not team-teach in one classroom, they find that planning together gives them new ways to think about how they are teaching and about what might be most helpful for their students. They also work closely with their teacher-librarian, Melanie Anastasiou, who supports them in finding engaging books for literature circles and sits in on literature circle conversations.

The Context

From Kindergarten on, students in the Early French Immersion Program are taught all subject areas in French; at the Intermediate level, they begin to receive instruction in English Language Arts 20 per cent of the time during the week. Both Stacey's and Lisa's classes are fully inclusive and have a high number of students who require extra academic support. Both want to encourage their students to think about and respond critically to the literature they are reading. To work toward their goal, they each have made the literature circle a part of their reading program, and decided to take a closer look at the texts they were using and their assessment practices. Their students read a variety of novels and have small-group discussions to share their thoughts about what they are reading. After each discussion, their students reflect in their reading journals. Stacey and Lisa circulate among the discussion groups to eavesdrop on conversations about the books and to provide support to groups as necessary.

This unit of study incorporates explicit learning intentions, using "I can..." statements, which are posted for the students to see, record, and use during the unit.

Learning Intentions

- I can describe criteria for a powerful response.
- I can write a powerful response, using criteria.
- I can use connections to deepen my understanding of what I am reading.
- I can engage in a meaningful conversation with my peers about books.
- I can use the criteria we co-created to describe a response.

The following notes highlight goals, processes, and expectations for implementing the literature circle concept in multi-level classrooms, no matter what language is used.

Essential Questions

Student Questions
- What is a powerful response?
- What makes a powerful **oral** response?
- What makes a powerful **written** response?
- How can I deepen my understanding of a text?

Teacher Question
- How can my assessment practices support student learning?

Key Thinking Skills
- Making connections
- Responding to literature
- Discussion
- Response-writing

Literature Circles
- *Discussions:* Students are asked to bring a powerful passage, event, or quote to share with their group; students use co-criteria for a good discussion in book groups as they participate.
- *Weekly Reading Responses:* Students write journal responses (personal reaction, a connection) to a key moment in the section of the book they read that week. When reviewing their students' journals, teachers can generate marks based on a four-point scale (see page 194).
  - Students write back and forth to a dialogue partner throughout the week, discussing the content of book, the questions they have, the connections they make, and their predictions for future chapters.
- *Ideagram (English)*: Students represent a theme from the book, using evidence (quotes, events, images) and connect it to what they have learned about the story, about the world, and/or about themselves.
- *Learning Journey (French)*: A dynamic way of retelling the story through key events in the life of a main character. Students use icons as metaphors to describe the problems and other critical moments that the protagonist encounters.

Theme
The text sets in English are chosen around the theme *determination*, which is of interest to the students perhaps because they bring background knowledge to the books they select. Having a familiar theme makes it easier for students to achieve the goal of engaging critically with the text.

In French Immersion, the teachers face the challenge of finding texts both interesting to the students and written at their language level. Because of this, the text sets are chosen precisely because they engage students' interest although they may not connect to a particular theme.

Lessons 1 and 2 — Rationale

Choosing a book to read aloud that connects to a topic or theme already being studied in the class reinforces learning. Books can be of different lengths; in this case, the French Immersion class heard a picture book, the English class read a short novel. As the teachers model their thinking — that is, how they make meaning of the text — the students are becoming involved in an apprenticeship model of learning. Students work with the master (the teacher), then work side by side (with their peers), then work independently. Because "making connections that help deepen understanding" is a key thinking skill for this unit of study, the teachers' modelling of their connections becomes the focus for the students. This process previews what the students will do independently later on in a literature circle.

Modelling

- Choose a picture book that connects with what is occurring in other areas of your class. Because these classes are learning about global citizenship in Social Studies at the same time, the French picture book is *Coton Blues* by Régine Joséphine, which is the story of a little girl who worked as a slave in the cotton fields by day and dreamed of her freedom by night. The English class hears a short chapter book, *Iqbal* by Francesco D'Adamo, which is the true story about a boy from Pakistan who was sent off to work at a carpet factory to pay off his family's debt. The reading of this text may require more than two classes.
- Read the picture book, pausing at key moments to share with the students your thinking about the passages. Model your think-alouds with examples of different types of connections: text-to-self, text-to-text, and text-to-world.

Lessons 3 and 4 — Rationale

Involving students in the assessment process is an essential component of student success.

Building criteria for oral responses

- When you plan to begin using literature circles, ask your students to help develop the criteria.
- Write on the board, "What makes a good literature circle discussion?" and ask for student input.
- Record students' suggestions and model how to create an assessment rubric using their suggestions.
- Figures 10.1 and 10.2 are examples of the criteria that Stacey's and Lisa's classes created for students' oral responses in literature circle discussions.

Figure 10.1 Criteria for oral responses developed by Stacey and her students

Criteria	Comments/Feedback
Be prepared • Has novel (and backup plan) • Powerful Passage (P.P.) marked in book • Assignment complete • TDT (Tease, Don't Tell) • Make sure you read the chapter selected	
Sharing your powerful passage • Eye contact • Speak loudly/clearly • Share something meaningful • Explain thinking in detail • Explain why you chose it • Explain any connections	
Responding to others • Listen respectfully • Look at speaker • Sit in a circle • Share and discuss opinions • Ask questions • Okay to agree/disagree (but support your thinking with evidence from book)	

Lessons 5 and 6—Rationale

Involving students in the co-creation of criteria in another form continues to build their understanding. Criteria answer the question What needs to be done? Criteria are best grouped into four or five categories rather than one long list. Choosing categories for criteria helps all students understand what is expected of them. Rubrics grow out of the criteria, adding in the aspect of quality, answering the question How well is this done? There is more than one way to create criteria and to build a rubric, as shown by these teachers.

Figure 10.2 Criteria and rubric for oral responses developed by Lisa and her students

Critères pour les réponses orales

Critères	Ne satisfait pas les attentes	Satisfait les attentes de façon minimale	Satisfait entièrement les attentes	Dépasse les attentes (toujours fait)
Être prêt • un moment choisi déjà • le devoir fini • garde à la fin un secret				
Partager le moment • regarde les membres du groupe • parle clairement • partage des idées significatives • explique en détails les liens personnels, aux autres textes ou au monde				
Répondre aux autres • écoute respectueusement • regarde la personne qui parle • assis dans le groupe • discute les idées présentées et explique les opinions • pose des questions				

Building criteria and rubrics for written responses

Building from experience
- Students have created the criteria for an oral response in lessons 3 and 4.
- Ask students to work in groups to develop criteria for a written response.
- Students brainstorm what a good written response should include.
- Students group their criteria into categories and share their thinking with the class.
- After receiving feedback from their peers and teacher, have students organize into small groups to create a rubric for a written response.
- Share rubrics with the class, then have the class vote on the most suitable rubric.
- Work together to refine the rubric. See example in Figure 10.3 for student-created criteria generated by Stacey and her class for a written response to books discussed in literature circle.

Figure 10.3 Criteria for written responses

My Thinking	Feedback/Comments

1. Explain why I chose the powerful passage:
   • use details from book and examples
   • include my feelings and emotions
   • explain my connections (personal/text/world)
2. TDT (Tease, don't tell)
   • When writing to my dialogue partner, don't give away too much of the story in case my partner has not read that far.	

Story Explanation	
1. Explain what happened in the book. 2. Describe the character (include feelings and descriptive words). 3. Explain how I relate to the character and how the characters relate to each other (e.g., sharing a similar experience). 4. Explain predictions for the future (e.g., what might happen next).	

Building from a performance standard

- Give the students a copy of a rubric for reading responses. We use the *BC Performance Standards* for this, which are easy to use and adapt. You can find them online at <http://www.bced.gov.bc.ca/perf_stands/reading_g5.pdf>. Use page 143 for the Grade 5 Reading scale.
- Have students work in pairs to read the standard and to discuss it, making an effort to understand as much as they can, then to ask clarifying questions.
- While circulating around the groups, discuss and respond to their questions to clarify the expectations.
- Provide each group with examples of reading responses to sort into appropriate levels, based on the criteria. For example, the *BC Performance Standards* outlines four levels of student achievement: Not Yet Within Expectations, Meets Expectations (Minimal Level), Fully Meets Expectations, and Exceeds Expectations. The samples should provide specific models of what the criteria describe; they should provide students with a good idea of how to meet the curricular expectations.
- Have students discuss which responses offer examples that meet the different criteria and in what ways.
- Once it appears that the students understand that the qualities make a powerful response according to the criteria, combine pairs of students to make groups of four.
- Give each new group another copy of the rubric (from the *BC Performance Standards*) so that they can rewrite the criteria in their own words.

Figure 10.4 Rubric of criteria

Rubrique

Ne satisfait pas encore aux attentes	
• le prof doit aider pour faire des liens personnels avec le texte • les réactions ou opinions sont simples et pas toujours claires • il n'y a pas d'exemples ni explications pour justifier la réponse • le minimum	
Satisfait aux attentes (de façon minimale)	
• fais des liens avec les expériences personnelles ou des autres livres • les réactions et opinions sont simples mais clairs • il y a de la difficulté à chercher des exemples pour justifier la réponse	
Satisfait entièrement aux attentes	
• fais des liens aux expériences personnelles et aux livres • donne des sentiments comme réaction au texte • il y a des exemples, des détails pour justifier ou soutenir la réponse	
Dépasse les attentes	
• crée des liens personnels, avec les autres livres, et ce qui se passe dans le monde • donne beaucoup de détails et explications logiques et claires pour justifier ou soutenir la réponse • demande des questions ou faire des comparaisons • fais un commentaire lié au thème du texte	

- Take all of their suggestions and compile them into a rubric that you and your students can both use for assessing their work. See Figure 10.4 for a sample rubric created by Lisa's French Immersion class for responses in literature circles.

Lessons 7 and 8—Rationale

Returning to the strategy of a think-aloud and having the students add their thinking to yours provides more direct teaching and support, which are necessary for all learners to succeed. The text chosen help build student understanding of a theme studied in other subjects. Writing a response to a common text is a natural next step toward independence, now that the criteria for success have been developed. It is necessary to teach students how to use the criteria, not just to co-create it, then assign its use.

Think-Aloud: Model and guided practice, Response-Writing with connections

- Model a think-aloud with a second picture book.
- During this think-aloud, focus on connections. Students will begin to add their connections to yours, moving to the guided practice stage. A text used in the French Immersion class is *Le Nouveau Monde* by Muriel Kerba (2006); in the English class, *Carpet Boy's Gift* by Pegi Deitz Shea (2003) is used.
- Review with the students the criteria for a powerful response in writing.
- Have the students write a response to the story, making a connection and elaborating on it.
- Remind students to refer to the criteria as a guide to what a powerful written response should look like.
- As a different format for focusing students' attention and supporting them as they make connections, use an overhead projector.
- Begin reading the text, and model the connections you make, using pictures and words on the overhead projector.
- Ask students to draw and describe the connections they are making with the text as they listen to the read-aloud.
- To conclude the lesson, do one of the following:
  - Choose responses as samples for assessment in the next lesson. Ask students to put an asterisk on their page if they are prepared to have their response used anonymously in the next day's lesson. Choose a range of responses.
  - Have students work in pairs to discuss the connections they made during the read-aloud.

Lesson 9—Rationale

Teaching to all students in a diverse classroom requires that teachers continue to guide their students in how to make the criteria work for them, and in how to use specific focused language when providing descriptive feedback to each other.

Criteria—Guided Practice

Learning intention: I can use the criteria we co-created to describe a response
- Remind students to be respectful when assessing their peers' responses.
- Organize students in pairs and give five sample responses.
- Once each pair agrees on the categorization of the samples, combine two pairs to form a group of four and have them compare their decisions. This activity allows students to discuss in depth, using

the descriptors, which responses meet the criteria minimally or fully, or that exceed the criteria. It is learning the descriptors, not the categorization, that most improves students' learning performance. Students must support their decision with evidence from the response. Figure 10.5 shows Nata and Sarah working together to match the responses with the category on their rubric.

- Share results as a class, and try to come to a group consensus, each group of students defending their choice with descriptive language from the criteria sheet and specific examples from the student samples. The goal of involving students so actively in the assessment process is to make sure that they understand the criteria, that they can use them, and that they will then take ownership of them.

- Most class members will willingly volunteer their samples to be placed on the overhead and shared with the group.

- Work through a few samples together, matching the written responses against the criteria, so that students can clearly see how their responses fit into the criteria. They will then be better able to articulate how their response successfully meets a criterion and where they should try to improve in other criteria.

Figure 10.5 Nata and Sarah match responses to a category on the rubric

Lesson 10—Rationale

Giving students their choice of books to read is more likely to keep them interested in reading. Knowing your students' interests as well as the range of reading abilities in the class really helps you when deciding the titles to include in a text set. Choose your text sets specifically with the class profile in mind, including their learning interests, and their needs. It is possible to present a range of texts with a range of different characters and settings and a range of difficulty. Students will read with much more enthusiasm and greater engagement when given a choice (see pages 195–196).

Literature Circles—Book choice, beginning to read

Learning Intentions: I can make a wise book choice. I can make connections as I read.

1. **Student choice after "selling" the books**
   - Introduce the literature circle novels today as a "book sell."
   - Read an interesting excerpt from each novel, give a brief description, and recommend the type of audience who might enjoy reading each novel.
   - Give the students three minutes to browse through each novel.
   - Have the students write their name and their top three book choices on a piece of paper.
   - Put these in a hat. Draw names randomly and distribute each student's first choice of novel.
   - In their book groups, students divide the novel into four sections for a four-week cycle; or, they meet briefly to decide on the minimum number of pages to read before the next class. Students can read ahead, but cannot reveal past the point determined during the discussions.
   - Homework is to read the set minimum number of pages, write down their thoughts, questions, and/or connections on a sticky note. Each student also chooses a powerful passage to share for next class.

2. **Student choice after the "book sell," with support for less able readers**
If your class has a wider range of diversity, arrange the book choices with more teacher direction.
   - Begin with the "book sell."
   - After you have read an excerpt from each novel and identified the target audience, invite students to peruse each novel before choosing their top three.
   - Organize the book groups based on their top three choices, not by random draw.
   - Keep a record of which students did not receive their top choice, and ensure that they do receive their first choice the next time.
   - In certain circumstances, you might provide books on tape as an option for students who need help or support in their learning. In other circumstances, pre-reading support should be arranged to allow all

students to successfully read the book that interests them and engage in meaningful conversations with their discussion group, regardless of their learning needs.

- Once they have their books, each book group must agree on an end point (a chapter or section) to read as homework for next class or meeting of their literature circle. Point out that the students are welcome to read beyond the end point, but that they are not expected to.
- Each member of each literature circle is to come to the discussion group with a powerful passage to share from the book.
- Students use sticky notes to record their thinking about the passage for the group discussion.
- Group members understand that they cannot share past the agreed-upon end point, once they are in their discussion groups.

Lesson 11—Rationale

In the small-group discussion, all students have an opportunity to speak and to be listened to. The discussion helps each student expand his or her thinking and understanding of the novel. There are different ways to organize the class for such a discussion. Whichever way you choose, it is critical to include all voices to allow each student the opportunity to learn how to talk to others and describe their thinking about a novel.

Literature Circle discussions

Learning Intention: I can have a meaningful discussion about a novel with my peers

1. Using the Say-Something strategy
   - Invite all groups to meet and discuss their chosen passages simultaneously.
   - While groups meet, choose two groups to facilitate and support, one after the other. At the next session, focus on another two.
   - Each member of the group is ready to share a powerful passage from the text.
   - Use the say-something strategy and have each member of the group make a comment about the powerful passage being shared at the time. This strategy encourages all students to speak. With continued modelling and practice, over time students will eventually be able to have more spontaneous discussions involving every group member.
   - After the discussions, have students write a response to their chosen passage, including not only their connections but also reflections on the comments made by others about their passage.

2. **Collaborating with the teacher-librarian or the resource teacher**
    - Invite one of the support teachers to work with you in class. This purposeful scheduling allows for all six of the book groups to meet for 15 minutes each in each 45-minute class block on the timetable. It also allows each teacher to participate as a member of each group, to model discussion strategies, to listen to the discussion groups, and to support students who need assistance.
    - Only two groups meet at one time with teacher support. The say-something strategy is used as groups meet.
    - Direct students to use the rubric that they created together to reflect on how well they are adhering to the criteria. As time goes on, their discussions in groups become more natural and fluid, and they require less modelling and support from teachers.

Figure 10.6 is a sample student's reflection on his participation in the literature circle discussion.

Figure 10.6

Oral Literature Circle Response   *april 17/06*

Criteria	Comments/Feedback *S. A.*
BE PREPARED ✓ Has novel (and backup plan) ✓ P.P. marked in book ✓ Assignment complete ✓ TDT (tease, don't tell) ✓ Make sure you read to decided chapter	I always am ready to share my P.P. even if I need to share with someone else. ☺☺
SHARING YOUR POWERFUL PASSAGE • Eye contact ✓ Speak loudly/clearly • Share something meaningful ✓ Explain thinking in detail ✓ Explain why you chose it... ✓ Explain any connections...	I share my P.P in a way that makes sense, but I need to work on eye contact and sharing something meaningful.
RESPONDING TO OTHERS ✓ Listen respectfully • Look at speaker ✓ Sit in a circle ✓ Share and discuss opinions ✓ Ask questions ✓ Okay to agree/disagree (but support your thinking with evidence from book)	I almost do every thing right here, but I need to look at the person speaking.

(Developed by the students of Div.4 – 2008)

- While teacher-facilitated discussion groups are meeting, have the other students write in their literature circle response books commenting on some aspect of the text. These journals take two different forms:
  1. A two-column journal entry (What Happened/My Thinking) responding to an event in their novel or to a powerful passage. On the left side of the page, they describe what happened in their own words or copy a powerful quote with page reference from their novel. On the right side of the page, they write down their thoughts about the event, including connections, questions, and predictions about the novel.
  2. Each student has a dialogue partner. Students write journal entries to their partner, sharing their thoughts and feelings about the book. They have the same dialogue partner each time, and they write back and forth answering each other's questions and responding to their connections and thoughts. These dialogue journals serve as another avenue in which students share their thinking.

Lesson 12—Rationale

Ultimately, it is the learner who most needs to know how to apply the criteria, give feedback, and begin to monitor his or her own learning. Knowing how to do this also sets the learners up to give feedback to their peers. Thus, students have many more opportunities to receive feedback and respond to it than they do when all the feedback comes from just the teacher.

Response: Self-assessment and peer-assessment

Learning intention: I can self-assess to see where I'm at and where I need to go.
- With more practice in using the criteria as a guide to writing more powerful responses, students can begin to use the criteria to assess their own response and then ask a peer to assess their response.
- Students might use colour-coding to indicate how the responses meets the criteria. Assign a colour to each criterion, which they can use to underline evidence in the responses that they believe meet the criteria.
- In addition, students might ask their peers to write a comment on sticky notes about one area in which they did well and one area that needs improvement, so that each student can readily see whether their piece of writing is powerful enough. Moreover, the written comments allow the teachers to see how well their students interpret the criteria.

Lesson 13—Rationale

To consolidate their learning, students enjoy a culminating activity. Both the Learning Journey and the Ideagram require inferential thinking and making connections among ideas. The Learning Journey has students revisit the plot using the metaphor of a journey. An Ideagram is a visual display that represents the theme of the novel. It is a creative collection of quotes, connections, personal responses, images, and significant events (Brownlie 2005). This activity helps students gain a deeper understanding of the novel as they pull information from the story to support their thinking.

Culminating activities: Student record-keeping and summative evaluation

Learning intention: I can be responsible for my own learning

- Have students become more responsible for their own learning by keeping track of the feedback given to them. Figure 10.7 is the graphic organizer that French Immersion students used to record the date, what they did well (*Je sais comment*—I know how to...) and what their next goal would be (*J'atteins mon but*—I am reaching my goal). In the English class, the students wrote in the Comments/Feedback section of their rubric about how they felt they were doing in relation to the criteria and what area/goal to focus on for the next response.
- Before students begin writing their next response, have them look over their feedback record to see what they need to focus on to improve their writing. This feedback record also gives you, the teacher, a quick reference for your students' progress.

Figure 10.7 Keeping track of feedback

Où suis-je? Où est-ce que je vais?

La Date	Je sais comment ...	J'atteins mon but

Learning Journey

- Students use traffic signs (i.e., stop, detour, uphill climb) to symbolize the key moments in the life of their main character, including both positive and negative events, and the learning he or she acquired on the journey through the novel (Brownlie 2005).
- Have students choose five key moments or events in the main character's life. For each one, they might select an appropriate icon or draw one that represents it.
- Then, have students write a brief summary of one event (one or two sentences), explain why it was important in the life of the main character, and make connections to the symbol.
- Encourage students to discuss the events with other members of their novel group. Figure 10.8 is the accompanying rubric. Figure 10.9 is Louis's learning journey.

Figure 10.8 Rubric created to guide students with the learning journey

Critères	Ne satisfait pas les attentes	Satisfait les attentes de façon minimale	Satisfait entièrement les attentes	Dépasse les attentes
La qualité des moments choisis	Pas lié du tout au développement du personnage principal	les moments sont simples, évidents	les moments choisis sont significatifs	les moments choisis sont significatifs et profonds
L'explication des moments	pas d'explication ou l'explication n'est pas du tout claire	les explications sont simples	les explications sont détaillées	les explications sont détaillées et profondes, soutenues par des exemples

Ideagram

- Give students time in their groups to identify a theme of their book.
- Once they have identified a theme, have students look back through their written responses for quotes, connections, and significant events that support and exemplify this theme.
- Have students collect their most powerful quotes, connections, and images and rewrite them to display on poster board for their presentation.
- Students might also include one or two sentences explaining how the quote or the event is related to the theme of the book.
- This activity usually helps students gain a deeper understanding of the novel, particularly when they are asked to pull information from the text to support their thoughts about the text. A sample Ideagram is highlighted in Figure 10.10.

Figure 10.9 Example of Louis's learning journey

Figure 10.10 A sample of an Ideagram, as students share with one another

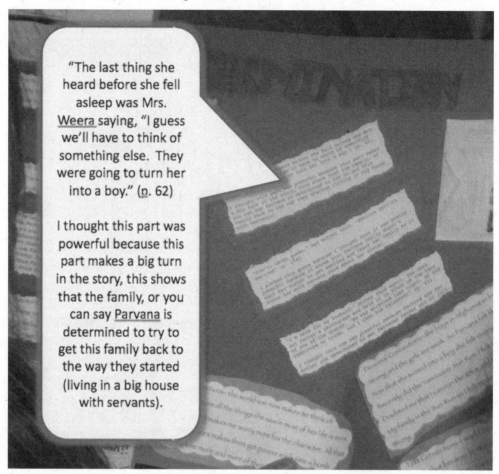

Assessment of Learning: Generating marks

Teachers give their students a grade based on the criteria they demonstrate. The criteria are organized into a rubric with a four-point scale. The letter grade assigned depends upon how the student's work relates to the criteria. If the work exceeds all or most criteria, the student receives an A. At the lower end, if the work fully met some criteria but only minimally met other criteria, the student received a C+. Students received marks only on work that had been modelled and on which, subsequently, they had been coached in guided practice situations.

Reflections

Stacey Wyatt: There were two key learnings for me. First, I made sure to create a text set that addressed the wide diversity within my classroom. There were novels that were easier to read, some at grade level (for lack of a better term) and others that were challenging both in content and reading level.

Students were supported in their book choice, not redirected toward an easier or more challenging text. Establishing this variety in text choice enabled all students to participate and experience success. Second, my involving students in developing the criteria for assessment allowed them to take ownership of what they were working on. It made their learning more meaningful and the goals more attainable because the students knew the expectations and were supported in working toward achieving them.

Lisa Chang: There were two key learnings for me. First, I found it critical to ensure that the content of the novels was relevant to my students while at the same time keeping the language level as appropriate as possible; otherwise, they had difficulty connecting to what they were reading. Their depth of reading comprehension was not going to improve if they did not enjoy what they were reading. Second, the learning process was more effective as a *partnership* between teacher and student. Students felt that, because they participated in developing the criteria, the process was fair and useful. One student said in a survey, "Je pense que les critères on a fait ensemble sont juste. C'est parce que nous (les enfants) ont créé ces critères. Donc, si le prof donne l'enfant un 1, l'enfant ne doit pas être fâché car le prof a marké la réponse par utilise les critères qu'il a crée."[1] The students took ownership of their learning, which made it more meaningful for them, and, therefore, they were making greater leaps in their learning.

Student text sets in English

The Breadwinner, Deborah Ellis

Among the Hidden, Margaret Peterson Haddix, Cliff Nielsen

The Report Card, Andrew Clements

Wringer, Jerry Spinelli

Esperanza Rising, Pam Munoz Ryan

Maniac Magee, Jerry Spinelli

Student text sets in French

Les Mille Oiseaux de Sadako, translated by Frédérique Fraisse

Tom et le gorille, translated by Florence Meyveres

Because of Winn-Dixie, Kate DiCamillo, translated by Brigitte Freger

Marion et le nouveau monde, Michèle Marineau

Louis Braille: l'enfant de la nuit, Margaret Davidson

---

1. Translation: "I think that the criteria we made together are fair. That's because we (the kids) created these criteria. So, if the teacher gives the child a 1, the child must not be mad because the teacher marked the response by using the criteria he created."

Le Miracle de Juliette, Pauline Gill

L'Odyssée miraculeuse d'Édouard, Kate DiCamillo, translated by Hélène Pilotto

Les Impatiences de Ping, Andrée Poulin

Le Message des biscuits chinois, Andrée-Anne Gratton

Chapter 11

Problem Solving in Geography

Grade 8—Humanities

Assessment FOR Learning	• World map and data interpretation pre-test • Quick-writes • Exit slips • Co-creating criteria for plausible interpretations • Co-creating criteria for PowerPoint • Co-creating criteria for oral presentations • Descriptive feedback • Peer assessment • Goal-setting
Gradual Release of Responsibility	• Think-alouds with statistical stories • Teacher modelling from concrete to abstract • Teacher modelling relationships and interactions with statistical indicators • Small-group practice with feedback • Independent application
Diverse Texts	• Atlases with country data sets, almanacs, reference books • Maps • Websites, PowerPoint, and keynote applications • Case studies from *Caring for Young People's Rights* • Images
Differentiation	• Open-ended activities • Paired students for reading and discussing • Scaling activites down or up by changing data sets or providing more images and maps as support
Assessment OF Learning	• PowerPoint slides • Statistical stories • Oral presentations
Essential Questions	• What story do these data or does this chart, graph, or map tell? Whose story? • What data are most revealing and representative of the quality of life? • How can I best represent these data to tell a meaningful story?

The Collaboration

Catriona Misfeldt believes that geography is more than factual knowledge and basic skills, more than memorizing capital cities, colouring maps and reading legends. She wants her grade 8 Humanities students to see the study of geography as an opportunity to problem solve, to address the impact of geographical facts on people's lives, to ask their own geography questions. Catriona believes that, because of her collaboration with other teachers and educational organizations, her thinking and teaching have grown. Catriona has worked with the Critical Thinking Consortium (TC^2)—a non-profit association of institutional partners, teaching professionals, and other educational organizations—for eight years. These experiences, coupled with her commitment to co-teaching and collaborative planning with teachers, have led to the co-development of many units that promote critical thinking and inquiry, build students' enduring understanding of key concepts, and meet the diverse needs of learners. For this unit, Catriona drafted her plans and then shared them with colleagues for feedback. The design of this unit also required students to collaborate with each other to apply the geographical ideas introduced through the analysis of statistics.

The Context

Two main issues prompted the creation of this unit. First, Catriona was dissatisfied with the way she was teaching geography—as a series of discrete, disconnected lessons that focused mainly on mapping skills rather than offering students the opportunity to assess, analyze, draw conclusions, and problem solve about geographical issues relevant to their lives. Geography was boring to teach and learn. Students were not actively engaged. There had to be a better way! Second, the students had difficulty in reading and understanding statistics and other text features such as tables, graphs, and pie charts in their Social Studies textbook.

With these goals in mind, she developed this unit in which students use statistics and graphic representations of data to explore and understand key geographic concepts and to further develop their skills in reading for information.

Essential Questions
- What stories do these data or this chart, graph, or map tell? Whose stories are they?
- What data are most revealing and representative of the quality of life?
- Which interpretation or conclusion is most plausible?
- How can I best represent these data so I can tell a meaningful story?

Geographic Thinking

- Determining geographical importance involves making judgments about the relative significance or value of a range of options and making decisions about what to report or leave out.
- Weighing evidence and offering interpretations requires students to consider how adequately the evidence justifies the interpretations offered and what interpretations of the evidence provided might be plausible.
- Exploring interactions involves considering how particular human and environmental factors and events influence and interact with each other across space and time.

Differentiation

- To plan the unit, begin with the end in mind and take into consideration the class's strengths, stretches, and interests in order to create open-ended activities that will provide entry points for all students.
- Pair students to read and discuss textual materials, data, ideas, or questions where possible. Require that they share the reading tasks.
- Most activities can be differentiated by scaling down or up their complexity or the quantity, by changing the data sets, or by providing such visuals as images and maps to support the interpretation of statistics.

Assessment of Learning

- Give a multimedia presentation in which students share the stories revealed by key statistical indicators of a selected country.

The Lessons

"Portals to Geographical Thinking" (Case and Clark 2008) is the reference text that Catriona used for this unit. It provides illustrative examples of three concepts, or "portals," to use as models to teach how to think like a geographer about data.

Thinking skills

- determining geographical importance
- using evidence to support interpretations
- examining interactions
- thinking critically about statistics
- drawing conclusions from analysis of the quality of life in developing and developed countries

Lesson 1—Rationale

Begin with an activity, an assessment for learning, that helps the teacher establish what the students know already about the content and what they need to learn. Then use this information to direct your instruction. Most of the research conducted in this unit comes from statistics and graphic representations of data so it is best to begin by assessing students' general knowledge of the world and their ability to interpret data in a chart or graph. A pre-test using both a world map and an activity requiring data interpretation provides a quick glimpse into students' knowledge of where the continents and major bodies of water are and their ability to read, understand, and interpret text features such as charts, maps, and graphs.

Assessing background knowledge

- Using a blank world map with Figure 11.1A, ask students to read and respond to the questions and instructions. They label from memory the continents, major bodies of water, lines of longitude and latitude, and the countries they will be studying over the course of the year.
- Choose a graphic representation from an atlas or textbook, such as the source described on Figure 11.1B. Ask students to describe the stories told by the selected graphic representation (e.g., What do you learn from the pie chart? What stories emerge from the trends across graphs?).
- Collect students' pre-tests and use the data to inform your instruction (e.g., What do students know? What do they not know? What are they confused about? What do I have to focus on? What will I teach first?).

Pre-Test Part 1: World Map

Read all instructions and questions with careful attention to details.

1. Write your name, class, and date in the top right-hand corner of the world map provided.

2. Draw a compass rose on the bottom right-hand corner of the world map.

3. Label the following lines of latitude and longitude.

a. Equator	b. Tropic of Cancer	c. Tropic of Capricorn
d. Prime Meridian	e. Arctic Circle	

4. Label the following continents:

a. North America	b. South America	c. Asia
d. Africa	e. Europe	f. Australia
g. Antarctica		

5. Label the following countries:

a. Canada	b. United States of America	c. Mexico
d. China	e. Japan	f. United Kingdom
g. India	h. Brazil	i. Russia

Bonus: What kind of map is this? Circle your answer.

Political   Physical   Relief

Figure 11.1B

Pre-Test Part 2: Interpreting Data

Use pages 26-27 in the *Pearson School Atlas* (Morrow 2004) to answer the questions.

1. What information is shown in the following two maps?
   a. Fish Habitats: West Coast
   b. Fish Habitats: East Coast

2. What stories do the maps tell?
   a.
   b.

3. What is shown in the following graphs?
   a. Volume
   b. Value of Catch

4. What trends do you notice across the graphs?

5. What story do these trends tell?

6. Name three things you learned from reading the graphs on Employment?

7. What stories do the Employment graphs tell?

8. What do the following pie charts show?
   a. Volume
   b. Value

9. Name two things you learned from reading the pie charts.

10. Read the overview of "Fishing in Canada." What is affecting the fish population in Canada?

Bonus: Name two types of graphs shown on pages 26-27.

Lesson 2—Rationale

Students co-create criteria for measuring "quality of life." As active participants in this process, they are more likely to internalize and apply the criteria. *Quality of life* is a key concept to be developed throughout the unit.

Connecting—Generating criteria or indicators for *quality of life*

This lesson is adapted from *Caring for Young People's Rights* (Case 2004). Invite students to reflect on whether or not they have a good life and what their reasons are for holding this opinion. Encourage them to go beyond superficial indicators (e.g., lots of money, nice clothes) and to consider factors such as nice place to live, nutritious food to eat, sense of purpose in life.

- Record the factors titled "Indicators for Quality of Life" on a chart and post it for reference.

Processing

- Have the students read the profiles of two young people who live in very different situations. One lives in a developed country, the other in a developing country. These profiles help illustrate the differences between the quality of life experienced in developing countries and that experienced in a developed country.
- Ask students to consider whether Canada is a developed or developing nation and whether developed or developing countries provide various factors that lead to a good life for the people who live there.
- Distribute a copy of "Emma," one of the case studies, to all the students (Figure 11.2). Using "Emma" as an anchor text, read the first paragraph aloud and model how to underline phrases in the text that might affect the quality of that person's life (e.g., the first two sentences in Emma's profile suggest that her father is angry and that there is tension or conflict). Direct the students to do the same.
- Introduce the second case study, "José," to the class (Figure 11.3).
- Offer students a choice between the familiar text "Emma" and the more challenging "José" text.
- When students have finished reading and underlining their assigned case study, pair them with a student who has read the other case study.
- Encourage partners to share their marked texts and discuss the quality of life for each youth.
- Direct students to record evidence related to factors that both positively and negatively impact the quality of life for each person on a comparison chart (Figure 11.4).

Figure 11.2

> ## Emma
>
> "I hate you. You're such an idiot!" The back door slammed loudly. Emma opened her eyes quickly and pulled up her soft comforter. Her heart was beating fast, and she had a knot in her stomach. It was her older sister who had yelled and slammed the door.
>
> "Lazy head, out of bed!" her father shouted from the bottom of the stairs. Heavy footsteps moved quickly through the house and then the front door opened and slammed shut. The car started and with a screech pulled away. Dad must be late for work. He often seemed angry now. Emma remembered happier times when he helped her with her homework and they would go to basketball games together. She wondered if it would ever be like that again.[1]

Figure 11.3

> ## José
>
> Turning over on the woven sleeping mat, José bumped into his younger brother. He could see the early morning light through the cracks in the stick wall of his family's home. The sticks broke easily but were a type of wood that the termites wouldn't eat.
>
> José could hear his mother feeding the chickens in the yard outside. Gently raising the thin bed sheet that kept the bugs off at night, Jose sat up and climbed over Salvador and his tiny sister Rosita. Careful not to wake them, he replaced the sheet and stepped on to the dirt floor.

Figure 11.4

Comparing Quality of Life

	Positive factors	**Negative factors**
Emma's life		
Jose's life		

---

1. Excerpt from *Caring for Young People's Rights*, a *TC²* publication (order online at <http://www.tc2.ca/wp/>). Used with permission of Roland Case, the author.

Lesson 3—Rationale

The exit slip helps students consolidate the key concepts of the class. It is an assessment for learning strategy used to provide the teacher with a quick view of what the students have understood and what topics require more instruction or refinement. The information from an exit slip sets up your instruction for the next class. This is the heart of responsive teaching.

Transforming

Critical question, refining criteria, Exit Slip: Comparing quality of life
- Pose the critical question Which person has the better quality of life?
- Direct students to indicate their decisions and provide relevant, supporting evidence in a short, written response.
- Invite students to share their decisions with supporting evidence.
- Discuss how being rich and having a good quality of life might be connected or how they might not be connected.
- Revise or add to the class list of "Indicators for Quality of Life" and add a star beside the factors that are the most important. Have students as a class try to agree on the eight to ten criteria that are most important for a good life.
- Have students complete an exit slip. Ask them to write down their definition of a good life, recalling as many indicators of a good life as possible. This will help you assess what stuck, what didn't, and what needs reviewing as illustrated in the following examples:

She would make her own dinner and watch TV a lot, has a cell phone, mom moved away, her sister yells at her, has a big screen TV and DVD *player.* —Samantha

Samantha recalled some of the details of Emma's life but did not list specific quality of life indicators nor show that she understood the concept. Further probing of the next class revealed that Samantha did not understand what a quality of life indicator was. She needed to be re-taught this concept and helped to see which category of indicators connected to the factors she listed.

A good life means barely any fighting, no sadness, no poverty. Quality of life indicators: family, education, some wealth, basic needs, shelter, clothing. —Connor

Connor's definition shows that he has a partial grasp of the concept, but his examples show a more complete understanding.

Lesson 4—Rationale

An Anticipation Guide helps focus students' reading before they read, and it supports all students, directing their thinking to information that they will encounter while reading. During their reading, students are more likely to pick out the textual information that connects to the statements on the Anticipation Guide. In the After Reading column, the students can compare what they learned and remember with what they thought before they read the text. Quick-Writes help assess students' insights, connections, and conclusions about the big ideas.

Connecting

Anticipation Guide, Quick-Write, Key concepts of the global village
- Prior to reading *If the World Were a Village* (Smith 2002), invite students to complete the left-hand column, Before Reading, of the Anticipation Guide (Figure 11.5A), agreeing or disagreeing with the statements that are based on the book they will be reading.
- Have students also make general predictions (Figure 11.5B) about two or three of the statistical indicators (e.g., literacy, electricity use) for continents discussed in the text (e.g., Asia, Africa, Europe).
- Prior to reading the book, take a quick tally of the number who agree and who disagree for each of the statements. Encourage students to defend their thinking.
- Read the book aloud, stopping to discuss the "stories" told on each page.
- Direct students to re-assess, as they are listening, the accuracy of the statements on the Anticipation Guide and mark their agreement or disagreement in the right-hand column.
- After the students have finished the book, have them read the Anticipation Guide statements aloud and discuss the ones for which they changed from agree or disagree, based on what they learned from the evidence presented in the text.
- As a class, discuss the concept of *global village*.
- End with a quick-write, asking students to reflect on the big ideas of the book (e.g., What are the big ideas about the concept of a *global village*? What is important about this concept? How does the concept of a *global village* connect to the quality of life indicators? What are the connections to the UN Millennium Goals?).[2]

---

2. *If the World Were a Village* has been made into an animated movie. An excerpt of this is available on YouTube, along with related movies, such as *The Miniature Earth*. You may wish to view these movies before reading the text to introduce the concept of *global village*.

Figure 11.5A

Name: _____

Class: _____

Date: _____

Anticipation Guide

What do you know about the world and its peoples?

1. Before reading the book, write an A (for Agree) or D (for Disagree) in the left-hand column beside each statement.

Before Reading A or D		After Reading A or D
	The world's population is about 6.2 billion people.	
	Over half of the world's people live in Canada and the United States.	
	Spanish is the most widely spoken language in the world.	
	25% of the world's people do not have easy access to clean drinking water.	
	More than half of the world's people are under the age of 30.	
	There is not enough food to feed everyone in the world.	
	Over half of the world's people are Christians.	
	Everyone in the world over the age of 7 knows how to read.	
	About 76% of the world's people have electricity.	
	Knowing what is happening in the world is important to be a good citizen.	

2. After reading the book, write an A (for Agree) or a D (for Disagree) in the right-hand column beside each statement.

Figure 11.5B

Name: _____

Class: _____

Date: _____

Predictions

Using your prior knowledge, make your best guesses as answers to the following topics about the "global village."

What do you know about the world's nationalities?

What do you know about schooling/literacy throughout the world?

What do you know about electricity consumption around the world?

Figure 11.6 shows several quick-writes. It is easy to see who fully understands the concept and who has incomplete understanding.

Figure 11.6 Examples of quick-writes

I understand global village to be an understanding of what is happening in the world and to accept that everyone is different. Also understanding that some places don't have enough of something like food and water and live in poverty. —*Alan*

My definition of a global village is that it's a metaphor showing the ways of the world. It is a way people can define and see races and cultures as if we were all in one village. — *Terri*

Global village is a way for you to see big stuff in a smaller way. Instead of looking at it like 1 million people you could look at it like 1 person. It's making the scale lower:

$$\frac{1,000}{10,000} = \frac{100}{1,000}$$

—*Charles*

Global village is about the idea of everyone who lives around the world should be like people in a village—have fast contacts and be friendly to one another no matter what nationalities or races. It's about everyone who lives in the world is the same and should be treated equally. — *Sandy*

Lesson 5—Rationale

Modelling by using think-alouds shows your students how to read specialized text. This text requires readers to make sense of statistics embedded in the text and data charts. The think-aloud shows how to use text features to better understand the statistical stories revealed by the data. The teacher models how to weigh the evidence and offer justified interpretations based on the evidence (e.g., statistical indicators) and consider what interpretations of the evidence provided might be plausible. The teacher also models how to see relationships and interactions among statistical indicators. After modelling, ask your students to do the same, first with their partners, then as individuals.

Most activities can be differentiated by being scaled down or up in complexity or number, or by changing the data sets. For example, a student with a significant cognitive impairment might analyze the stories behind data in their immediate world, such as the number of girls and boys in the class, and learn to represent these numbers in a bar graph; the intent and understandings remain, but the content changes. Alternatively, provide visuals such as images and maps to support the statistics.

Processing

Think-Aloud with information text, modelling and guided practice, representing stories with graphics

- Project the introduction of *If the World Were a Village* on an overhead to the class.
- Conduct a Think-Aloud, modelling how to mark the text and read the statistics to better understand the information.
- Introduce the geographical concepts of *evidence* and *interpretation*. Ask students to consider what plausible (most likely) interpretations might be made from the evidence.
- Discuss how the images support and/or extend the story told by the statistics.
- Invite partners to select one of the themes from the book (e.g., religion, schooling, electricity). Distribute copies of the selected texts and direct partners to mark their texts and interpret the stories told by the text, the data, and the images.
- Return to the introduction. Again, using a think-aloud, model to the class two or three ways of representing in graphic formats the stories told in the statistics (e.g., image, bar graph, pie chart, line graph).
- Discuss the advantages and disadvantages of each type of visual representation, then discuss which one would best represent the story told by the data.
- Invite partners to collaborate and create three different visual ways to show their information, then star the best one.
- Ask two pairs to share their stories and best visual representation of the data with each other.
- For homework, ask students to work individually through the above process using a new theme.

Lesson 6—Rationale

A framework such as What? So What? Now What? helps students move from a literal understanding to an inferential understanding and then to action. Rather than just recite data, they can now analyze data.

Processing

What? So What? Now What? and Quality of Life PPT Slide

- If students do not know how to make slides in a PowerPoint or Keynote presentation, teach them how to do so before starting this lesson. To complete the task, students have to be able to create a new slide, type in a title, add text to pre-set templates, select charts or graphs, enter data correctly, and insert text boxes and pictures. Use the Gradual Release of Responsibility process to model this, or print a step-by-step guide and pair experts with novices. The amount of support you have to provide depends on the needs of your students. If they are learning a new skill, keep the actual product simple.

- Introduce the framework What? So What? Now What? to the class (see Figure 11.7).
- Using the statistical stories and visual representations you generated from the introduction in Lesson 4, model how to apply the framework to the data. For example:
  - *What?* Write an important fact (or facts) about the story.
  - *So What?* Tell the story of your fact (or facts). Explain why it is important (e.g., why we should care or pay attention to it).
  - *Now What?* Explain how your fact (or facts) connects to quality of life. Describe what we need to think about, say, or do as a result of the fact(s) to make a difference.

Figure 11.7 Framework for selecting statistics: What? So What? Now What?

Name _____ Blk. _____

Which statistics tell the *real story* of the quality of life for people living in your selected country?

Country: _____

Important statistic or fact (What)	What story does it tell? (So What?)	How does this connect to quality of life? (Now What?)

Lesson 7—Rationale

Give students an opportunity to practise creating a slide with others and alone. While they are working together and deciding which slides are the most effective, they gain a better understanding of the criteria. Their self-assessment allows them to personalize the learning and to set learning goals for their next PowerPoint slide before being judged on it. They learn how to create a slide while using their curriculum content. As a result of their sharing and analysis of slides, they also begin to consider how particular human and environmental factors and events influence and interact with each other across space and time (e.g., How might the number of doctors per person relate to the infant mortality rate?).

Transforming

Creating PowerPoint or Keynote slides, generating criteria
- Students work in partners to create a slide for either the statistical stories and visual representations that they generated for the first theme or the one completed for homework.
- Direct students to include the following in their slides:
  - a title
  - a key visual (graph or chart) showing the statistics
  - an image that reflects the topic
  - a What? So What? Now What? reflection
- Ask pairs to print, then tape, their completed slides to the chalkboard or a blank wall.
- As a class, sort the more effective slides from the less effective slides.
- Use the two sets to generate the criteria for an effective presentation slide (e.g., insightful, visually appealing, revealing). Work with the class to state what each criterion means.
- Invite students to individually evaluate their own slides against the class set of criteria and make notes on what they need to tweak in their next one. Figure 11.8 is a simple checklist for students to use in their self-assessment.

Figure 11.8 Self-assessment on PPT Slide

Criteria	Assessment			What needs tweaking?
Insightful means...	√ (fully met)	~ (partially met)	X (did not meet)	Next time,
Visually appealing means...	√ (fully met)	~ (partially met)	X (did not meet)	Next time,
Revealing means...	√ (fully met)	~ (partially met)	X (did not meet)	Next time,

Lesson 8—Rationale

Much content learning requires specific and technical vocabulary. Highlighting and introducing this vocabulary prior to reading enhances your students' ability to read and reason with the information in the text. Preview the data sets in the atlas that students will be using to determine 15 to 18 words to select. If students can think about what they know about the words before they read, it is easier for them to refine or adapt this initial understanding with new information from the text.

Connecting

Chart for Before Reading/After Reading, Word Wall, Exit Slip

- Before students begin to analyze statistical indicators for developing countries, select key terms such as *population density, gross domestic product, birth rate, literacy, human development index,* and *primary industry.*
- Create a Before Reading/After Reading comparison chart that lists each of the terms (see Figure 11.9).
- Invite partners to discuss each term. Then have them record their meanings on the chart.
- Randomly select students to share their thinking and discuss how they arrived at their predictions in a class discussion.
- Assign each pair one of the terms and direct them to research it, using the atlas as a resource.
- Partners create a flash card that includes the word (printed clearly and in large letters) and its definition. Allow students choice in how they represent their definitions (e.g., writing, illustrating, computer graphics).
- After partners have shared their completed flashcards with the class, create a Word Wall with them. This will serve as a useful class resource for the remainder of the unit.
- As a quick assessment of their understanding of these terms, ask students to write the following on a triple-2 exit slip:
  - the definition for two words they really understand and could explain to someone else
  - two words that they really do not understand
  - two words that confuse them
- For homework, assign students to independently complete the After Reading column. Make atlases available for reference.

Figure 11.9 Understanding world statistics

Name: _____

Date: _____

Understanding World Statistics

Terms	Before Reading	After Reading
Gross Domestic Product (GDP)		
Literacy		
Developed country		
Developing country		
(HDI) Human Development Index		
Infant mortality rate		
Labour force		
Population density		
Primary industry		
Urban		
Rural		
Foreign debt		
Fertility rate		
Birth rate		
Commercial energy use		

Lesson 9—Rationale

Students have enough background statistical knowledge to begin to use what they know to compare Canada with a developing country that they select. The comparison with Canada provides a frame of reference and a familiar context for students to better understand the statistics and make plausible interpretations. Using a think-aloud again shows students how to slow their reading down, making it purposeful and thoughtful with their goal in mind—the specific information for which they are reading.

Connecting

Modelling, Think-Aloud, data chart, geographical evidence and interpretation

In this lesson, students will analyze and interpret key statistical indicators for Canada and a selected developing country.

- Create a Facts at a Glance data chart that indicates key facts for a variety of developing countries and Canada using the data sets in the atlas as reference (be sure to check the currency of information). [3]
- Project the Facts at a Glance chart for the class to view.
- Present students with a copy of the Facts at a Glance handout and direct their attention to the Canadian statistical indicators.
- Remind students that, by reading and understanding statistical indicators, they can learn more about a country, the nature of its problems, and the quality of life of its citizens.
- Reveal the facts one at a time and conduct a think-aloud discussing the stories revealed by the facts—what they mean and why the information is important (e.g., what significance it might have in the students' daily lives, what it reveals about Canada's quality of life, the relationship between the facts).
- Draw students' attention to the units of measurement used to describe each indicator. Explain how these units help us make sense of the information and determine what is significant or insignificant in the bigger picture.
- Use a wall map of the world, an atlas, and/or images of the selected countries such as those found in *Material World* to help students visualize the statistics and consider the context.[4]
- After working through three or four examples, invite students to analyze the remaining facts in a whole-class discussion.
- Encourage them to expand on their thoughts, provide specific answers, and justify their analyses with evidence (e.g., "I think that … has poor medical care because…").
- When the group analysis is complete, summarize orally the conclusions that might be drawn from the facts about the quality of life in Canada.

---

3. *Caring for Young People's Rights* has such a chart. Also, the Canadian International Development Agency website allows you to download Facts at a Glance, comparing Canada with a selected developing country.

4. World Mapper re-sizes regions of the world according to the topic of interest.

- Present the statistical indicators for the selected developing country.
- Repeat the above process.
- The numbers provide an access point for most students, especially those for whom English is not their first language. Providing the context and the comparison to Canada is key to ensuring that the students can make meaning from the numbers.

Lesson 10 — Rationale

Formative assessment improves student learning. It is important to discuss with the class that they are learning to become better analyzers of statistics and draw more plausible conclusions from the data. Although the process may seem to take a long time (one to two minutes per student), the individual feedback "in public" is a powerful learning experience in formative assessment. Students learn from each other's stories and get better at describing their own conclusions. A teacher's later descriptive feedback to students provides additional insights that students can use in future activities.

Processing

Data chart, graphic organizer, formative feedback

- For independent application, direct students to write "statistical stories" of three to five facts for another developing country of their choice. Students who require support may benefit from creating new stories, using either of the two countries worked through as a class or a developing country similar in profile to the modelled example.
- Ask students to share their stories with each other. Then invite them to share their stories aloud with the class.
- After each presentation, identify and explicitly point out what aspect(s) of the story were clearly identified and how they might revise those aspects of the analysis that were less clear (e.g., confusions, misinterpretations, errors).
- Students now apply their analysis skills independently by comparing Canada with their profiled country (they may choose to stick with the same country they researched in lesson 8 or select a new one).
- Create and photocopy for each student, a comparison organizer (e.g., Figure 11.10A is an open organizer, Figure 11.10B provides more support) that lists key statistical indicators and leaves room for students to record relevant information for both Canada and their selected country.
- Students collect the data, analyze the information, and write the statistical stories revealed by the facts of their developing country.
- Collect and assess the stories with the students, highlighting plausible analyses and underlining aspects of their stories that are problematic (e.g., inaccurate or show misunderstanding).

Figure 11.10A Example of an open comparison organizer

Name: _____

Class: _____

Comparing us and them

	Canada	Profiled Country
Population		
Land area		
Population growth rate		
Education (literacy rate; students per teacher)		
Life expectancy		
Infant mortality rate		
Access to clean water		
Health care (e.g., doctors per person; hospital beds per person)		
Climate (e.g., temperature, average rain fall)		
Major landforms and bodies of water		
Land use		
Environmental issues		
Official languages		
Conflicts		
Economic status (e.g., GDP, poverty rate, gross domestic income, employment)		
Communications (e.g., Internet users, telephones, TVs, cars)		
Energy consumption		

Figure 11.10B Example of a structured comparison organizer

Name: _____

Class: _____

Comparing us and them

	Canada	Profiled Country
Population	33,390,000	
Land area	9,093,507 sq km	
Population growth rate	0.87 %	
Education (literacy rate; students per teacher)	Literacy rate: Students/teacher:	
Life expectancy	80 years	
Infant mortality rate	5/1,000	
Access to clean water		
Health care (e.g., doctors per person; hospital beds per person)	Doctors/person: Hospital beds/person:	
Climate (e.g., temperature, average rain fall)		
Major landforms and bodies of water	Pacific Ocean, Atlantic Ocean, mountains, prairies	
Land use	Farm land: 5% Crops: 0.65% Other: 95%	
Environmental issues	Air & water pollution; over-fishing; deforestation	
Official languages		
Conflicts		
Economic status (e.g., GDP, poverty rate, gross domestic income, employment)	Population in poverty: 16% Gross domestic income: $35,700 US GDP: 1.2 trillion dollars	
Communications (e.g., Internet users, telephones, TVs, cars)	People/car: 2 People/radio: 1 People/telephone: 2 People/TV: 2	
Energy consumption		

- Ask students to rewrite or retell the sections of their stories that are problematic.

Lesson 11—Rationale

The formative assessment process supports you as a responsive teacher. Before students complete a summative assessment, use the information gained from your formative assessments to provide additional instruction.

Processing

Geographic interactions, kinesthetic activity, reflection questions

- Read through students' statistical stories and notice if the students require additional instruction. Catriona found that most students did not have adequate background information about many of the underlying issues related to the statistical indicators, nor did they automatically see how the issues were interconnected.
- With an adjusted target in mind, find two activities that address the issue. Catriona found on the website of the Facing the Future Organization two articles useful for building an understanding of geographic interactions:
  1. viewing the Global Issues interactive website
  2. completing the Making Global Connections lesson plan[5]
- Invite students to consider the criteria for what makes a global issue (i.e., significant, trans-national, persistent, interconnected).
- Assign students an issue (e.g., poverty, consumption, population growth, environment, technology, culture, media, energy use).
- Have students stand in a circle and take turns passing a ball of yarn to a classmate across the circle. As they do so, ask them to state how their issues are connected (e.g., Health care is connected to poverty because most people in the world who live in poverty do not have access to basic healthcare).
- Once the web is completed, students reflect on what happens when a piece of the yarn is tugged on (e.g., feel the tension) and how that tug might signify or represent connections between global issues.
- Reflection questions in the lesson plan provide a valid formative assessment of student understanding of why and how global issues interact with one another.

---

5. The first offers an overview of global issues (e.g., rich/poor gap; economy; food and water security; health; population) in two versions *60 Second Tours*, which shows key images and facts, and *Issues in Depth*, which shows the same key images but provides more detailed information. This is useful for differentiation and/or is a helpful teacher resource.

Lessons 12 and 13—Rationale

Students have had a number of opportunities to learn and practise how to represent the selected data visually in multiple formats (e.g., bar graph, pie chart, diagram) and using print and non-print sources. They are now ready to apply it to their final project.

Processing

Individual research, choosing an image

- Book two library periods for students to research current, key statistical indicators for a country of their choice.
- On the first day, encourage students to explore print resources (e.g., almanacs, atlases, reference books).
- On the second day, have students access recommended websites.
- At this stage in the unit, students create their own note-making organizer. For support, give the choice of a blank comparison chart template or a partially filled comparison chart (see Figures 11.10A and 11.10B, pages 217 and 218). Encourage students to use an appropriate option for them. Because statistics are easy to record, students with difficulties in written output complete the task with relative ease. The challenge for some students is to ensure that their information is current.
- The final task/product requires students to find a representative and revealing image that best shows the quality of life in their selected country.
- Discuss each criterion (e.g., What does *representative and revealing* mean?)
- Invite students to select (from a handful of images about their own city, province, or country) which image fully meets the criteria. Ask students to defend their choice. This helps them thoughtfully select their own images.

Lesson 14—Rationale

Determining geographical importance involves making judgments about the relative significance or value of a range of options as well as making decisions about what to report or leave out (e.g., Which seven statistics best represent the quality of life in the selected country?). Students now have sufficient background and skill to be able to complete this activity independently.

Transforming

Geographical importance, What?/So What? template

- Review the Facts at a Glance for Canada used in Lesson 9 on geographical importance. Geographers often make judgments about the relative importance of data—what to report, what to leave out, what to study.

- Invite students to select the seven statistics that are most representative of quality of life in Canada.
- Return to conduct a think-aloud and model how to determine the importance of a given statistic.
- Encourage students to read over their statistics and select the seven that best tell the real story of the quality of life for people living in their selected countries.
- Have students record their top seven statistics, describe what story they tell, and develop a So What? for each statistic (e.g., Why is this important? How does it connect to quality of life? What other indicators are there?).
- Notice that the process is not new to the students, but choosing their top seven statistics for the template is (see Figure 11.9, page 214). Some students may need to have an example modelled and displayed as they work through their own analyses.

Lesson 15—Rationale

Students are now ready to integrate their learning into a final project. The concepts of geographic thinking have been introduced to the whole class using simple, concrete, or familiar scenarios. Moving into small groups, then independent application of these concepts, has involved them in more abstract, decontextualized scenarios. They are ready to address several essential questions in their project:

- What data are most revealing and representative of the quality of life?
- Which interpretation or conclusion is most plausible?
- How can I best represent this data so it tells a meaningful story?

Transforming

The culminating PPT and oral presentation

- Set the stage for the culminating project:

  "You have been selected by the United Nations to create a short multimedia presentation about the quality of life in a developing country. Your presentation must include an oral component. Information presented must be clear, revealing, and show insight into relevant issues."
- Armed with their analyses, students complete an individual PowerPoint slide presentation that summarizes the statistical stories about the quality of life in their selected countries.
- As in lesson 5, completed slides must include the stories, a representative and revealing image, a key graphic, and a thoughtful So What? Students who would benefit from an extension can include a Now What? For some students, reporting the stories for three statistics is adequate.

- If students do not have access to appropriate technology to practise their oral accompaniment to their presentation, have them print off black and white copies in class.

Lesson 16—Rationale

The goal is to give students practice giving and receiving feedback, to have them reflect on their own strengths and weaknesses in making presentations, and to encourage them to continually refine their oral presentation skills.

Generating criteria, peer assessment, goal-setting—Preparing for final presentation

- Invite students to consider what a powerful presentation looks like and sounds like. Have the class generate the criteria for a powerful presentation in terms of both the content (What is on the slide) and the delivery (how it is presented).
- Once the criteria are established, pair students. Direct partners to take turns practising their presentations, then evaluating each others' presentations using the agreed-upon criteria and orally noting a star (something their partners did well) and a pointer (something they need to work on). Figure 11.11 provides an example of giving feedback.
- Invite students to set individual goals for their next presentation.
- Have students switch partners and repeat the process two or three more times.

Figure 11.11 Example of form for giving constructive feedback on oral presentations

Oral presentations: Giving constructive feedback

1. Listen to your classmates' presentations. For each speaker, identify:

☆
a star

something they did well: Say: "I like the way you…" OR "You did a good job of…"

➔
a pointer

something they can improve: Say: "Try…" OR "The next step might be…"

Voice	Eye Contact	Posture	Delivery
• Speak in a clear, loud voice. • Speak with expression.	• Look at your audience. • DO NOT just read your notes.	• Stand straight. • Do not lean on the board/wall.	• Engage your audience through use of gestures, facial expressions, or other props/visuals.

2. Share your feedback in a respectful way.
   - Incorporate your classmates' feedback, then practise, practise, practise!
   - Remember, in addition to being assessed on these criteria, you will also be assessed on how polished your presentation is.

Figure 11.12 Example of the rubric for a keynote presentation, completed by a student and assessed by the teacher

Name _Veronika a._ Blk. _E/D_

If the World Were a Village Keynote Slide

	Good start	Fully Meeting Expectations	Exceeding Expectations
Revealing	• slide tells a brief or incomplete story about the topic; • images & graphics do not support or enhance the text in a meaningful way	• some aspects of the story are clearly told in the slide; key information is missing or misinterpreted • images & graphics relate to the topic but may not fully support or enhance the story	• slide clearly tells an accurate & full story about the topic • images & graphics are carefully selected to meaningfully support and enhance the story
Insightful	• no/few plausible inferences are drawn about the story behind the statistics • vague or superficial connections are made to quality of life • surface understanding of the big ideas	• some plausible inferences are drawn about the story behind the statistics; may have some misconceptions • 1–2 connections are made to the quality of life but these may not be clearly explained, meaningful or supported • 1 or 2 big ideas are touch upon	• all inferences are plausible • 3 or more meaningful, sophisticated, supported connections are made to the quality of life; students identifies the interconnectedness between stated connections • deep understanding of the big ideas
Visually appealing	• visually cluttered; hard to read/understand • graphics, titles & headings do not effectively support the story • colour, background, fonts do not clearly support the message; they detract from the message and distract the reader	• most information is clearly laid out and easy to read/understand; some confusion exists • graphics, titles &/or headings may be missing or misleading • colour, background, fonts support the message but may, in places, detract from the message or distract the reader	• well laid out and easy to read/understand • graphics, titles, headings are used effectively • colour, background, fonts compliment & enhance the message

Handwritten annotations:
11.5 / 15 B

Veronika,
your graph is clear & easy to read.
You touch on the issue of inequal distribution.
What other story can you tell about how the food is shared?

Comments: I really liked how I did my connections in "NOW WHAT".

Lesson 17

Tranforming—Final presentations, summative assessment, self-assessment

- Evaluate student presentations using the Statistical Stories Assessment. Figure 11.12 is an example of a rubric for evaluating a Keynote presentation, as scored by a teacher.
- Invite students to reflect on their own presentations.

Catriona's Reflections

Designing the unit around essential concepts in geography and the skills involved in reading for information challenged me to create lesson sequences that would help students develop a good understanding of the knowledge and skills required to evaluate, analyze, and interpret the statistics involved. The focus on data and graphic representations as opposed to text made the unit accessible for all students. Intentionally designing activities and assessments around students' interests, needs, and strengths resulted in high motivation and engagement. Gradually releasing responsibility to students when introducing new concepts or processes forced me to slow down to the pace of student learning and not make assumptions about what the students knew how to do or not do. Students enjoyed the collaborative nature of tasks and representing their understandings in a variety of ways. Ongoing formative assessments such as exit slips and quick-writes provided me with instant feedback on students' understandings and/or misunderstandings, with little effort and time expended in marking. I also found that specific, on-the-spot feedback on statistical stories resulted in stronger final products. I was excited about the increased risks that my students were taking with their thinking. They grappled with data sets to analyze and interpret statistics and looked for connections among the issues. Geography was, at last, fun to learn and teach!

Chapter 12

Online Literature Circles: Students and Teachers Learning Together

Grades 4–12—English

Literature Circles
- Choice of diverse texts
- Read at own pace
- Online discussion
- Discussion forum
- Criteria for good discussion posts

Use of Student Exemplars
- View and discuss before posting
- Use one another's posts

Modelling and Guided Practice
- Response to literature circle questions
- Generating questions for posts
- 1:1 in student-teacher conferencing

Connecting/ Processing/ Transforming
- Literature circle questions

One-to-One Strategic Tutoring
- Written responses (posts)
- Conferences about reading

Assessment FOR Learning
- Learning intentions
- Clear criteria
- Descriptive feedback
- Self-assessment
- Peer-assessment
- Ownership

Diversity
- Diverse texts
- Models and exemplars
- Flexible time
- Re-posting and interaction

The Collaboration

Terry Taylor teaches at Lucerne Elementary Secondary School, a rural school in New Denver, British Columbia. Terry teaches English Language Arts to multi-age classes. She is passionate about using online interactive learning to promote student engagement in reading and writing. Beginning with her first partner, Shelley Little, another grade 12 teacher 400 km away in Invermere, then partnering with Kari Kroker 100 km away in Nelson, she explored how to best use online literature circles. Using Moodle, an asynchronous course management software, students in both schools read from the same books in their literature circles, responded online to their reading in discussion forums, taking advantage of their access to different perspectives and communities. A research project of the Network of Performance-Based Schools showed improved results in reading and writing for all learners involved in the online literature circles in both schools. Subsequent partnerships have been as wide-ranging as multi-grade (4-5-6) classes to all middle and secondary grades of English classes in urban and in rural communities. Terry, Shelly, and Kari are committed to using the principles of diversity and student learning discussed by Allington (2001) and Brownlie (2005)—that is, they offer students their choice of novels and questions, use diverse texts to foster inclusion, and also increase student access to texts and the volume of texts they read. They have also provided an additional piece to the puzzle—how to connect teachers and kids online so as to enhance collaborative opportunities and diminish the impact of physical boundaries.

The Context

The teacher's goals in an online literature circle are simple: use technology, choose texts thoughtfully, encourage reading, and engage all students in high-quality literary conversations. Since the literature circles are online, the circle for conversation is extended beyond the classroom. Students can be linked with others reading the same book in very different contexts, whether small or large schools, urban or rural, north or south; so the possibilities are endless. The "conversation" in the online discussion forum is written as students respond to weekly prompts. This gives students the opportunity to draft their response before posting it, to read others' responses to their posts, to read others' posts and respond again, all of which helps enrich their understanding of the text and deepen their thinking. Teachers engage in reflective collaborative practice as they teach their own students face to face in the classroom as well as team teach online. Terry has noticed intense engagement from the students, increased number of texts read by students, and improved writing skills. Her students are reading more than ever and are enthusiastic about joining both the "virtual coffeehouse" and the discussion forums about their novels.

Key Structures

Literature Circles

- Online literature circles can work within a school or a single class or link classrooms together from different schools and school districts.
- Students choose from a diverse list of six to eight novels or non-fiction texts selected to mirror their interests and their reading levels.
- Students read one or more or all of the books—at their own pace for the specified length of time.
- A literature circle can run for four to six weeks. During this time, students read their books, discuss their ideas, and respond both online and in the classroom, showing their thinking and understanding of what they've been reading.
- Each week, every student "posts" a written response to the online discussion forum and also reads their peers' ideas about the books in the forums.
- Discussion forum posts can be done in response to topics posed by the teachers or to questions generated by students in the circle.
- Criteria for good discussion posts are set by students with their teacher after the students have read other models and seen exemplars with reference to the *BC Performance Standards* (2002). The summative assessment of the discussion forums might use the Performance Standard four-point scale or English 10 and the English 12 Holistic Scoring Guide six-point scale.
- Discussion forum posts may be used as assessment *for* or *of* learning, but that depends on the instruction goals and learning intentions established. Summative assessment develops from comment-only descriptive feedback.
- The "virtual coffeehouse" allows students to connect socially and learn appropriate online etiquette as they persuade others about topics they initiate; for example, "Trucks, vans or cars?" "Who's the best NHL hockey team?" or "My favourite movie is *Phantom of the Opera*."
- The coffeehouse encourages students to increase the amount of their reading and writing as they scour the coffeehouse for each other's responses to opinions offered.
- Online literature circles can include the online reflection journals, online collaborative group projects, and other assignments.
- The "teacher forum" is private and allows teachers to plan collaboratively and communicate.

Use of Student Exemplars

- Before students begin their own responses in the discussion forums, they view samples of previous discussion forums and discuss these exemplars along with criteria.

- As they read their novels, students read what the other students in the circle think. They may also analyze these responses using the criteria discussed, pose questions, respond to the questions of others, and check their understanding of their novel by reading other students' work.
- Students tell us that one reason they are so engaged by online literature circles is they relate to the rich variety of exemplars from other students in the discussion forums.

Modelling and Guided Practice

- Teachers explicitly model how to respond to questions and topics in the circles. The modelling moves to guided practice where students can work with others to form their own thoughtful posts to the discussion forum. One-to-one modelling happens when students and teachers conference on student work.
- Teachers model literary questions. Typically, by week two or three of the cycle online, students begin to pose their own questions, and their peers respond to one another's ideas, which results in greater student ownership.

Connecting, Processing, Transforming

- The teachers' questions are formed with the intention of providing the opportunity for students to access prior knowledge, to connect their understanding of their reading, and to transform their thoughts and form their own insights.

One-to-One Strategic Tutoring

- As students work on their posts to the online discussions or as they read, teachers may have one-to-one conferences with each student about their reading, thinking, and written responses, which becomes a core part of teaching strategies in these online literature circles.

Assessment for Learning

- **Learning intentions**—The learning intentions are on the homepage of the Moodle site, and are clearly stated and easily accessible for student reference at any time.
- **Clear criteria**—Students and teachers collaboratively develop the criteria for assessment.
- **Descriptive feedback**—Feedback is given by students to one another in the discussion forums, as well as by teachers in small-group discussions and one-to-one as students work.
- **Self-assessment**—A core aspect of the success of these circles results from students continually assessing their work in reference to the other students' samples that they see in the discussion forums. Students set learning goals in their journals for online learning, identify their strengths, their areas of focus, and their reflections on their learning.

They copy and paste powerful sentences or ideas from the forums into their learning journals to identify their learning journey, and show the before-and-after progress in their understanding. More formal teacher-directed self-assessments with learning goals for improvement are set as outcomes and also embedded in the design.

- **Peer assessment**—Peers give one another informal feedback in the discussion forums as they discuss one another's ideas and as they work together discussing books in the classroom. Structuring formal opportunities for students to give written descriptive feedback based on criteria to their peers in their circle is also useful.
- **Ownership**—Student ownership is key in the instructional design of Online Literature Circles. Students choose their own novels, choose the topics or prompts they wish to respond to, create their own thoughtful questions that others respond to, and give feedback to their peers. Ownership is a core part of the engagement process.

Diversity

- Diverse texts reach a range of interests and reading abilities.
- Models and exemplars scaffold struggling students, as do the one-on-one conferences.
- Time for reflection, observation, and thinking allows all students to participate in the literary conversation when they are ready.
- Multiple opportunities to re-post to the discussion forums, opportunities to use descriptive feedback to improve their performance, and the interactive nature of the online discussion topics all encourage students to do their best.

So… how do you begin? How do you attain the student focus shown in Figure 12.1?

Figure 12.1 English 11/12 students reading during online literature circle time. Can't hear a pin drop.

Step-by-Step Guide to Online Literature Circles.

Step 1: Find a teaching colleague, and partner your two classes

- Consider teacher colleagues who teach the same grade or range of grades. Trust, teaching style, and shared values are important factors when choosing a partner teacher and class for an online literature circle. These circles provide great opportunities for students to work together, and for teachers to collaborate and team-teach.
- Most of the work is "asynchronous." This means that students don't have to be online at the same time to talk about their books with one another. As a result, variations in secondary school timetables, schedules, and other commitments are supported. Whether the school is on a secondary semester or a linear timetable, the circles can fit into the school schedule and students can participate when their schedule allows.
- Elementary classes find that it is easy to work together in circle by scheduling to fit into their school day.
- The circles work effectively in multi-graded classrooms and for classes with a diverse range of learners. They are as effective in big schools as in small ones. Students from large and small school contexts say that their online literature circle enhances their learning community.

Figure 12.2 shows the set-up on Moodle for a grade 5/6/7 online literature circle between two schools in School District 10. The two teachers chose to have all their students do a predicting and questioning response in week 2. In the subsequent weeks of this circle, students had a choice of two or three topics on which to respond.

Figure 12.2

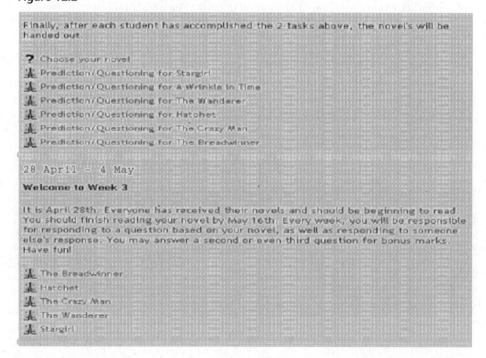

Step 2: Choose the books for the Online Literature Circle, keeping the class context and diversity in mind

- Just as for a face-to-face literature circle (Brownlie 2005), select between six and eight books to offer your students. Some students will read all of the books; some will read only one.
- Teachers determine whether a thematic focus or a curricular goal is key in the choice of titles. They might also ask students to give suggestions for titles (see Student Resources, page 249).
- Choose at least one book that every student in the class is able to read. Think of the learners in the classroom and select a range of texts to match student interests and reading levels. If students are highly interested in a book, they can read some texts above their usual level. Non-fiction or creative non-fiction excites some struggling readers, as do graphic novels. Books with a lower reading level but with provocative "big ideas" can challenge students to read thoughtfully and extend the discussions.
- Choose at least one text with a focus on Aboriginal themes. Good books with Aboriginal characters and voice or written by Aboriginal authors extend the learning of all students. First Nations students may choose to read these books, but non-Aboriginal students are frequently the ones engaged by powerful Aboriginal literature and stories that are offered in the text set.
- Choose Canadian content and Canadian writers, and whenever possible, choose writers who live in the community or in the region, province, or territory. When you can tie the Canadian connection into author visits or writers' festivals, the excitement for reading Canadian authors is intensified. The *BC English 8-12 English Language Arts* IRP (2006) requires that students read at least one major Canadian work each year, and the online literature circle is a wonderful way to include Canadian voices in the classroom.
- Choose diversity in culture and gender. Integrating multicultural voice and diversity in gender mirrors the students who represent many cultures and identities in today's classrooms. Reading books that showcase diversity and promote understanding of others helps all learners gain a sense of belonging and fosters appreciation of ethnicity and social justice issues.
- Choose graphic novels or non-fiction text. Many readers appreciate the inclusion of text with graphic features or real-life connections. For some students, this reflects their interests, but for all who read the aptly chosen books in these genres, thinking is also deepened.

Figure 12.3 shows two examples of text lists that demonstrate inclusion of gender, Canadian content, non-fiction or graphic novels, Aboriginal voice, and multicultural authors.

Figure 12.3 Sample online literature circle texts

English 11/12	English 9/10
The Song of Kahunsha by Anosh Irani	*Perepolis* by Marjane Satrapi
Three Day Road by Joseph Boyden	*Men of Stone* by Gayle Friesen
Wuthering Heights by Jane Eyre	*The Book Thief* by Markus Zusak
Into the Wild by Jon Krakauer	*A Swift Pure Cry* by Siobhan Dowd
Harry Potter and the Deathly Hollows by JK Rowling	*The Hobbit* by JRR Tolkien
The Republic of Nothing by Lesley Choyce	*The Absolutely True Diary of a Part-time Indian* by Sherman Alexie

Step 3: Set up a Moodle site and choose the structures to host online discussions

No need to be a geek to participate in an online reading discussion or have a degree in Computer Science or a membership on <geek.com>. Try one or both of the following suggestions:

1. Invest in online course management software to host or manage discussion forums.
   - Discussion forums are the heart of the work that students do; both the literature discussions and the coffeehouse discussion forums support students as they engage in "grand conversations" about their books.
   - Teachers use a private-teacher-discussion forum to plan and discuss their teaching.
   - Teachers can also assign groups of students to their own discussion forums to work on collaborative projects.

Figure 12.4 shows the layout on Moodle for a grade 7/8 literature circle between two schools in two different districts. The teachers chose to structure the discussion forums so that each week the students click on the title of their novel and then respond to one of the three questions in that forum.

Moodle is open-source course-management software, which means it is free. Moodle provides the structure for the discussion forums and online coffeehouse. Online learning journals can be downloaded from <www.moodle.org>. Thousands of schools, colleges, and universities across the world use this software. It looks slick, requires minimal technical skill, is easy for students and teachers to use, and does the job of managing all

Figure 12.4

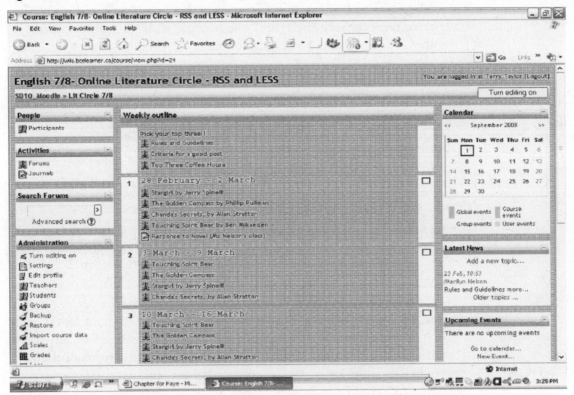

the different questions and discussion threads in an easy-to-navigate manner. Moodle also has a journal feature where students can write out their thoughts so that only they and the teacher can read their entries on their thinking or learning. This feature is a powerful way to increase student reflection and ownership of their learning process. Moodle also has a grade book—that is, students see only their own grades, while the teacher can see the grades of all students. WebCT or other commercial applications would also work. Blogs might also facilitate participation in an online literature circle, but managing the many threaded conversations would be cumbersome.

2. Have someone with IT knowledge and authority install the Moodle software and work with others who have experience.

- The technology person for the school district or someone with administrative privileges installs the software to a district server—or to a school server. They download the Moodle program (or whatever software you are using) to the server, and then assign the teachers privileges as a "teacher" or "administrator" so they can develop the course-discussion forums, coffeehouses, learning journals, or other assignments, as well as create links to websites and exemplars.

- Another option is to partner with a school or district that already has Moodle in place. If students from two schools are working together in an online literature circle, only one Moodle server is needed. In fact, the discussions *should* be hosted on just one school or district server so the students can connect with one another.
- When launching an online literature circle for the first time, it is not a bad plan to piggyback on someone else's experience and to use their server to host the discussion forums. For example, in Figure 12.6, School District 10 hosts the circle on their Moodle server, and students from LV Rogers in Nelson and Lucerne School in New Denver have access to the same discussion forums to talk about their books.

Step 4: Set up the structure of the Online Literature Circle

- Decide how many weeks the circle will run. Ideally, four to six weeks works for most schools. Consider what length and timing are best for both teaching partners.
- Write up questions for discussions forums — usually two or three questions each week for each book in the text set for the circle. The teachers post the questions on the Moodle site for students on the Sunday night of each week; students can post their responses any time between that Sunday night and the following Sunday for each week.
- Share the workload. Often, as team teachers, we each create two or three questions per novel per week for only half of the novels, while our teaching partner is responsible for creating the questions for the remaining ones. Teachers learn from seeing the thoughtful questions that other teachers create. Teachers each assess their own students and give them each descriptive feedback.
- Create a virtual coffeehouse for students to meet and discuss ideas not directly related to their reading. A coffeehouse helps students feel more engaged with online peers and increases the fun factor. Clear learning intentions, with a task for the coffeehouse and an expectation that each student will contribute an opinion, make the coffeehouse more successful (see Figure 12.5).

Figure 12.5 An example of "top three" coffeehouse tasks for grades 7 to 12

Top Three Coffeehouse

What do you think?

What are your top three? Top three books, movies, vacation destinations, causes, songs, bands, people who have changed your life, sports, accomplishments, failures, heroes, ideas, philosophies, philosophers, computer games, poets, nonsense words, words that dance, characters from Canadian literature, foods...

State. Persuade. Support. Debate.

By April 14, post your ultimate top three...choose the one post or create a final post that encapsulates the best argued points and ideas for your top three.

Join the conversation. Listen in. Respond to others' ideas respectfully.

Step 5: Determine learning intentions and connect these with discussion-forum questions

- Decide on your learning intentions and connect these to the questions for the students. Is there a thematic thread across the books? An overarching idea that connects them? Are there certain skills in reading, responding to literature, or writing that teachers want to address through the literature circle process? If so, embed these themes or skills into the discussion forum questions.

Discussion-forum questions should require deep thinking. Figure 12.6 shows sample questions from a variety of teachers.

Figure 12.6

Grade 7/8 from LUCERNE (New Denver) and ROSSLAND
Touching Spirit Bear by Ben Mikaelsen
"Trust and Be Trusted"—question written by Gary Parkstrom, Lucerne School, New Denver

After his experience with the Spirit Bear, Cole struggles with trust. Give two examples from the novel. Do you believe Cole should be trusted now that he has had a near-death experience? Justify your answer with evidence from the novel, and your own personal experiences.

GRADE 7/8 from LUCERNE (New Denver) and ROSSLAND
Chanda's Secrets by Allan Stratton
"AIDS"—question written by Marilyn Nelson, Rossland Secondary School, Rossland

AIDS is introduced in this first section. How do different characters talk about and respond to it? What information do you get about how AIDS patients are treated socially? Is this different than how they are treated in our society? Support your answer.

GRADE 10/11/12 from LV ROGERS (Nelson) and LUCERNE (New Denver)
the curious incident of the dog in the nighttime by Mark Haddon
"Pythagoras"—question written by Kari Kroker, LV Rogers Secondary, Nelson

There are many references to Pythagoras. In fact, Pythagoras is so important to Christopher that he is in the appendix. What do you know about Pythagoras? Are there any connections to Christopher?

GRADE 7 from RANDERSON RIDGE (Nanaimo) and NAKUSP ELEMENTARY
Ice Dragon by George R.R. Martin
"Character"—question written by Leslie Leitch, Nakusp Elementary School, Nakusp

How is Adara's relationship with her father different from his relationship with her sister, Teri? How does that affect your impression of their father?

Figure 12.6 (cont'd)

GRADE 5/6/7 from NAKUSP ELEMENTARY (Nakusp) and EDGEWOOD ELEMENTARY
The Wanderer by Sharon Creech

Question written by Katrina Sumrall, Lucerne Elementary Secondary, New Denver (note that the question permits student response in image format as illustrated in Figure 12.7.)

Using the Internet, can you locate a map of where they are sailing and insert it in as an answer?

Figure 12.7

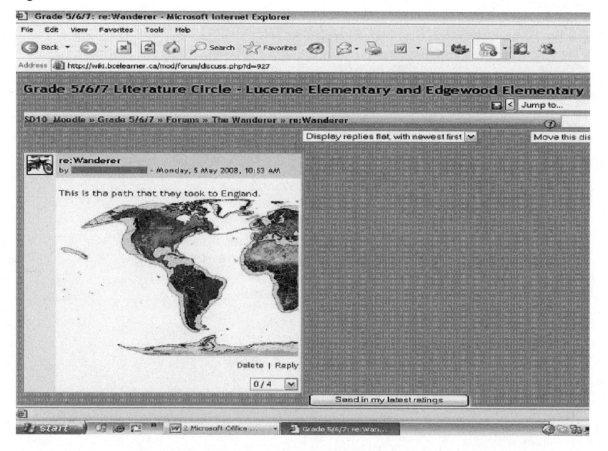

Step 6: Create your class in Moodle, and add student names; create the structure

- Structure your online literature circle as a course in Moodle or other software. The number of weeks and the structure of the forums all need to be created. It is easy to learn how to do this. The teacher role on Moodle allows a teacher to create course elements.

- Create a separate forum for each novel in each week of the online literature circle. This makes it easy for students to find their forums. In each week, all the titles of the novels in the text set will appear. Decide how many forums will receive descriptive feedback before a forum is graded. Students can see only their own grades in Moodle; teachers can see all student grades and enter the student-specific marks.
- Using the class lists from both classes in the circle, enter the students' names and create usernames. Set a default first-login password. These tasks may be done by a technical administrator in your district, or, teachers can be given the role of an "administrator" on the Moodle site to complete this enrolment function. As well, you may use an enrollment key that allows students to self-register.
- Decide whether an online learning journal (a journal wherein students reflect on their learning) is helpful and, if so, add one to the online literature circle Moodle course.

Step 7: Establish clear rules and guidelines

- Establish the rules for the students (see Figures 12.8 and 12.9 for sample rules and guidelines).
- Communicate the rules and guidelines clearly to the students before beginning.
- Educate students about the differences between their work online for school and their contributions to social networking sites and chat rooms that may occur on their own time. Online literature circles provide an opportunity to teach students about formal English as opposed to MSN-speak, to discuss "tone" in digital communications, and to learn the consequences of harassment or cyber-bullying.
- We have found that these circles are very safe because every word is monitored by the teachers and other students. All posts are documented and recorded, and all students know the rules. Being transparent with students about this information is key; it helps them to know that their words are read and monitored, as are those of other students.

Figure 12.8 Sample rules for a grade 5/6/7 Online Literature Circle

1. When writing or posting anything, you must always use proper English.
2. Remember the rules of grammar. Edit before you post.
3. For many of you, it will work best if you write first on a Word document.
4. Think about your audience and write with that in mind.
5. When responding to someone else's opinion, be sensitive to their viewpoint.

Figure 12.9 English 9/10—Rules to live by in a digital environment

1. **Be aware of your audience.** This is a school course using school technology and school servers and read by students and teachers. Think "appropriate" language. Stay focused on the topic. Think and review before you hit "send" or "post to forum."

2. **Be aware of your purpose in writing.** The reason for the forum is to engage in a dialogue with other students about novels that you have read. There may be differences in opinion in interpretation and analysis, but your purpose is to use evidence from the text to substantiate your point of view and thoughts on the novel. The task is a literary discussion rooted in the ideas from your books.

3. **Be aware of tone.** The only appropriate tone in this forum is one of respect and tolerance for the ideas of others. You may disagree and have an alternate viewpoint, but please in every post be aware of the impact of the words that you choose and the impact of the tone that you take. Be persuasive; don't be mean-spirited. In the same way that putdowns or a disrespectful tone of voice is unacceptable in a classroom, our virtual classroom must be a place where all students feel safe to express their ideas and where all students communicate in a respectful manner.

4. **Be aware of the limitations of the technology.** Digital communication is sometimes a challenging medium. Words can be misinterpreted and tone can be volatile. Graphics such as italics, capital letters and font size take on communication values in the digital world that are magnified. Words have greater connotation and magnitude in the absence of a two-way real-time conversation. There's no way to gauge facial expressions, response, or emotions to modify our communication, so email and discussions online can be easily misunderstood and conflicts can easily escalate.

5. **Be aware that there is a fine line between having a strong opinion and being abusive or harassing.** We need to be mindful of what defines workplace harassment in a digital environment. It's not okay to be disrespectful in this medium in our society and in the adult (and school) world. There are significant consequences for stepping over this line at school and in our society.

Step 8: Orient students to Moodle and show models or samples of discussion-forum posts

- Using a LCD projector or screen, show students the Moodle site and explain the concept of online literature circles. Introduce the partner class, and check out their school website and context.
- Show students:
  - how to log on to the Moodle site, how to change their password, and how to enroll themselves

- how to post to the discussion forums
- that they have one hour to make any edits or changes after submitting to the forum
- the benefits of drafting in Word or checking carefully for grammar and spelling, as there's no spell-check in Moodle
- how to interact respectfully in the coffeehouse
- rules and guidelines for online literature circles and the consequences for breaking the rules

- Show samples of student work at each point of your rubric scale. We use the *BC Performance Standards for Reading*, or *English 10 Holistic Marking Scale for Reading*. These allow students to see how they can contribute to the discussion forums; they also prepare them to consider criteria for their own work. Use School District 10's Moodle site or other online exemplars to help students visualize what their own work can look like.

- Encourage students to use images as well as text to communicate their ideas—especially in the coffeehouse. Teachers can also write questions that require a visual or graphic response.

- Inform students that they can choose which questions they will respond to each week on the discussion forum about their novel. Invite students to create their own questions and respond to their own or their peers' questions.

Figure 12.10 shows a sample discussion forum post on Moodle. This discussion forum is based on Vancouver writer Anosh Irani's, *Song of Kahunsha*. The teacher's question is listed first, then the student's response.

Figure 12.10 Sample discussion forum

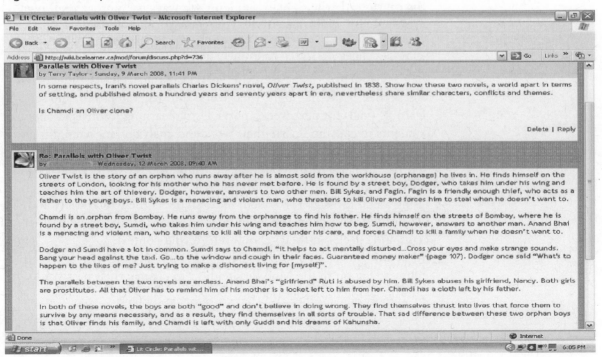

Step 9: Set criteria with students

- After seeing and discussing exemplars and performance standards in reading and writing, negotiate the criteria for a good forum post with the students.
- A length guideline is helpful in an online environment. Whether the goal is a paragraph, 250 words, or a multi-paragraph response, students respond in more depth if there is a stated expectation about length.
- Discuss using evidence from the text and show exemplars integrating quotations and evidence.

Step 10: Beginning the Online Literature Circle with students

- Have students read the first chapter or two of their book and then start working online.
- Give students a small task to allow them to navigate the online experience. Make a post to the coffeehouse, write about their favourite movies or books, or change their avatar—these are all ways to get things rolling. Some teachers devote the first week to getting students and teachers comfortable with Moodle and the technology, and with communicating with online peers, while others start with the discussion forums right away.
- Look at the week 1 discussion forum posts written by the online partner class, and, using the criteria, have students make suggestions about what works and does not work in these posts. What strengths are evident and how can reading others' work help improve our own? What is one thing that the writer could improve? Using the other classes' exemplars as an assessment-for-learning activity with the rubric and criteria helps students see ways to improve their own learning with some objectivity. This process then scaffolds them to use the discussion forums as exemplars for their own work as they engage in the literature circle.
- Self assessment—using the criteria and the rubric, have students self-assess their work, highlight what works and what does not, and set learning goals for next week's posts. Using learning journals to allow students to copy and paste their work and analyze their strengths and learning goals is an effective strategy. Continue to use the learning journal regularly to allow students to show and tell as they self-assess their work in the online literature circle.

Step 11: Reflect and plan for learning

- Assess what works and what does not, and adjust your practice accordingly.
- Follow the assess/plan/teach cycle with your teaching partner throughout the project. The teacher forums are a great way for teachers to support one another and share insights and plans.

- Use assessment for learning and other metacognitive strategies with students to help them improve their thinking and learning.

Why Online Literature Circles work

Online Literature Circles work because they...

- connect students with learning outside the borders of the classroom, school and district
- use high-quality diverse texts (non-fiction and literature) to engage students at their level, using their interests
- engage students as social learners in high-quality literary conversations through online discussion forums
- allow students to work at their own pace, including asynchronously, at home or school, and with control over their learning
- encourage students to edit and revise their work—within 60 minutes online—or by resubmitting their work once it has improved
- build reading and writing skills using daily student models and exemplars in the online discussion forums
- encourage metacognitive reflection: online literature circles allow students to journal online about their thinking, to reflect on their changing understanding of what they read, and to consider how they are learning and how to set goals to improve their reading skills and strategies
- employ Assessment for Learning strategies
- create genuine audience and purpose for reading and writing
- motivate students to read (since they chose their book)
- motivate students to edit their work (since their peers are reading their thoughts and they have multiple opportunities to edit and re-submit their work)
- motivate students to read what their peers think—they want to hear what other readers have to say
- allow everyone's "voice" to be heard; not just the vocal students contribute to the discussion—Everyone does
- involve deep learning for *all* students; struggling readers are scaffolded for success through exemplars and self-paced structures; talented readers are challenged by a wide range of books and an expanded learning

Terry's Reflections

It takes a few weeks before most teachers feel fluent in using online literature circles, but the process is easy to learn. Some teachers find that it is best to partner with someone who has done it before. Truly, one of the best parts of the experience from a professional point of view is being able to "team teach" with colleagues from within a school, across a school district, or around the province. Check out School District # 10's online literature circles at <http://wiki.bcelearner.ca> or <www.onlinelearner.ca> to see examples of how to set up the literary forums, see sample student responses and criteria, view questions, see student feedback, and view student-created PowerPoints.

The last word is theirs: What students say about the Online Literature Circle

- "It is very interesting how people think about certain things differently. And …it helps me to understand the story better.… Other people's ideas give me more ideas that can improve my reading. I can develop my understanding of the story too. Also, I feel that it's very good to have my *own* opinion about the book."
- "… you didn't get put on the spot and have to be quick on your feet."
- "It was fun and original being able to talk to other people I don't know about our thoughts on things…"
- "I liked that I could type it up at any time of the night. I especially liked that because that is when I am the most creative."
- "I really like using the Moodle site because I can get ideas from other people and share my work with others. It gives shy people the chance to show their work when they usually wouldn't. I hope we can continue using the site next term. It was very helpful. I like being able to see other people's comments on my work."

Professional References

Alvermann, D.E. 2001. Effective literacy instruction for adolescents. Executive summary and paper commissioned by the National Reading Conference. Chicago: National Reading Conference.

Allington, Richard L. 2001. *What really matters for struggling readers: Designing research-based programs.* Glenview, IL: Pearson Education, Addison-Wesley Educational Publishers.

Atwell, Nancie. 1998. *In the middle: New understanding about writing, reading, and learning,* 2nd ed. Portsmouth, NH: Heinemann, Boynton/Coo Imprint.

Atwell, Nancie. 2002. *Lessons that change writers.* Portsmouth, NH: Heinemann.

Biancarosa, G., and C.E. Snow. 2004, 2006. *Reading next: A vision for action and research in middle and high school literacy: A report to Carnegie Corporation of New York,* 2nd ed. Washington DC: Alliance for Excellent Education.

Black, Paul, Chris Harrison, Clara Lee, Bethan Marshall, and Dylan Wiliam. 2003. *Assessment for learning: Putting it into practice.* McGraw Hill Education International, Maidenhead: Open University Press.

Black, Paul, and Dylan Wiliam. 1998. Assessment and classroom learning. Assessment Research Group: *Assessment in Education,* 5 (1): 7–74.

British Columbia Ministry of Education. 2002. *BC Performance Standards for Reading and Writing,* rev. ed. Victoria, BC: Student Assessment and Program Evaluation Branch. Retrieved February 2, 2009, from: <http://www.bced.gov.bc.ca/perf_stands/>.

British Columbia Ministry of Education. 2006. *English Language Arts, Kindergarten to Grade 7: Integrated Resource Package.* Victoria, BC: British Columbia Ministry of Education.

Brownlie, F. 2009. Adolescent literacy assessment: Finding out what you need to know. In *Adolescent literacy, field tested,* 117–125, by S.R. Parris, D. Fisher, and K. Headley, eds. Newark, DE: International Reading Association.

Brownlie, F. 2005. *Grand conversations, thoughtful responses: A unique approach to literature circles.* Winnipeg, MB: Portage & Main Press.

Brownlie, F. 2004. *Literacy in the Middle Years: Part 1*, webcast. Retrieved January 18, 2009, from: <http://www.bced.gov.bc.ca/literacy/webcast.htm>.

Brownlie, F., C. Feniak, and V. McCarthy. 2000. *Instruction and assessment of ESL learners: Promoting success in your classroom.* Winnipeg, MB: Portage and Main Press.

Brownlie, F., and C. Feniak. 1998. *Student diversity: Addressing the needs of all learners in inclusive classrooms.* Markham, ON: Pembroke Publishers Limited.

Brownlie, F., C. Feniak, and L. Schnellert. 2006. *Student diversity: Classroom strategies to meet the learning needs of all students,* 2nd ed. Markham, ON. Pembroke Publishers Ltd.

Butler, D.L., L. Schnellert, and S.C. Cartier. 2005. Adolescents' engagement in "reading to learn": Bridging from assessment to instruction. *BC Educational Leadership Research,* 2. Retrieved December 2, 2005, from: <http://slc.educ.ubc.ca/eJournal/index.htm>http://slc.educ.ubc.ca/eJournal/index.htm>.

Butler, D.L., and L. Schnellert. 2008. Teachers working to achieve valued outcomes for students: Making meaningful links between research and practice. *Education Canada,* 48 (5): 36–40.

Cameron, Caren. 2007. *Informed assessment practices*: Webcast # 3 of 6. Retrieved January 18, 2009, from: <http://bcelc.insinc.com/webcastseries/20080116/>.

Cameron, C., C. Politano, J. Paquin, and K. Gregory. 2004. *Practical ideas to spark up the year, 4-8.* Winnipeg: Portage & Main Press.

Carnegie Corporation of New York. 2004, 2006. *Reading next: A vision for action and research in middle and high school literacy: A report.* G. Biancarosa, and C.E. Snow. Washington, DC: Alliance for Excellent Education.

Carnegie Corporation of New York. 2007. *Writing next: Effective strategies to improve writing of adolescents in middle and high schools: A report.* Steve Graham and Dolores Perin. Washington, DC: Alliance for Excellent Education. Retrieved August 17, 2009, from: <http://www.all4ed.org/publications/WritingNext/WritingNext.pdf>.

Case, R., ed. 2004. *Caring for young people's rights.* Vancouver: The Critical Thinking Consortium. Website: <http://www.tc2.ca/wp/>.

Case, R., and P. Clark, eds. 2008. Portals of Geographical Thinking. In *The anthology of social studies: Issues and strategies for elementary teachers,* vol. 1. Vancouver: Pacific Educational Press.

CIA Fact Book 2009. CIA Facts at a Glance. Retrieved November 12, 2008, from: <http://www.acdi-cida.gc.ca/CIDAWEB/acdicida.nsf/En/NIC-5482847-GN3>.

Clark, P., and R. McKay. 1992. *Canada revisited: A social and political history of Canada to 1911.* Edmonton: Arnold Publishing Ltd.

Clarke, P., T. Owens, and R. Sutton. 2006. *Creating independent learners: A practical guide to assessment for learners, 7–9*. Winnipeg: Portage & Main Press.

Doty, J.K., G.N. Cameron, and M.L. Barton. 2003. *Teaching reading in social studies*. Aurora, CO: McREL.

Earl, Lorna. 2001. Assessment as learning. In *The keys to effective schools*, Willis D. Hawley, ed. National Education Association, Thousand Oaks, CA: Corwin Press.

Facing the Future. Website accessed January 11, 2009: <http://www.facingthefuture.org>.

Frey, N., D. Fisher, and K. Moore. 2005. *Designing responsive curriculum: Planning lessons that work*. Lanham, MD: Rowman & Littlefield Education.

Fullan, Michael. 2001. *Leading in a culture of change*. San Francisco: Jossey-Bass.

Fullan, Michael. 2004. *Leadership and sustainability*. Thousand Oaks, CA: Corwin Press.

Gladwell, Malcolm. 2008. *Outliers*. New York: Little, Brown and Company.

Graham, Steve, and Dolores Perin. 2007. *Writing next: Effective strategies to improve writing of adolescents in middle and high schools*. A report to Carnegie Corporation of New York. Washington, DC: Alliance for Excellent Education. Retrieved August 17, 2009, from: <http://www.all4ed.org/publications/WritingNext/WritingNext.pdf>.

Gregory, K., C. Cameron, and A Davies. 1997. *Knowing what counts: Setting and using criteria*. Winnipeg: Portage & Main Press.

Hattie, John, and Helen Timperley. 2007. The power of feedback. *Review of Educational Research*, 77 (1): 81–112.

Helin, Calvin. 2008. *Surfing the demographic tsunami: Indigenous education in the 21st century*. Presented at the 3rd annual Rural Schools Conference, Richmond, BC.

Hitchcock, C., A. Meyer, D. Rose, and R. Jackson. 2002. Providing new access to the general curriculum: Universal design for learning. *Teaching Exceptional Children*, 35 (2): 8–17.

Hourcade, Jack, and Joanne Bauwens. 2002. *Cooperative teaching: Re-building and sharing the schoolhouse*, 2nd ed. Austin, TX: Pro-Ed.

Keene, Ellin. 2008. *To understand: New horizons in reading comprehension*. Portsmouth, NH: Heinemann.

Lenz, B.K., and D.D. Deshler, with B. Kissam. 2004. *Teaching content to all: Evidenced practices for middle and high school settings*. New York: Allyn & Bacon.

Liston, Daniel, P., 2004. The lure of learning in teaching. *Teachers' College Record*, 106 (3): 459–486.

Menzel, P. 2004. *Material world: A global family portrait*. San Francisco: Sierra Club Books.

Moodle (open source software package). Website accessed June 10, 2009: <http://www.moodle.org>.

Noël, Michel. 2003. *Le Kitchimanitou.* Montréal: Hurtubise HMH, collection Plus Éditions.

Online Literature Circles: (wiki). Retrieved April 20, 2009, from: <http://wiki.bcelearner.ca>. See also <http://www.elearningbc.com/> and <http://www.newmediabc.com/>.

Pearson. P.D., and M.C. Gallagher. 1983. The instruction of reading comprehension. *Contemporary Educational Psychology*, 8: 317–344.

Peterson, Shelley Stagg. 2003. *Writing across the curriculum: All teachers teach writing*, rev. ed. Winnipeg: Portage & Main Press.

Ritchhart, R., and D. Perkins. 2008. Making thinking visible. *Educational Leadership*, 65 (5): 57–61.

Robinson, V.M.J. 2007. School leadership and student outcomes: What works? *ACEL* #41, October 2007.

Rose, D.H., and A. Meyer. 2002. *Teaching every student in the Digital Age: Universal Design for Learning.* Alexandria, VA: ASCD.

Schnellert, L. 2004. Strengthening student writing network: Teachers meeting with teachers to share with and support one another. *Update: The Journal of BC Teachers of English Language Arts*, 46 (2).

Schnellert, L., D.L. Butler, and S. Higginson. 2008. Co-constructors of data, co-constructors of meaning: Teacher professional development in an age of accountability. *Teaching and Teacher Education*, 24 (3): 725–750.

Schnellert, L., M. Datoo, K. Ediger, and J. Panas. 2009. *Pulling together: How to integrate inquiry, assessment and instruction in today's English classroom.* Markham, ON: Pembroke Publishers Ltd.

Schnellert, L., and N. Widdess. 2005. Student-generated criteria, free verse poetry, and residential schools. *Update: The Journal of BC Teachers of English Language Arts*, 47 (2): 19–28.

Smith, D.J. 2002. *If the world were a village: A book about the world's people.* Toronto: Kids Can Press.

Smith, Frank. 2004. *Understanding reading*. Mahwah, NJ: Lawrence Erlbaum Associates.

Smith, Frank. 2006. *Reading without nonsense*. New York: Teachers' College Press.

Smith, Michael W., and Jeff D. Wilhelm. 2002. *Reading don't fix no chevys: The role of literacy in the lives of young men.* Portsmouth, NH: Heinemann.

Smith, Michael W., and Jeff D. Wilhelm. 2006. *Going with the flow: How to engage boys (and girls) in their literacy learning.* Portsmouth, NH: Heinemann.

Statistics Canada. 2006 Census. Website accessed January 29, 2009: <http:www.statcan.gc.ca>.

Turpel-Lafond, Mary Ellen (BC Representative for Children and Youth). Making Connections Conference, November 2008. Richmond, BC.

United Nations. Cyber School Bus, "InfoNation." Website accessed January 29, 2009: <http://cyberschoolbus.un.org/infonation3/menu/advanced.asp>.

Villa, R., J. Thousand, and A. Nevin. 2004. *A guide to co-teaching: Practical tips for facilitating student learning.* Thousand Oaks, CA: Corwin Press.

Wiggins, Grant, and Jay McTighe. 2001. *Understanding by design.* New Jersey: Prentice Hall Inc.

Wilhelm, Jeffrey. 2007. *Engaging readers and writers with inquiry.* New York: Scholastic.

Wilhelm, Jeffrey D., Tanya Baker, and Julie Dube. 2001. *Strategic reading: Guiding adolescents to lifelong literacy.* Portsmouth, NH: Heinemann.

Willms, Doug. 2002. *Vulnerable children.* Edmonton: University of Alberta Press.

Worldmapper. Website accessed February 16, 2009: <http://www.sasi.group.shef.ac.uk/worldmapper/index.html>.

Student Resources

Chapter Reference	Novels, Text Sets, and Textbooks
Ch. 12	Alexie, Sherman. 2007. *The absolutely true diary of a part-time Indian*. Boston: Little Brown & Company.
Ch. 6	Anderson, Laurie Halse. 1999. *Speak*. New York: Farrar, Straus & Giroux.
Ch. 6	Bell, William. 1990. *Forbidden city*. Toronto: Doubleday Canada.
Ch. 6	Bo, Ben. 1998. *The edge*. Minneapolis, MN: Lerner Publications.
Ch. 12	Boyden, Joseph. 2005. *Three day road*. Toronto: Penguin Group.
Ch. 12	Brontë, Charlotte. 1847. *Jane Eyre*. New York: Penguin Classics.
Ch. 12	Brontë, Emily. 1847. *Wuthering Heights*. New York: Penguin Classics.
Ch. 11	Case, Roland, ed. 2004. *Caring for young people's rights*. Vancouver: The Critical Thinking Consortium (TC²).
Ch. 11	Case, Roland, and Penney Clark, eds. 2008. *The anthology of social studies: Issues and strategies for elementary teachers (Volume I)*. Vancouver: Pacific Educational Press.
Ch. 11	Case, Roland, and Penney Clark, eds. 2008. *The anthology of social studies: Issues and strategies for secondary teachers (Volume II)*. Vancouver: Pacific Educational Press.
Ch. 9	Choi, Sook Nyul. 1991. *Year of impossible goodbyes*. Boston: Houghton Mifflin.
Ch. 12	Choyce, Lesley. 2007. *The republic of nothing*. Fredericton, NB: Goose Lane Editions.
Ch. 8	Clark, Penney, and Roberta McKay. 1992. *Canada revisited: A social and political history of Canada to 1911*. Edmonton: Arnold Publishing.
Ch. 10	Clements, Andrew. 2006. *The report card*. New York: Aladdin.
Ch. 12	Creech, Sharon. 2002. *The wanderer*. New York: Harper Collins.
Ch. 10	D'Adamo, Francesco. 2003. *Iqbal*. New York: Atheneum Books for Young Readers.
Ch. 10	Davidson, Margaret. 2002. *Louis Braille: L'Enfant de la nuit*. Paris: Gallimard Jeunesse.
Ch. 10	DiCamillo, Kate (tr. by Brigitte Freger). 2004. *Because of Winn-Dixie*. New York: Scholastic.
Ch. 10	DiCamillo, Kate (tr. by Hélène Pilotto). 2006. *L'Odyssée miraculeuse d'Édouard*. Toronto: Scholastic.
Ch. 12	Dowd, Siobhan. 2006. *A swift pure cry*. United Kingdom: David Fichling Books.

Ch. 7	Ellis, Carol. 1995. "The dare," in *Bad behaviour*, ed. Mary Higgins Clark. San Diego: Harcourt Brace & World.
Ch. 10	Ellis, Deborah. 2000. *The breadwinner*. Toronto: Douglas & McIntyre.
Ch. 6	Ellis, Deborah. 2002. *Parvana's journey*. Toronto: Douglas & McIntyre.
Ch. 6	Ellis, Deborah. 2003. *Mud city*. Toronto: Douglas & McIntyre.
Ch. 6	Farmer, Nancy. 2002. *House of the scorpion*. New York; Atheneum Books for Young Readers.
Ch. 6	Finn, Perdita. 1972. *Julie of the wolves*. New York: Harper & Row.
Ch. 10	Fraisse, Frédérique, tr. 2003. *Les mille oiseaux de Sadako*. Toulouse: Milan Poche.
Ch. 12	Friesen, Gayle. 2002. *Men of stone*. Toronto: Kids Can Press
Ch. 10	Gill, Pauline. 2007. *Le miracle de Juliette*. Quebec: Éditions du Phoenix.
Ch. 10	Gratton, Andrée-Anne. 1998. *Le message des biscuits chinois*. Montreal: Boréal.
Ch. 10	Haddix, Margaret Peterson. 1998. *Among the hidden*. New York: Simon & Schuster Books for Young Readers.
Ch. 10, 12	Haddon, Mark. 2003. *The curious incident of the dog in the nighttime*. Toronto: Random House Canada, Anchor Canada.
Ch. 6	Haworth-Attard, Barbara. 2003. *Theories of relativity*. Toronto: Harper Collins Canada.
Ch. 6	Hehner, Barbara. 2004. *The tunnel king*. Toronto: Harper Collins Canada.
Ch. 6	Hughes, Monica. 1990. *Invitation to the game*. Toronto: Harper Collins Canada.
Ch. 12	Irani, Anosh. 2006. *The song of Kahunsha*. Toronto: Random House Canada, Doubleday.
Ch. 10	Joséphine, Régine. 2007. *Coton Blues*. Rouen, France: Gecko Jeunesse.
Ch. 10	Kerba, Muriel. 2006. *Un nouveau monde*. Paris: Gautier-Languereau.
Ch. 6	Krakauer, Jon. 1997. *Into thin air*. New York: Random House, Villard.
Ch. 12	Krakauer, Jon. 1996. *Into the wild*. New York: Villard.
Ch. 6	Laird, Elizabeth. 2003. *The garbage king*. London: Macmillan Children's Books.
Ch. 6	Lawrence, Iain. 1998. *The wreckers*. New York: Delacorte Press.
Ch. 3	Lerman, Rory S. illustr. Alison Bartlett. 1997. *Charlie's checklist*. New York: Orchard Books.
Ch. 6	Lowry, Lois. 2000. *Gathering blue*. Boston: Houghton Mifflin Books for Children.
Ch. 10	Marineau, Michèle. 2002. *Marion et le nouveau monde*. Quebec: Dominique et compagnie.
Ch. 6	Marsden, John. 1993. *Tomorrow, when the war began*. London: Macmillan.
Ch. 12	Martin, George R.R. 2007. *Ice dragon*. New York: Tom Doherty Associates.
Ch. 6	Matthews, Laura S. 2004. *Fish*. New York: Random House.
Ch. 11	Menzel, Peter and Charles Mann. 1995. *Material world: A global family portrait*. San Francisco: Sierra Club Books.
Ch. 5	Meyer, Stephenie. 2005. *Twilight*. New York: Little, Brown & Co.
Ch. 10	Meyeres, Florence, tr. 2005. *Tom et le gorille*. Paris: Gallimard Jeunesse (original *Tom and the Gorilla*, by Jeanne Willis).
Ch. 5, 12	Mikaelsen, Ben. 2001. *Touching spirit bear*. New York: Harper Trophy.
Ch. 8	Morrow, Robert. 2004. *Pearson school atlas*. Toronto: Pearson Education Canada.

Ch. 6	Nicholson, William. 2000. *The wind singer* (first volume of *Wind on Fire* trilogy). Mammoth Books, Random House Australia.
Ch. 8	Noël, Michel. 2003. *Le Kitchimanitou.* Montreal: Éditions Hurtubise HMH, collection Plus.
Ch. 9	Park, Linda Sue. 2001. *A single shard.* New York: Clarion Books.
Ch. 6	Philbrick, Rodman. 1998. *Max the mighty.* New York: Blue Sky Press.
Ch. 10	Poulin, Andrée. 2005. *Les impatiences de Ping.* Quebec: Québec Amérique.
Ch. 5	Rowling, J.K. 1998. *Harry Potter and the chamber of secrets.* London: Bloomberg.
Ch. 12	Rowling, J.K. 2007. *Harry Potter and the deathly gallows.* London: Bloomsbury.
Ch. 10	Ryan, Pam Munoz. 2000. *Esperanza rising.* New York: Scholastic Press.
Ch. 12	Satrapi, Marjane. 2003. *Persepolis.* Toronto: Random House of Canada.
Ch. 10	Shea, Pegi Dietz. 2003. *The carpet boy's gift.* Gardiner, ME: Tilbury House, Publishers.
Ch. 11	Smith, David J. 2002. *If the world were a village: A book about the world's people.* From the *CitizenKid* series. Toronto: Kids Can Press, Inc.
Ch. 10	Spinelli, Jerry. 1990. *Maniac Magee.* Boston: Little, Brown.
Ch. 10	Spinelli, Jerry. 1997. *Wringer.* New York: Harper Collins.
Ch. 9	Stone, Jeff. 2006. *Tiger.* New York: Yearling.
Ch. 10, 12	Stratton, Allan. 2004. *Chanda's secrets.* Toronto: Annick Press.
Ch. 12	Tolkien, J.R.R. 1937. *The hobbit.* Boston: Houghton Mifflin.
Ch. 9	Toutant, Arnold and Susan Doyle. 2000. "The Three Gorges Dam," in *Outlooks 7: Ancient Worlds.* Toronto: Oxford University Press.
Ch. 6	Trueman, Terry. 2000. *Stuck in neutral.* New York: Harper Collins.
Ch. 9	Watkins, Yoko Kawashima. 1986. *So far from the bamboo grove.* New York: Harper Collins, Lothrop, Lee and Shepard.
Ch. 6	White, Robb. 1973. *Deathwatch.* New York: Bantam Doubleday Dell Books for Young Readers.
Ch. 6	Wiesel, Elie. 1985. *Night.* New York: Aronson.
Ch. 9	Ye, Ting-Xing. 2003. *Throwaway daughter.* Toronto: Doubleday Canada.
Ch. 12	Zusak, Markus. 2005. *The book thief.* Australia: Picador.
Chapter Reference	**Websites for Students**
Ch. 11	*CIA Fact Book 2009.* CIA Facts at a Glance. Retrieved November 12, 2008, from website: <http://www.acdi-cida.gc.ca/CIDAWEB/acdicida.nsf/En/NIC-5482847-GN3>.
Ch. 11	Facing the Future. Website accessed January 11, 2009: <http://www.facingthefuture.org>.
Ch. 11	United Nations Cyber School Bus, Infonation. Website accessed January 29, 2009: <http://cyberschoolbus.un.org/infonation3/menu/advanced.asp>.
Ch. 11	World Mapper. Website accessed February 16, 2009: <http://www.sasi.group.shef.ac.uk/worldmapper/index.html>.

Chapter-by-Chapter Index